The Best Interviews from *The Missouri Review* and the American Audio Prose Library

Edited by Kay Bonetti, Greg Michalson, Speer Morgan, Jo Sapp, and Sam Stowers

University of Missouri Press • Columbia and London

University of Missouri Press, Columbia, Missouri 65201
Printed and bound in the United States of America

5 4 3 2 1 01 00 99 98 97

Library of Congress Cataloging-in-Publication Data

Conversations with American novelists / edited by Kay Bonetti . . . [et al.].
p. cm.
Contents: Robert Stone—Jamaica Kincaid—Jim Harrison—Tom McGuane—Louise Erdrich and Michael Dorris—John Edgar Wideman—Robb Forman Dew—Rosellen Brown—Peter Matthiessen—Scott Turow—Margaret Walker—Linda Hogan—Robert Olen Butler—Jessica Hagedorn—Larry Brown.
Includes bibliographical references (p.).
ISBN 0-8262-1136-4 (paper : alk. paper)
1. Novelists, American—20th century—Interviews. 2. American fiction—20th century—History and criticism—Theory, etc. 3. Fiction—Authorship. I. Bonetti, Kay.
PS379.C665 1997
813'.5409—dc21 97-33393
CIP

⊗™ This paper meets the requirements of the American National Standard for Permanence of Paper for Printed Library Materials, Z39.48, 1984.

Text Design: Mindy Shouse
Jacket Design: Stephanie Foley
Typesetter: BOOKCOMP
Printer and Binder: Thomson-Shore, Inc.
Typeface: Garamond

Contents

Conversations with American Novelists

Introduction

There are plenty of ways for author interviews to go awry. Interviewers may be preoccupied by some issue or ideology. They may want to interrogate a writer about the "real meaning" behind his or her work. Worse still, the conversation sometimes devolves to facile news pegs, which dates it. Or one may catch authors when they are on tour, flogging their current wares—a time when the fevers of selling can temporarily numb the artist.

In our hunt for good interviews, *The Missouri Review* was fortunately able to strike up a working relationship with a kindred literary enterprise. Two years after we opened for business in 1978, Kay Bonetti started the American Audio Prose Library. The purpose of her project was to produce recordings of interviews and readings by distinguished fiction writers and, in addition, produce public-radio programming from this material. Kay's ideas about why readers read and writers write coincided with ours. She avoided the trendy and the flattering. Her sensibility was as democratic as ours. So long as the writing was excellent, she interviewed writers of best-sellers as well as literary novels, and the venerable as well as the newly hatched. Before the current rhetoric of multiculturalism, Kay realized that much of what was valuable in American fiction came from writers who were considered to be of minority or regional interest. Thus, the selections of the American Audio Prose Library represented the work of African American, Native American, and minority men and women from various locales.

Our final print interviews are primarily drawn from hours of tape recordings between Kay and the writers. Consequently, we have extensively edited the original material, though in all cases the author has been an active partner in the process. Each writer has his or her own oral style, and occasionally that transcribes into good solid sentences and paragraphs. The spoken rhetoric of Robert Stone and Tom McGuane, for instance, is particularly lucid in print. But just as often speech that sounds sensible, even elegant, to the ear reads quite otherwise. Our intent has been to remain as true as possible to a particular author's spoken style and rhythm, to maintain the sense of conversational speech so that the reader can "hear," as much as is possible in print, the author's voice.

What you will find in this collection is how each writer in his or her particular way transforms the stuff of life and personal circumstance into the art of fiction. The interviews are interesting for what they reveal about each writer's background and sense of craft. All discuss in some way how they have approached learning their craft and finding their subjects and voices. What becomes clear is how the accumulated experiences and concerns of childhood and family, home and landscape, education and local culture combine to form the writer's ideas about fiction. They show what the writer has discovered about what matters enough in this world, in the words of Jim Harrison, "to build a sentence out of it." To pick just one example, Antiguan-born Jamaica Kincaid—a product of the British-colonial educational system—speaks of how she had to write her way through and out of the English of Milton and Wordsworth in order to find the voice in which she could explore what she only gradually came to realize was her true subject: the relationship between the powerful and the powerless, with the nature of the mother-daughter relationship forming the surface of her work and serving as her metaphor for this larger issue.

No small selection of writers is entirely characteristic of an age, but among these writers there are certain representative threads. Except for Margaret Walker, who is a product of the school of social protest of the thirties, all of them have achieved a special mark in the novel since the 1960s. They are chronologically postmodern, to use the designation of college English departments. In literary studies postmodernism is one of those words that professors will argue about until they decide it is no longer an issue, but its simplest definition refers to the latter part (one-half to one-third, again a point of much disagreement) of this century.

The beat writing that emerged in the 1950s provides a convenient dividing line between modernism and what followed. The serious modernist, under the spell of Henry James and James Joyce, tried to pack his work with complexity and seamless refinement, to become invisible behind flawless, self-contained texts that hummed away with all wheels and springs in marvelous balance and, most of all, avoided any taint of the didactic or political. A look at any list of the most notable works of fiction of the first half of the twentieth century shows that modernism, defined this way, in fact covers only a small portion of the important books of the period. Yet, most serious writers did continue to look to the great refined interior novelists as their model of high art.

Beat writing arose from a grab bag of sources, literary and nonliterary, including down-and-outer and leftist writing of the thirties, wino romanticism, the larger bohemian scene that developed during and after World War II in New York and Paris, non-Western religious thought, pornography, and crime fiction. In literature, this exotic flower had a surprisingly wide and ongoing influence. It made much of the genteel literature of the day seem dated. It reintroduced a celebration of America-as-melting-pot and the sweep of the American landscape. It emphasized literature as performance and belonging to the public. For better or for worse, it planted the seeds of confessionalism.

There are other markers that both divide the times of these writers from what came before and, judging from their interviews, had a loosening effect on the hold of modernism: the Civil Rights movement and the growth of black power, which profoundly reshaped not just the face of African American literature, but also the sensibilities of writers such as Robb Forman Dew, Larry Brown, and Rosellen Brown; the sixties, of which Robert Stone says, "sometimes I feel like I went to a party one day in 1963 and the party spilled out and rolled down the street until it covered the whole country and changed the world"; the rebirth of feminism and comparable movements that opened up space for writing by women and minorities; and, of course, the Vietnam War, which reshaped the war novel and politicized the culture as pervasively as the Civil War and the Great Depression. It was also during this time that international literature burgeoned, especially Spanish American, and, with it, the influence in this country of magical realism. And finally, this era has seen the flowering of what is now called creative nonfiction, which has had a profound impact upon the novel.

In his essay "The Literature of Replenishment," John Barth writes that his "ideal postmodernist author neither merely repudiates nor imitates either his twentieth-century modernist parents or his nineteenth-century pre-modernist grandparents. He has the first half of our century under his belt, but not on his back. Without lapsing into moral or artistic simplism . . . he nevertheless aspires to a fiction more democratic in its appeal. . . ." Indeed, despite the genuine grandeur of the best work of writers such as Joyce and Faulkner, modernism was a room where one went to play ornate parlor games to forget the horrors of a world that spawned the two world wars. Looked at through the least flattering lens, its practitioners were cultural priests offering up mythology, fatalism, and obscurantism. The great accomplishments of writers such as Ralph Ellison, Vladimir Nabokov, Robert Penn Warren, and the early work of Saul Bellow notwithstanding, American fiction was ready for different influences by the mid-fifties. One of the books that broke the mold was Jack Kerouac's *On The Road* (1957). Kerouac's novel was spontaneous, personal, revealing, and about as lacking in irony as it could be, and for many it served as a blast of fresh air in the stale atmosphere of late modernism.

In one way or another, all these writers fit this mold. Their work is accessible: "I think that the sort of burnt-earth successes of modernism have left prestigious writing quite inaccessible to normal readers. . . . I'm a little bit dour now when it comes to books which are terribly brilliant by some sort of smart-set consensus, but which nobody I know can read," says Tom McGuane. The craftsmanship of these writers is impeccable. As Rosellen Brown describes it, "The charge you give yourself is self-fulfilling, self-delighting. You are shaping the best story or novel or poem possible." And, "All serious writers are their own audiences, with all the books of the past looking over their shoulders. If our readers' pleasure coincides with our own, that's all the better."

These writers are most of all overwhelmingly pragmatic with respect to shaping their work in terms of the modernist "rules" about narrative voice, point of view, and structure. Robert Stone, speaking of a particular section of *A Flag for Sunrise,* said: "Yeah, it violates point of view. . . . But I thought it was necessary to get that perspective. . . . I worried about it a bit, but I thought if it was an effective scene, and had its element of verisimilitude, then I would put it there and keep it there." And when asked about writers who still insist that politics, morality, and transmitting cultural values is a thing of the past in fiction, that the only serious writers are those who are purely pushing language to its ultimate, Stone replies, "I don't feel that I have any part in that argument, because I think that you're supposed to do both. A well-intentioned writer with a broad moral vision who can't write very well isn't very interesting. A writer who can write well but who has no subjects and isn't interested in reflecting life and people's lives isn't very interesting either."

All writers of fine fiction have more or less followed the dictum of writing as discovery, and form following function. But writers such as Jamaica Kincaid and Jessica Hagedorn profess consciously to "subvert" traditional notions of form and, as Hagedorn says, "what is considered fiction." Adds Jamaica Kincaid: "Whatever a novel is, I'm not it, and whatever a short story is, I'm not it. If I had to follow these forms, I couldn't write. I'm really interested in breaking the form." Jessica Hagedorn invents news clippings, press releases, and historical writing about the Philippines that she intersperses with ones that are real. Jim Harrison in *Sundog* creates a faux memoir that uses a fictional "Jim Harrison" as its narrator.

Which brings us to what might be one of the most striking and representative aspects of the work discussed in this collection of conversations: a refusal to be bound by modernist assumptions about what the proper province of fiction is. These writers are increasingly less likely to imagine themselves to be practicing a "pure" activity, unconnected to politics, society, and history. Even writers of domestic dramas, such as Rosellen Brown and Robb Foreman Dew, weave them within the fabric of the culture at large, the times their characters are living in, even the world of work, as do writers Peter Matthiessen, Robert Stone, Robert Olen Butler, and Larry Brown.

In addition to an urge toward relevancy, fiction nowadays is demonstrably more multicultural and multiracial. The market itself has given the lie to editors and publishers who claim that ethnic fiction (meaning fiction about anybody but middle-class whites) will not sell to a large-enough audience. No matter how many market analyses a nervous editor may trot out, he or she will have a hard time today making a convincing argument that there is no market for novels about Vietnamese people (Robert Olen Butler), blacks (Margaret Walker and John Edgar Wideman), Filipinos (Jessica Hagedorn), Native Americans (Louise Erdrich, Michael Dorris, and Linda Hogan), immigrants (Jamaica Kincaid), or poor and blue-collar whites (Larry Brown).

Another thread among these writers is a concern for history, both modern and distant, embedded not just in the milieu of their fictions, but as a direct aspect of the narrative and subject: Jessica Hagedorn writes about forty years of Filipino history; Louise Erdrich and Michael Dorris about the destruction and diaspora of the Chippewa and Modoc peoples; Robert Olen Butler (and Robert Stone) about the lives of those caught up in the Vietnam War and its outcome; Linda Hogan about the stealing of oil and land rights in Oklahoma; John Edgar Wideman about his family history in Homewood and before; and Margaret Walker, in her great novel *Jubilee,* about antebellum slavery and its aftermath.

Henry James, perhaps the greatest of the "interior" novelists, nevertheless admonished the doctrinaire that we must ask, finally, if a novel is "valid, in a word, is it genuine, is it sincere, the result of some direct impression or perception of life." James believed that "experience, as I see it, is our apprehension and our measure of what happens to us as social creatures." In other words, the novel answers to the whole of its culture. Certainly, the work of these writers meets that measure. They understand what fiction is good at, including the search for a more useful and subtle understanding of life as lived. Incorporating what they find useful from earlier novelists, they tell their stories in a relatively accessible fashion, stories whose ultimate reference is not themselves but the world.

Robert Stone

Robert Stone, born in 1937, is in many ways an old-fashioned, big-theme novelist in the tradition of Joseph Conrad or Herman Melville. He writes novels of high drama, adventure literature that works on a theological level, often involving large historical developments and the crucible of individual morality. Proceeding from a biblical framework—he describes the Bible as "America's book"—his work has an eerie, apocalyptic flavor in its pursuit of the numinous, "seeking some kind of transcendental ground." His subjects are drawn from the corruptions of war and politics—the residue of Vietnam, political maneuvering in the Cold War, civil war in Central America, the culture of drugs and the drug trade. Almost always, the moral center of his novels is a woman, and it has been said that he writes better as a man about women than any other American writer. Children of Light *was conceived as a tribute to the novelist Kate Chopin's* The Awakening.

Stone is the author of A Hall of Mirrors *(1966),* Dog Soldiers *(1974),* A Flag for Sunrise *(1981),* Children of Light *(1986),* Outerbridge Reach *(1992), and* Bear and His Daughter *(1997). This interview was conducted in Laguna Beach, California, in 1982, just after publication of* A Flag for Sunrise, *perhaps his most critically acclaimed book.*

INTERVIEWER: You're the kind of writer who is associated with the long haul, the big form. You have such a large vision that I was a little startled at the presence of short stories in your canon. How much do you work in the short story form?

STONE: Well, I started out writing quite a few. I find that I'm difficult to satisfy in terms of my own stories. I think I have destroyed many more than I have ever submitted. My stories are rather different from my novels. They're a bit more surreal; perhaps there's more humor in the short stories. The concerns, though, are the same. Perhaps I find I don't have the opportunity to really address those concerns in what I consider to be a serious way, in the story, in quite the same way that I can get to them in the novel, because in the novel I can go off in different directions. I can find resonances by setting up things like parallel structures where two different sets of people are doing totally different versions of the same thing, whereas in the short story everything must be particularly impacted. So I'm always waiting for some story to occur to me that I consider to be inevitable. Because I don't actively pursue the form but rather wait to be struck by some story that will come together in my mind, I don't do many.

INTERVIEWER: You said that the concerns were the same and by that did you mean the thematic concerns of your short stories?

STONE: I think there's a common element in everything I've ever written. I started out in my first book and I think I was working my way toward the main subjects that I deal with. All of them touch on these subjects, and they are subjects that a great many educated people today don't take very seriously. I'm concerned with basic ontology, with questions that are perhaps more religious than political. I write about the presence or the absence of God and the significance that the question of God's absence or presence has on people's lives. People's pursuit of the numinous, their desire for some kind of transcendent ground, seems to me to be a very large part of the human experience. It isn't something that is very often addressed in academic or literary or educated circles generally, but I think it's something that occurs in the lives of most people, even though they don't often talk about it.

INTERVIEWER: Is this just your personal material, or do you see those issues as the fundamental business of the novelist?

STONE: Well, I suppose every novelist finds his fundamental business, decides what his fundamental business is. That, I think, is mine.

INTERVIEWER: What does that say to you about the fact that most contemporary novelists are somewhat embarrassed by this kind of subject matter, or consciously avoid it?

STONE: Well, I understand why novelists do. It's very dangerous territory. It's very easy to be fatuous about transcendence and spiritual values.

There's an awful lot of fatuous and sentimental stuff written about people's hunger for areas beyond their own ken. This is an area that you really can't fake. You come to it with either active belief or active disbelief or a position which takes its dynamics from somewhere in between. It has to concern you. If it doesn't, then you can't write about it. You can't, I think, effectively write about people's hunger for transcendence unless it's something that you yourself experience. It can't be done secondhand; it can't be rendered warmed-over.

INTERVIEWER: You said that you think this is a central issue in most people's lives and I was wondering if you see yourself as writing to try to understand your culture within this frame of reference, or are you just trying to get down what you see? The phrase that comes to mind is Whitman's injunction to vivify the contemporary fact.

STONE: Well, of course I'm trying to do that. I'm writing about the American experience. It's very hard for me to keep politics out of what I write. I'm not an ideologue. I don't have an ideology, and yet I find it difficult to leave politics alone, I suppose because politics in America—politics of course anywhere—is the vehicle through which people attempt to act out their moral vision. I'm trying to render the American experience, which is particular, as there are specifically national ways of perceiving the world. The United States is a country which has always liked to see itself as representing a certain moral position. It's one of the countries in the world, like India and the Soviet Union and various others, that claim to represent a high moral purpose. At the same time, the United States and the people in it are very aware of the ways in which this claim to high moral purpose is compromised. This tension between the ways in which our pretensions, our protestations, of high moral purposes are compromised by the contradictions within the society is, in fact, the very stuff of American politics and a very large part of the American experience. We are all brought up with the idea that history, human events, is a kind of moral story. In this culture the basic book is the Bible. That's *the* book. And if you're brought up on the Bible, and even if we don't come from religious backgrounds, most of us have absorbed some of its basic assumptions from this society, and one of the basic assumptions is that history moves to a purpose. There is such a thing as progress. The will of God, the will of history, is represented in human events. There is a moral charge to a historical event. That's something we have always assumed. Everyone who's ever written about our history seems to have accepted that politicians have, of course, vulgarized it and utter moral prophecy all the time. But there's this constant assumption of high moral purpose by the practitioners of American politics. I think probably a bit more here than in other countries. Of course all politicians claim to represent historical progress. The way in which it's done in America, though, is rather special. I think we do it more shamelessly. Our politicians engage in moralizing more shamelessly. Our newspapers, our media, talk a lot about morality. In fact, it seems that just lately there's more talk of moral purpose and morality in general than perhaps we've ever had before. There's not a hell of a lot of it being practiced, as far as I can see, but there certainly is a lot of talk about it. And, I mean, this is one of the things I'm trying to render. The contradiction between this high moral purpose and American reality.

INTERVIEWER: The last line of one of your stories reads, "Momma's deluded." Do you think that there are any of your characters which are *not* deluded in some way or another?

STONE: Yes. There's always a character who is seeing as clearly as he or she can. Very often that character—I think, for example, Justin, in *A Flag for Sunrise*—really has a great deal of common sense. And she makes a rational decision to commit herself. She is a person given to commitment. She is, I think, an American who represents some of the best things about America, but she is undermined by the situation in which she finds herself. She's undermined by the other characters. Very often, I think, there are characters in my novels who are *not* deluded, who are as close to clarity as one gets. Frequently they find themselves, as in life, just undermined by these inescapable ambiguities that are involved in their relations with other people, or with the social situation in which they find themselves. It is very, very difficult to act morally and rationally at the same time. Usually one gives in the face of the other. One has to be a bit of an athlete of perception and a person of great strength and integrity to succeed in doing both.

INTERVIEWER: It just seems that the undermining is so complete in your novels that one might at the end come away wondering if, as one critic said in reference to *A Hall of Mirrors,* the message is "despair and die." And yet other readers have said that despite all the horrible things that are done by people to one another in the name of some of the finest ideals in Western culture, one cannot come away from your novels with a sense of a black vision about the universe. That it's just simply not there. How do you explain these two radically opposing views of your vision on the part of many close and careful readers?

STONE: *Always* in these novels people are trying to get out of the box they're in. As in life, they don't often succeed very well. But they are always catching glimmers of something outside themselves that may be able to save them. They are always looking for the areas in each other that are positive. They are looking for love. They don't often get it, or if they get it, they run into its multiple faces and are confused. But my message is not despair; my message is, find out how bad it gets and begin from there. These people are looking for a place to start from. They pay the price of that. But what I'm not saying is that every time you try to do something worthwhile, disaster descends on you; what I'm trying to underline is the great price one pays for action in the face of things as they are. I'm trying to define the tremendous difficulty of setting out to act decently. I mean, most people, even the worst of them, have some level in which they want to see themselves as decent people. They have aspirations. There is always, I think, an imminence of a breakthrough. And what I'm writing about—basically what's in the white space, perhaps—is that breakthrough. What form it takes, I don't know. The characters don't know. But they're vaguely aware of it. They're getting some sense that there's a level in which one can break out of this box. They don't succeed in doing it; I can't have them succeed because I don't know how they'll be able to do it. I just don't know any more than they do. But every time I get in with those people, sit down and write them and get in with them, and they take on a certain reality for me, I am with them in their struggle to break through to something beyond the frustration of our social situation and our individual selves.

INTERVIEWER: So then you do see Rheinhardt at the end of *Hall of Mirrors,* Marge and Converse at the end of *Dog Soldiers,* and Holliwell at the end of *A Flag for Sunrise* as being on that moment? It seems to be most clearly articulated in *A Flag for Sunrise.* Holliwell looks into the sun and sees the eye of the universe and has that universal perception that what the eye is seeing is in fact what your eye is seeing in that eye. It's a very compassionate vision of a young child standing there holding a Coke can; you see them, in fact, as children at birth at that point?

STONE: Well, I've always been taken with something that Malraux wrote in *Antimemoirs.* He talks about speaking with this old priest and he asks what the priest's sense of human life is, since he spent sixty years or so listening to confessions. And the priest says, "Well, in the first place, people are much more unhappy than one might think. And in the second, there is no such thing as a grown-up." In a way, I think that's true. We're not going to get anywhere by overlooking the difficulties that life presents us. We have got to start from an acceptance of the fact that we find ourselves beset, by our own natures which are imperfect, and by a world which is imperfect. We cannot simply decide to overlook and transcend these things in a casual way. If we try to do that we end up compounding our situation. I mean that's why revolutions, for the most part, turn on themselves and fail. It's why complacent moralism ends up being vapid and useless. It's why prophets almost always undo themselves and are finally revealed as agents of dualism. We have to accept the human condition for what it is. And my understanding of the human condition is something like this: there was this mud, this substance. It somehow came into existence. Over a period of millennia, it became conscious of itself. It stood up on legs and started walking around, and talking and thinking and having aspirations of one kind or another. Now this is a miracle, that the very mud of the earth could somehow come to consciousness. There is some kind of positive significance there. In what I write, I try to be aware of that, and that's why I think I'm not pushing a message of despair, because I try to have everything happen in these books against the background of that miracle. That's an unspoken positive dimension. We are just mud, finally, that has become conscious of itself. That's a tough condition.

INTERVIEWER: But "the jewel is in the lotus."

STONE: "The jewel is in the lotus." What the nature of the jewel is, I don't know, but I believe with Egan that it is.

INTERVIEWER: But I wonder if the "despair and die" readers of Robert Stone are seeing another side of the coin. You were saying earlier that we believe in a progressive sense in Western culture. That's it in a nutshell, isn't it? Our conflict with an Eastern sensibility, as in *A Passage to India,* the muddle of India, the inattention to vaccinations, to taking care of disease, to the things that we all grew up in this culture with. I wonder if the "despair and die" readers of Robert Stone are having difficulties with perceiving those two worldviews as being present in your work?

STONE: Well, I think so because people who interpret the underlying message in my writing as "despair and die" are mistaken. I mean that is not what I'm telling people, that's not what I'm writing about. I'm not writing about how the world is just too awful for words. The very act of writing is a positive act. The dynamic that's present in most of what I write is *perception,* and I believe in the value of perception. I believe in a perception that faces things as they are, that looks it all in the eye. I believe very much in common sense. I think certainly it is better to have vaccinations and plumbing and leisure and affluence for working people and farming people, and the more that you can accomplish in that direction the better things will be. But embracing the philosophy that somehow, automatically, God is on our side, and things are just going to get better because that's the structure of history, I think that's a big mistake. That's what I want to bring into question. I mean, what I am pushing for is that what keeps us going is our perception, our ability to reason down to basics, to somehow not delude ourselves into thinking we are more than what we are.

INTERVIEWER: The terms "allegory" and "morality play" get called up over and over again in reference to your novels. What affinities do you feel with those forms, or, if not the forms, the way of looking at the world which those forms represent?

STONE: Well, allegory is something that you do almost unconsciously. The best allegories are not deliberate, but are stumbled on. In a way, I think it's less a matter of allegory than metaphor. Individual lives can often be taken for metaphors for the universal situation. So it's not so much—I don't know how much I employ allegory. But I certainly do use certain situations as metaphors for the "basic situation" as I see it.

INTERVIEWER: Is there a suggestiveness in your names, for instance, "Holliwell"?

STONE: Yeah, sure, Holliwell is twofold. He's Frank Merriwell gone to seed. But his name also literally means "a holy well."

INTERVIEWER: Not a hollow well.

STONE: No. Well, there's a kind of hollowness too. I mean you can't always control what's coming into your mind. I was thinking of Frank Merriwell and I was thinking of holy wells, in the sense of somebody making a pilgrimage to a holy well. There are all kinds of holy wells. There's the kind that he is, in fact, named after, the ones in the British Isles, and then there are the holy sacrificial wells of the Mayans, which are less attractive in their origins. But there's a certain kind of hollowness in that name, too.

INTERVIEWER: Who's Frank Merriwell?

STONE: Oh, he was the guy who played for Yale in those old books—*Frank Merriwell at Yale.* He was an all-purpose, all-American sportsman at Yale in books that I think were written in the 1890s. An all-American hero of popular fiction in the nineties.

INTERVIEWER: What about Pablo Tabor? The word "tabor" means "drum."

STONE: It also is the name of an extreme Hussite leader in the wars of religion, about the time of the Reformation. The Taborites were a kind of peasant army who fought the local nobility and also fought the church. They were one of the extreme factions in the religious wars of central Europe.

INTERVIEWER: What about Rainey and Rheinhardt? Morgan Rainey and Rheinhardt.

STONE: Well, with Rheinhardt I was thinking of Django Reinhardt, the gypsy guitarist. I was writing about a musician. And Rainey was a name that I just associated with the Gulf Coast, and the Gulf Coast sounds.

INTERVIEWER: Morgan Rainey is one of these characters of clarity, is he not? I would question whether or not he was deluded by drugs or booze as opposed to ideals.

STONE: It's his own nature, his own rather masochistic vision of virtue that undoes him. I think the clearest-thinking person in that book is Geraldine, who is totally a victim of circumstances. She sees things clearly enough. Rheinhardt seems to promise something to her that she very much wants, but she is the clearest-eyed of the characters in the book. She's most completely a victim of circumstances.

INTERVIEWER: Let's go back to *A Flag for Sunrise.* There's the Pablo/Negus episode versus the Pablo/Holliwell episode. I want to know if you see a moral difference between those two episodes. In the first we have Pablo and Negus as the last survivors of the whole Callahan crew. Then you have Holliwell, the last survivor of the revolutionaries and the missionary-camp characters—the two survivors. In the first of the two, Pablo throws Negus overboard, and in the second Holliwell throws Pablo overboard.

STONE: It's that they're in situations where it's impossible, trust is impossible. They're impelled by fear and ignorance to destroy each other, which is a situation that a lot of the world is in, or close to being in, right now, so there in their individual relationships they just echo. Not to be too portentous about it, their situation is a bit like the situation in which the nations of the world find themselves right now. They're operating on ignorance and fear. Even Holliwell finally gives in to his own fear.

INTERVIEWER: I'm maybe most fascinated by the character of Pablo in *A Flag for Sunrise.* To me, he's the most problematic character in terms of the way people read you. To me, Pablo is one of the scariest people I've ever run across in the world of fiction. My feeling when Holliwell threw him overboard was that Holliwell knew exactly what to do if he was going to survive. And indeed he didn't dare go to sleep or Pablo would probably kill him at that point. On the other hand, in some ways we might see Pablo as one of the positive characters in this book, and see Holliwell as a "hollow man," that his act is selfish, stupid, and self-indulgent at that point.

STONE: Well, I think both of those things are true. There's meant to be room there for—I mean, it's all true. Pablo is really crazy and dangerous. On the other hand, Pablo really means well. He always sees himself as a victim. I mean, when he is going to steal something, he's stealing because he thinks he's entitled. He sees the other people in the world as enormously powerful, and himself as a constant victim. If he steals something, it's only him trying to get his own back.

INTERVIEWER: But he's a speed freak.

STONE: He's a speed freak, he's a sociopath. He sees himself as meaning well. He sees himself as constantly having to defend himself by violence. At that point in the book, he really thinks that he has found a friend, just before Holliwell kills him. His belief is that he's completing his spiritual education, which he really believes in. He thinks he's found a friend who has addressed one of the central problems of his, Pablo's, life. Of course, he hasn't found a friend. He's found his ultimate enemy. And although it is wise for Holliwell to kill him, it is much safer for Holliwell to kill this dangerous speed freak, it is also Holliwell finding himself in the last position that he ever would think to find himself, as assassin, as murderer. So he is guilty of Pablo's murder, even though his doing it was not an altogether unwise act of self-preservation. And although Pablo, an hour later, might decide that killing Holliwell was absolutely necessary, he at that moment thinks he's found a friend. Okay, I'm making a comment on how it is with people.

INTERVIEWER: You've mentioned common sense several times, and yet it seems to me that one of the central things about your novels that is absolutely pertinent to the condition of experience that most people of our generation find themselves in is that common sense doesn't seem to mean a darn thing.

STONE: That's the trouble, because people go for the answers that have capital letters. Common sense is very hard to bring to bear. It's like common decency. Common decency and common sense are very hard to bring to bear on the large scale.

INTERVIEWER: It's just that all the time, as people commit acts of decency in the world of your novels, anything good or bad could come out of it at any time. The good things that happen are random.

STONE: Right. As with so many things in history in general, and your history and my history.

INTERVIEWER: But I think thus the confusion that readers come up against—

STONE: Right.

INTERVIEWER: —in trying to figure out the nature of your vision. They know it's there, it's present everywhere, and you know it's not bogus. But it's very difficult to understand.

STONE: I can see where people might mistake what I am doing for the rather trivial exercise of saying that life is tough and no good. But it's just as trivial to say life is shit as it is to say life is roses. I mean, I pursue those questions because I'm interested in possible answers. But I really have to deal with the world and render the world as I experience it. I see a great deal of human life limited, poisoned, frustrated, by fear and ignorance and the violence that comes from it. And I feel, consequently, that I have to address it. And I think some of the people I write about are constantly trying to get above that and get around it somehow. They're always seeing these glimmers of transcendence which may be something, in fact, that is beyond ordinary life, or it may be the better part of their own natures, or it may be the promise of care, love, concern from other people.

INTERVIEWER: You're praised for being a writer in whom craft and vision meet, and yet it seems that lines in the contemporary fiction scene are drawn nowadays between the two. I think particularly of the running debate between William Gass and John Gardner over the question of "moral fiction." To what extent, in your view, is language per se the business of the novelist?

STONE: I don't know what the business of the novelist is if it isn't language. The way I learned it, you're supposed to have both. You're supposed to be able to write and you're supposed to be able to think. Language is the medium, the music. Language makes the spell, it makes the situation, it makes the characters. You can't somehow get around the level of language in literature. It *is* language. It's a way of using language to invoke issues, individuals. I mean, music can constitute a vision, and painting can constitute a vision, and literature constitutes a vision. You can't have good paintings without paint, skillfully applied. You can't have music without a sense of sound, and you can't have literature without being able to wrangle the language.

INTERVIEWER: What do you think about that debate, though, of the writers who insist that politics, morality, transmitting social values and things, that that's a thing of the past as far as fiction is concerned, and that the only serious writers are those who are purely pushing language to its ultimate?

STONE: I don't feel that I have any part in that argument, because I think that you're supposed to do both. A well-intentioned writer with a broad moral vision who can't write very well isn't very interesting. A writer who can write well but who has no subjects and isn't interested in reflecting life and people's lives isn't very interesting either.

INTERVIEWER: One general criticism of your work, although critics seem hard-pressed to find things to criticize in your work, is that it's too heavily plotted. Number one, how do you plot your novels, and from whom, if anyone, do you think you most learned plotting; and number two, do you think that's ever a legitimate criticism of a writer?

STONE: Well, my favorite novels were in the grand tradition, in the old tradition. I think you have to tell a story. That's one of the reasons that people read books: they want to have a story. I would argue with a sensibility so refined that it can take its satisfactions beyond the level of storytelling. I yield to no one in my admiration for Beckett. But Beckett is a teller of stories, too. That it's heavily plotted, well, I do believe in plot. And I suppose I learned to some degree from all the nineteenth-century masters. I think I have some roots there that moved me very much when I was younger, when I was reading.

INTERVIEWER: Care to name some names?

STONE: If I name the names, I feel like I'm trying to put myself in the same league with these people, which I'm not. I learned a lot from Conrad. I loved Stendhal, Flaubert. Certainly in the novels of the early twentieth century there's a great deal of story, of plotting. The plot in *The Great Gatsby* is a tremendously important part of the novel, and that's the American novel that at this moment, I most admire. Its plot, which is so heavy with metaphor, is a very important part of its effect. So situation and plot, for me, are metaphor. I have to entertain myself while I am writing a novel, and in order to entertain myself, I have to tell a story, to keep the illusion of human event going. I don't *like* plot all that much. I sometimes find having to go back and say to myself, he does this because she did that because he did that, is a little tiresome, but you do try to recapitulate human causality.

INTERVIEWER: A lot of people have brought up Graham Greene in reference to your work, and yet you've not mentioned him today in this list of writers.

STONE: I rather like *The Power and the Glory,* but Greene—the trouble with Graham Greene—is he was one of the writers who, when I went to school, I was adjured to read. I went to a Catholic school and he was a Catholic writer. But I never read a lot of Greene in the years that I was reading the writers who influenced me a great deal. I think our concerns are really very different. There's some superficial resemblances. Especially in *A Flag for Sunrise,* you have the idea of a priest staggering around drunk under a palm tree. The whiskey priest. But I think that's all very superficial. I don't think there are any stylistic influences. Admirers of Greene would say that's because Greene is so much better a writer than I am. I myself don't agree with that assessment.

INTERVIEWER: How do you plot your novels, or should I ask, what's the germ?

STONE: I start with the situation and then I have the people. I believe that, in a novel, character is literally fate. Once you know who the people are, you know what's going to happen. I know the beginning in the situation, and I usually know the end. I don't always know what's in the middle. I find out as I go along. It comes out of the people.

INTERVIEWER: But you do have an end.

STONE: Usually have an end in mind, yeah.

INTERVIEWER: That's very different.

STONE: I don't know. Maybe it is. I've never really asked other novelists how they do it. I can surprise myself sometimes. I didn't know, for example, that that quarrel between Dieter and Hicks was going to break out. The day I started writing that piece I didn't realize that was going to happen. It just developed as I wrote the dialogue and imagined myself into the situation. I'd have to say also that Dickens is a writer who I think had an enormous influence on me and who was, in a way, a *haluciné,* inasmuch as he could see his characters and his situations, he could really *see* them and he makes the reader do the same. Dickens very much entertained himself and his readers with plot, and so do I.

INTERVIEWER: Of course you're an extremely different writer from somebody like Henry James. But when you said that character is fate, that's what he thought, too. And you know the novel that he felt was his largest failure was *The American,* and that's what he said was wrong, that he started with an ending. He felt that there's a certain inevitability, but that things have to play themselves out and by definition, if you start with an ending, you're going to come up violating the novel's sense of felt life.

STONE: You have to be flexible; you can't be rigid. You can find your way to a different ending. I mean it's nice to have the ending there even if you don't use it, if you see what I mean.

INTERVIEWER: But you started, for instance, with that idea of Holliwell in the boat at the end, and casting the jewel from Pablo's pocket—

STONE: No, not that precisely. I think I had a general sense of how things were going to end up, well for Justin, anyway.

INTERVIEWER: That does seem inevitable.

STONE: Well, plotting this was quite different then than it would have been now, because when this was all mapped out, there was no revolution in Nicaragua, let alone in El Salvador. So this all precedes. It comes out of trips to Central America that I had made in the middle seventies.

INTERVIEWER: *A Flag for Sunrise* preceded the facts of what's going on down there now?

STONE: Yeah. But you didn't have to be incredibly prescient to see all this going on. I mean, the Church was already getting itself in trouble by organizing cooperatives and so forth. No American missionaries had been killed or anything like that, nor had the archbishop been killed. In fact, Duarte was a good guy back in the middle seventies. He had been denied the presidency after the election, and there were riots in El Salvador in his behalf at that point. So, it's true that it preceded all these—the headlines, considerably, and the revolutions. But I don't lay claim to any great prescience.

INTERVIEWER: This is so often true, in fiction, that fiction precedes reality. It happens a lot.

STONE: Yeah, it does.

INTERVIEWER: Some critics feel that you lost control of the structure in both *Hall of Mirrors* and *Dog Soldiers.* Do you think that's true, or are you satisfied with how they turned out structurally?

STONE: Yeah, I guess I lost control of their structure. I'm pretty satisfied with the way they turned out. I didn't have a sense of being out of control.

INTERVIEWER: What about that middle scene in *A Flag for Sunrise*? It's the only time we see the revolutionaries, other than glimpses of Godoy. Some readers have questions about that scene, the way it comes and goes and you never see any of those people again.

STONE: It violates the traditional mode of the novel. I wanted a look at the revolutionaries. I wanted to put everything in the perspective of the revolution itself. And I wanted to make it—I wanted to also employ what I knew about political forces in Central America. Certainly it is a violation of the traditional mode of the novel, but I figured I could get away with it, and I think I did. I think it's worthwhile.

INTERVIEWER: By traditional, you mean the organic expectations of—

STONE: Yeah, it violates point of view. It violates the tradition of consistent point of view. It violates the structure inasmuch as we go from one central character to another and move along in time, and all of a sudden in the middle of this book we have these other characters planning a revolution. But I thought it was necessary to get that perspective and to put them in, and so I did, without—well, I won't say without worrying about it too much, I worried about it a bit, but I thought if it was an effective scene, and had its element of verisimilitude, then I would put it there and keep it there.

INTERVIEWER: What about the Mennonite boy? The same question has come up with the Mennonite. Some readers see him as being really only there to illuminate some central flaw or some central delusion in Egan's character at the end, and yet he runs all the way through. Did you feel you were taking a chance at all with him?

STONE: Yes, I did. I had him there, I think, to represent yet another manifestation of humanity in extremis, in delusion.

INTERVIEWER: What about the fact that some eight years or so has come between the three novels? Does that mean that you work slowly, or does that mean other things have taken your time, or that you rest for a while?

STONE: It's about seven years between them—biblical cycles. It means that I work very slowly and carefully, that I really have to spend a lot of time with plot, that I'm inefficient, my method of working is inefficient. It probably means that I'm lazy. I feel like I'm working all the time. I can't imagine how I can work so much, put out so much effort, and come up with only three novels. I do tend to put everything into the novel. I think I could've made more novels out of the material, if I wanted to write novels in a different style. But because I seem to be enslaved to the idea of the grand novel that I imprinted as an impressionable kid, it just takes me that long to do it.

INTERVIEWER: How long has it taken?

STONE: Well, in fact, I think I did *Dog Soldiers* in about two and a half years. The expanse of time between publication is seven years, but I did that one in two and a half years. I really didn't know what I was going to do next. I was working as a freelance journalist and so forth. I *was* doing other things. But when I got down to it, it took me two and a half years. *A Flag for Sunrise* took me a long time, I don't know, four years or so—too long, longer than it should've taken. I'm not pleased with having this space of time between novels.

INTERVIEWER: What is your routine? How do you work?

STONE: I get up in the morning. I get up really early, and I work as long as I can, I try to get as many pages done, either in rough or smooth. I do two versions. First I do it in rough, then I do it in smooth, then I rewrite the whole thing. But I always start in the morning. I don't usually work at night.

INTERVIEWER: Did you get a whole draft of *A Flag for Sunrise* before you went back and started retouching anything, or did you work in pieces of it?

STONE: I rewrite everything at least once. Then I'll leave a section that I think has some problems, and when I get some time I'll go back and work on it. I did that with the Naftali section in *A Flag for Sunrise.* I must've done that about six or seven times. Then when I have the whole thing done, I go through it and try to find what I think is wrong structurally or in terms of the writing in a given section and make myself a checklist and go through the whole book and do rewrites as I see them to be necessary.

INTERVIEWER: Many of your book jackets refer to, and I'm quoting, your "heavy involvement in the counter-culture in the 60s." Would you mind—what was your heavy involvement in the counterculture in the sixties?

STONE: Well, I—my heavy involvement with the counterculture is—I don't know. I was a friend, and still am a friend, of Ken Kesey's and was around California when the Kesey gang was there. Many of my friends are from those days, who I sort of grew up with, or grew old with, or whatever. I was just another character with literary ambitions. Sometimes I feel like I went to a party one day in 1963 and the party spilled out and rolled down the street until it covered the whole country and changed the world.

INTERVIEWER: How'd you come to meet those guys?

STONE: I had a fellowship at Stanford and I lived near Perry Lane where it was all going on, and Ken lived there. As I say, I went to a party one day, and that was the counterculture.

INTERVIEWER: What's the story with you and the military?

STONE: I joined the navy when I was seventeen. I was in the service till I was twenty-one.

INTERVIEWER: Where'd you then go to school?

STONE: Started at NYU. I went there for less than a year and left, and went south, and worked a whole lot of crazy jobs and wanted to write and really didn't. I wrote a lot of poetry and read it to jazz in the days of poetry and jazz down in New Orleans. And it was quite a while, I think, before I was able to get enough of the sense of life lived in time to begin a novel. But

I finally did, about 1961, begin to write *Hall of Mirrors.* Of course that was interrupted by my "heavy involvement in the counter-culture." I was being involved in the counterculture when I should have been writing. So it took me kind of a while to finish that.

INTERVIEWER: Going back before that, what is your family background, and where you're from, and where you went to school before you went to college?

STONE: I went to Catholic schools in New York. My mother's family had been in the rug business in Brooklyn for generations. My grandfather was fairly well known, a guy named Alex Grant who was a legendary figure on the Brooklyn waterfront. He was a chief engineer and captain of a tugboat. A lot of his relatives and my relatives worked on tugs, worked on the New York waterfront.

INTERVIEWER: When did you start to write? Or when did you have a sense of vocation? When did you receive the call?

STONE: Oh, I think fairly early on, although I wasn't in a position to recognize it. I always liked to write, but it took me years to decide that it was something I might be able to make my living doing. But as soon as I reached the point that I saw that I had made no provisions for any kind of alternative career and had no academic credentials of any kind, and was barely capable of delivering a day's work for a day's pay in any area other than making up stories or putting one word in front of another, then I had a vocation, I mean I had a vocation or else. I had pretty much burned my bridges.

INTERVIEWER: When did this happen?

STONE: Oh, I guess in my early twenties.

INTERVIEWER: Was that when you began *A Hall of Mirrors*?

STONE: Yeah. More toward my mid-twenties. But I was a would-be writer from the time I was out of the service, which was when I was twenty-one.

INTERVIEWER: Are you a practicing religious person in the formal sense? Are you a Catholic?

STONE: Not in the formal sense. Sometimes it seems to me that I am some kind of Catholic. I hadn't made my Easter duty last year, so technically—I think you still have to do that. You're supposed to go to church, take

Communion at least once a year, so I haven't done that. So I'm sort of a fellow traveler of Christianity.

INTERVIEWER: One reviewer has pointed out that you write with a lot more care and regard for both women and children than is common of most men of your generation. How do you account for that?

STONE: Well, I was raised pretty much by a woman. My mother was the parent who really raised me. I was a father fairly young. I don't know. I never found myself in an adversary relationship with women. I believe that a certain amount of tension between the sexes is not altogether a bad thing. But I think there is a surprising amount of woman-hating on the part of a great many men, and maybe a lot of man-hating on the part of a lot of women. I was not caught up in that. I have not felt threatened by women as a group of people. On the contrary, I've always felt pretty good about women. I was real fond of my mother, who was a character. I never hesitated to write about women characters and I hope I won't hesitate to do it. The human condition is universal.

INTERVIEWER: Do you feel an affinity with any particular novelists or group of novelists among your contemporaries? How do you place yourself—with your friends such as Ken Kesey or with writers like Toni Morrison or the South American writers, the magical realists?

STONE: I don't have any sense of being part of a school. Most of us, of my generation, have read largely the same writers, were influenced by them in different ways, and then went off to do totally different things. I don't feel part of any party or group. I don't oppose one way of writing and advocate another. As I feel that I'm without political ideology—not without political opinions, but without political ideology—I also don't feel myself as belonging to any literary camp or opposing any literary camp. I don't mean to be sort of, you know, universally and superserviceably agreeable; I just don't feel that I'm part of a group or camp or school, one as opposed to another.

INTERVIEWER: Do you enjoy the act of writing?

STONE: Yes, I do.

INTERVIEWER: Is there an aspect of writing to slake off dread?

STONE: Well, you do it because you need to do it. It's too hard to do if you don't need to do it. People who write are driven. Otherwise nobody would do it. I mean, I was warned when I began writing that it was very, very hard. I thought it was easy. I thought, well, you don't have to show up anywhere and go to work, and you can make up stories, and so forth. But I was warned, rightly, that it was very, very hard work. All writers who regularly write, I think, are driven.

Jamaica Kincaid

Jamaica Kincaid was born Elaine Potter Richardson in 1949 in St. John's Antigua, West Indies, the daughter of a cabinetmaker. At the age of seventeen she left Antigua for New York to work as an au pair. Shortly thereafter she struck out on her own, eventually finding her way onto the staff of the New Yorker *as a regular contributor in the 1970s to "The Talk of the Town" through her association with the writer George Trow, an experience she says taught her to write. She eventually married composer Allen Shawn of the* New Yorker *Shawns, and currently lives in Bennington, Vermont, where this interview was conducted in April 1991.*

Kincaid's career as a fiction writer began in 1983 with At the Bottom of the River, *a collection of stories about her girlhood in Antigua. Her writing offers a vivid reminder of the perennial vitality and value of autobiographical fiction. Her novel* Annie John *(1985) chronicles an intense relationship between a mother and daughter, including a closely observed psychological portrait of the division that can come between a mother and daughter at puberty. Its motifs are love, defiance, ambivalence, and rebellion. The novel* Lucy *(1990) begins where* Annie John *ended and follows her to her life in New York. Kincaid's most recent work is* The Autobiography of My Mother *(1996). Her stories are filled with dialects of the West Indies, Europe, and America. Sometimes imitating the structure of Caribbean folktales, they are lyrical and surrealistic, moving from finely detailed realism into memory and dream. Henry Louis Gates Jr. has said of her that she writes "like she invented the English language."*

INTERVIEWER: Ms. Kincaid, in the novel *Lucy,* you give Lucy Josephine Potter one of your birth names and your own birthday. How closely do the facts of Lucy's biography match your own?

KINCAID: She had to have a birth date so why not mine? She was going to have a name that would refer to the slave part of her history, so why not my own? I write about myself for the most part, and about things that have happened to me. Everything I say is true, and everything I say is not true. You couldn't admit any of it to a court of law. It would not be good evidence.

INTERVIEWER: Your father, like Lucy's, was a cabinetmaker, and your own mother married a much older man with whom she had three sons several years after you were born.

KINCAID: Yes, that is true. But here's an example of something that is true and not true: in "The Long Rain" the girl has an illness—a rite of passage, I guess you might call it—when she's fourteen years old. I had an illness like that when I was seven years old, and I was writing about that illness. I root my fear of rodents in that time of my life. I used to lie on my bed and look up at the ceiling, and I saw hundreds of rats running around the ceiling. It must have been only one or two, but they seemed to go around like a merry-go-round. It must have been a hallucination. I was left alone, and like the girl I did get up and wash and powder the photographs, but some of the photographs described in the book could not have existed when I was seven years old. The confirmation photograph, for instance, did not exist. I don't aim to be factual. I aim to be true to something, but it's not necessarily the facts.

INTERVIEWER: Where did the story of the green figs and the black snake come from?

KINCAID: That was a story my mother told me about herself, but the outcome of that story as it is in the book is not what really happened. I tried to write a story about my mother and myself, and there were incidents that I perceived as betrayal, at the time, though I don't necessarily believe that now. In my writing I suppose I'm trying to understand how I got to be the person I am. The truth is important, but it's a certain kind of truth.

INTERVIEWER: Even though *Annie John* begins and ends chronologically, it's not built on a linear model. A single one-time happening recurs in several episodes, taken from different points of view, within different contexts. Did you conceive of it as a novel or as a sequence of short stories?

KINCAID: I didn't conceive of it as either one. I just write. I come to the end, I start again. I come to the end, I start again. And then sometimes I come to the end, and there is no starting again. In my mind there is no question of who will do what and when. Sometimes I've written the end of something before I've written the beginning. Whatever a novel is, I'm not it, and whatever a short story is, I'm not it. If I had to follow these forms, I couldn't write. I'm really interested in breaking the form.

INTERVIEWER: It is interesting that a story your mother told about herself as a girl—walking home with a bunch of green figs on her head in which a snake is hiding—becomes a parable that the mother tells the daughter in *Annie John,* to try to induce her to confess.

KINCAID: What did I know? I was writing this story and I had a lot of information about my family and their history, and I used it in this way. My mother used to tell me a lot of things about herself. It's perhaps one of the ways in which I became a writer. Why I used that incident, I can't really say. It was conscious and it was not conscious. A psychiatrist would see that it's not an accident that I picked that particular one to speak of seduction and treachery. As we know, the serpent is associated with betrayal.

INTERVIEWER: In *Annie John,* Annie is praised by her teachers, and she even holds them spellbound with her writing at one point. When you were a girl in Antigua, did you have teachers who encouraged you and thought that you were special?

KINCAID: Yes and no. I was considered a bright child. I was always first, second, or third, and when I was third it was considered disappointing. But to say people encouraged me, no. No one was encouraged. Some of us might go off to the University of the West Indies to study, or to England, but then what would we do? There's nothing in Antigua. I am from a poor family, and most of the girls who went off to university were from privileged families. Only boys could go off to university if they were from my background. If I had been a boy, there's no question that I would have been singled out.

INTERVIEWER: So it was that you were a girl, as much as anything, that narrowed your opportunities?

KINCAID: It was. I can see that now. The other day I was reading the newspaper from my home—the government is very corrupt—everybody's always got their face in the newspaper for some terrible thing—and one of the pictures was a boy I used to go to school with. He and his brother once beat me up because I came in ahead of one of them in an exam. They thought that I had cheated; if I hadn't come in ahead of them, whatever glittering prize—a book of poetry or something—would have gone to one of them.

INTERVIEWER: You had to have cheated because you were a girl.

KINCAID: I had to have cheated. But what happened to him? He's a member of the cabinet. There's a girl that I went to school with who in fact is the "Gwen" character in *Annie John.* She was a brilliant, brilliant girl but nothing much happened to her. She's a supervisor somewhere. There's no question, if she and I were boys, that we would have fared much better. As it turns out, for me, it didn't matter.

INTERVIEWER: You grew up in the British-colonial tradition, reading John Milton's *Paradise Lost* and the Bible. Are you conscious of the ways in which that kind of literature has had an impact on your work?

KINCAID: People have told me so, and when I read it out loud, I become aware of the influence of the things I read as a child—images from Christian mythology and *Paradise Lost.* All of this has left me very uncomfortable with ambiguity. My sense of the world is that things are right and wrong, and that when you're wrong you get thrown into a dark pit and you pay forever. You try very hard not to do a wrong thing, and if you do, there's very little forgiveness. I was brought up to understand that English traditions were right and mine were wrong. Within the life of an English person there was always clarity, and within an English culture there was always clarity, but within my life and culture was ambiguity. A person who is dead in England is dead. A person where I come from who is dead might not be dead. I was taught to think of ambiguity as magic, a shadiness and an illegitimacy, not the real thing of Western civilization.

INTERVIEWER: That's the way you were taught, and so now that's your inclination.

KINCAID: Yes, yes. The thing that I am branded with and the thing that I am denounced for, I now claim as my own. I am illegitimate, I am ambiguous. In some way I actually claim the right to ambiguity, and the right to clarity. It does me no good to say, "Well, I reject this and I reject that." I feel free to use everything, or not, as I choose. I was forced to memorize John Milton and that was a very painful thing. But I'm not going to make myself forget John Milton because it involves a painful thing. I find John Milton very beautiful, and I'm glad that I know it. I'm sorry that the circumstances of how I got to know it were so horrid, but, since I know it, I know it and I claim every right to use it.

INTERVIEWER: One book that seems to incorporate different cultural expectations and interpretations of the same events is *Lucy.* In one scene Lucy tells Louis and Mariah her dream. Their response, the Western white response, is to look at each other and say, "Freud lives," or words to that effect.

KINCAID: The people in Lucy's society live for dreaming. They believe that waking life is informed by dream life. Where I come from some people act only on their dreams. All their nonsleeping actions are based on what happened to them when they were asleep. Louis and Mariah were in fact saying that her perception of the world was not valid, that she needed Freud.

INTERVIEWER: My Milton professor once described the imagery in John Milton as being "highly visual, nonvisual" imagery—because of Milton's blindness. You couldn't draw a picture of what John Milton describes, yet it is highly visual. Do you feel an affinity between that notion and the style of *At the Bottom of the River*?

KINCAID: One of the things that inspired me to write was English poets, even though I had never seen England. It's as if I were a blind person too. When I was about ten years old I read *Jane Eyre,* and at one point she describes the evening as the "gloaming." She's describing something English, something I would never see until I was thirty-odd years old. I got stuck on that word, and eventually found a way to use it in *At the Bottom of the River.* Then I was free of it. It was important for me to have written those stories, because it freed me of an obsession with a certain kind of language. I memorized Wordsworth when I was a child, Keats, all sorts of things. It was an attempt to make me into a certain kind of person, the kind of person they had no use for, anyway. An educated black person. I got stuck with a lot of things, so I ended up using them.

INTERVIEWER: So you see *At the Bottom of the River* as a kind of catharsis?

KINCAID: I would not have ever, ever been able to say, "You know, I really need to write this, I really need to get rid of these images," but that's what I was doing. A sort of desire for a perfect place, a perfect situation, comes from English romantic poetry. It described a perfection which one longed for, and of course the perfection that one longed for was England. I longed for England myself. These things were a big influence, and it was important for me to get rid of them. Then I could actually look at the place I'm from.

INTERVIEWER: And what did you find there?

KINCAID: In the place I'm from you don't have much room. You have the sea. If you step on the sea, you sink. The only thing the sea can do is take you away. People living on a tiny island are not expected to have deep thoughts about how they live, their right to live. You can have little conflicts, disagreements about what side of the street to walk on, but you cannot disagree that perhaps there should not be a street there. You cannot disagree about fundamental things, which is what an artist would do. All they're left with is a kind of pastoral beauty, a kind of natural beauty, and wonderful trinkets. They make nice hats. They catch fish in an old-fashioned way. It's all aesthetic, but it has no thinking to it. They cannot think. They will not allow themselves to think. They might have to change things, and they can't bear it.

INTERVIEWER: Was it necessary for you to leave Antigua to become a writer?

KINCAID: Oh, absolutely. It's no accident that most West Indian writers do not live in the West Indies all the time. It's the source of their art, but they can't live there. The place is full of the most sewerlike corruption you ever saw. The ones who live there become obsessed with politics, and almost always stop writing. And you can't blame them, you know. There is simply no way to stay there and write. People there don't really read. They have cable television, thanks to America. You couldn't make a living there, you couldn't be supported economically, to begin with. But you wouldn't be supported spiritually, either. These are not places that support people. I was attempting to do this thing that, as far as I know, no one in Antigua had attempted to do. Part of the reason I changed my name was so that they wouldn't know I was writing. I was afraid I would be laughed at, though it would not have stopped me. Nothing has made me not do what I wanted to do.

INTERVIEWER: So you changed your name to disguise yourself so that you could write. How did you pick the name Jamaica Kincaid?

KINCAID: It had no significance other than it was useful, to protect me from things. It was one of those things you do in the middle of the night. In those days we used to smoke marijuana or drink. I can't remember which one we were doing. If someone should say, "Well, you know she used to smoke marijuana," they should know that I don't mind that anybody knows. I try not to have too many secrets.

INTERVIEWER: You're not going to try to get appointed to the Supreme Court?

KINCAID: Or become secretary of defense. Or marry the president. My husband is not going to be the president. It was just one of many things I was doing in my life to make a break with my past.

INTERVIEWER: Perhaps I am identifying you too strongly with your characters, but Lucy talks about the fact that she realizes she's inventing herself when she starts studying photography, and you too studied photography at a certain point after you got here.

KINCAID: I didn't have the words for it, but yes, I was inventing myself. I didn't make up a past that I didn't have. I just made my present different from my past. How did I really do that? Just a few years off the banana boat basically, and there I was doing one crazy thing after another. How was I not afraid? The crucial thing was that I would not communicate with my family. Somehow I knew that was the key to anything I wanted to make of myself. I could not be with people who knew me so well that they knew just what I was capable of. I had to be with people who thought whatever I said went.

INTERVIEWER: Do you feel like you were running for your life in the fiction by telling the mother/daughter story from different perspectives?

KINCAID: It was the thing I knew. Quite possibly if I had had another kind of life I would not have been moved to write. That was the immediate thing, the immediate oppression, I knew. I wanted to free myself of that.

INTERVIEWER: It must have taken a great amount of focus and self-determination to become a writer.

KINCAID: I wouldn't describe myself as someone with focus and self-determination. Those are words and descriptions I shy away from. I consider them, in fact, sort of false. I find ambition to achieve unpleasant. The ambition I have is to write well. I don't have an ambition to be successful. I have an ambition to eat, which I find quite different from an ambition to be successful though I think in America the two are rather bonded together.

INTERVIEWER: When you came to the United States to be a maid did you have an agenda?

KINCAID: No. I did not know what would happen to me. I was just leaving, with great bitterness in my heart—a very hard heart— toward everybody I'd ever known, but I could not have articulated why. It's a mystery to my family why I feel this way, because they see nothing wrong with what happened to me. If I had remained a servant, I would not have been surprised. I would have been in great agony, but I would not have been surprised. I knew that I wanted something, but I did not know what. I knew I did not want convention. I wanted to risk something.

INTERVIEWER: You've done a very American thing. Like Huck Finn, you "lit out for the territory."

KINCAID: What good luck it was that I did light out for American territory and not Britain. I do not think that I would have been allowed this act of self-invention, which is very American, in Europe—certainly not in English-speaking Europe. When I came to America, I came from a place where most of the people looked like me, so I wasn't too concerned with the color of my skin. If I'd gone to England I could only have been concerned with the color of my skin.

INTERVIEWER: More so than here?

KINCAID: Much more so. I was not used to American racial attitudes, so whenever they were directed at me I did not recognize them, and if I didn't recognize them they were meaningless. I had no feeling about my own race. No feeling about my color. I didn't like it or not like it; I just accepted it the way I accept my eyes. I'm sure people denied me things because of the color of my skin, but I didn't know it, so I just went on. That was not my problem. I didn't know that there were very few black people writing for the *New Yorker*, so I wasn't troubled by that. I actually knew nothing about the *New Yorker*—its history, or its prominence in American literature—when I was taken to meet the editor. I was just a fool treading where angels feared to go.

INTERVIEWER: You wrote the "Talk of the Town" column for about four years. How did this come to be?

KINCAID: How did I come to write for the *New Yorker*? George Trow befriended me—I think that is how I would put it—and was very generous and kind and loving. He thought I was funny, and he would take me around to parties. I was so grateful, because I was very poor. Sometimes the only meal I ate was those little cocktail things. He would write about me in "Talk of the Town." He took me to meet Mr. Shawn, and I started to write for the *New Yorker.* I gave George my impressions of an event, and they appeared in the magazine just as I wrote them. That was how I discovered what my own writing was. It was just all a matter of luck, chance.

INTERVIEWER: Were you George Trow's "sassy black friend"?

KINCAID: I was his "sassy black friend," which didn't offend me at all. I seemed to be sassy, I said these things that he thought were sassy, and I was black.

INTERVIEWER: How do you think the writing that you did for "The Talk of the Town" prepared you for the fiction?

KINCAID: It did two things. It showed me how to write, and it allowed me to write in my own voice. The *New Yorker* no longer has that kind of power, but at one time it could take any individual piece of writing, no matter how eccentric the writing was, and without changing so much as a punctuation mark, the piece became the standard of the *New Yorker.* It had such power of personality. So there I was, writing anonymously in this strange voice, and it looked like the *New Yorker.* It was a wonderful thing for me because I was edited by this brilliant editor, this brilliant man, Mr. William Shawn, who became my father-in-law.

INTERVIEWER: Later. We have to say later.

KINCAID: Yes, he was very keen on not appearing to practice nepotism. Anyway, I had this wonderful editor and what I had to do to keep him interested was write clearly and keep my personality. And I did it. I could make him understand what I had to say. I doubt very much that I would have turned out to be the writer I am without him. He often bought my bad "Talk" stories, and didn't print them, but paid me for them, just so I could have some money to live on. The *New Yorker,* you know, used to support writers. Sometimes it didn't work out, but some of us kept on going. I wrote many very weird "Talk" stories that appeared in the *New Yorker,* very experimental "Talk" stories, and it was from them that I learned how to do the stories in *At the Bottom of the River.* Sometimes

I was doing both; I was writing weird stories and I was writing *At the Bottom of the River.*

INTERVIEWER: At what point were you Jamaica Kincaid, in "Talk of the Town"?

KINCAID: By the time I made the effort to write I had changed my name, so I was never anything but Jamaica Kincaid as a writer.

INTERVIEWER: And "my sassy black friend" before that.

KINCAID: That's true. But it would be "our sassy black friend, Jamaica Kincaid," I was always named.

INTERVIEWER: I read that there was a bit of controversy, at least among people privately, about the Louis character in *Lucy* being too close to an actual writer on the staff of the *New Yorker.* Did that surface in a public controversy at all?

KINCAID: I must say when I read that, it was a surprise to me. If it was a controversy among my friends, they didn't tell me. Everyone likes to think that everything is really telling them something about someone, but I never write about other people. I'm not that interested in other people at all. The people that I really want to say anything about are people at home, and even so, I muddle up characters. The true characters in *Lucy* are the mother and Lucy. Apparently it's the stock-in-trade of West Indian writers to write about their childhoods. Merle Hodge's *Crick Crack, Monkey* is a wonderful book, and it's about a Caribbean childhood, too, not unlike mine. It's true that women sometimes fall victim to a kind of narcissism. Certainly it's true in the West Indies. I went to a conference of West Indian women writers, very learned, brilliant women. Many of them said, "I know I should give my paper, but I'm going to tell you about myself instead." It was at that moment I realized that my mother wasn't that unusual. I don't know if this sense of "Here I am, let me tell you about me" is universal to women, but it's a very West Indian trait. Maybe it is because she's confined to home and family that there's a great love of self as an aesthetic thing among West Indian women. It must be said they're very beautiful women.

INTERVIEWER: The critic Henry Louis Gates Jr. says that you, like Toni Morrison, "never feel the necessity of claiming the existence of a black world, or a female sensibility," that you assume them both as a given.

KINCAID: That is very true. I don't really write about men unless they have something to do with a woman. I was just reading an African writer who described black people as black. I couldn't tell whether he meant it as race or skin color. I didn't understand what he meant.

INTERVIEWER: There's also an acceptance of androgyny in your books, a completely frank treatment of adolescent sexuality between girls. "Gwen and I will get married," says Annie John. There it is, and no big deal is made of it.

KINCAID: I grew up with a great acceptance of female bonding. The greatest loves that I knew, and the greatest quarrels, the greatest enmities I knew were between women. I was very interested in feelings between these people, and I just wasn't going to worry about whether they were homosexuals or not. If they are, well good for them.

INTERVIEWER: Another thing that you do with absolute matter-of-factness is to take the imagery of patriarchal literature—God, we all know, is a man and so is Lucifer—and without any ado, God, by God, becomes a woman.

KINCAID: I am writing about power and powerlessness and I think that these things have no sex. They have only their nature. I have never met a man more impressive than my mother. When Ronald Reagan was announcing the invasion of Grenada, at his side was Eugenie Charles, the prime minister of Dominique. If you were from Mars, you would think that she was the leader of the powerful country and he was the leader of the weak country. My mother is like that—grand and impressive. I've never met any man with that sort of personal power.

INTERVIEWER: You've talked about your mother and the stories that she tells as being a part of what makes you a writer now, and yet you've also commented that it would never occur to people like her to step back from their experience and create a work of art. Can you elaborate on that?

KINCAID: I started to write out of reasons that were, I thought, peculiar to me—I was lazy and I wasn't really interested in being educated in a way that would suit other people. I was interested in knowing things that pleased me. For instance, I often read books on astronomy but it doesn't interest me to go to school to study astronomy. I became a writer because I could live a life that pleased me. I liked to investigate my own life. I liked to talk about my mother, her family, my life, what happened to me, historically, in my childhood, and I could only get to them in this way. I do not know why I am able to step outside and look. I certainly don't have more courage than they do, more education, more brilliance. My mother is an extremely brilliant woman. I do not know what it is that made, in me, the desire to do this thing and to seek satisfaction for that desire.

INTERVIEWER: Have you come to the point in your life where you're comfortable with the enriching things about you that come from your mother?

KINCAID: Absolutely. There are many things about her that I've consciously tried to adopt, that I love. Sometimes I only write in her voice. I think the voice of Lucy is very much her voice. Her voice as a piece of literature is the most fabulous thing you ever read or heard. She is a person in her own right, but careless with her gifts. That's very painful to me to watch.

INTERVIEWER: How do you mean that?

KINCAID: I perhaps am a writer because of her, in a very specific way. For instance, I love books because of her. She gave me an Oxford dictionary for my seventh birthday. She had taught me to read when I was three and a half years old. There are many things that should have allowed her to free herself from her situation and perhaps one of them would have been to have no children at all, including me. But you see her with these marvelous gifts and sense of self—people who have less of this than she have done things, ruled the world for instance. She's in her seventies and she's quite something. If she roused herself she could do quite a bit.

INTERVIEWER: Have you ever felt that a part of why you write is to win your mother's approval?

KINCAID: When I first started, among the things I wanted to do was to say, "Aren't you sorry that no greater effort was made over my education? Or over my life?" But as I've gotten older I am fairly sure that that's not a part of my life anymore. I didn't see her for twenty years, so the desire for her approval was greater in her absence. Then as we saw each other and spoke, I realized there was a certain chasm that could not really be closed; I just grew to accept her. I also wanted my children to know my mother, because whatever my differences are with her, I wanted them to feel a part of this person, and if possible to realize that some of the dynamics in my life were related. I didn't want her to die without closing that circle.

INTERVIEWER: If you suddenly won your mother's total and unconditional approval, would you still be writing?

KINCAID: Now you've frightened me. I think it's not possible, but I no longer really want that. We're just two grown-up people living the life we chose to live. It would be nice if she understood certain things about me. On the other hand, she's in her seventies, she needn't make any new arrangements if she doesn't want to, and, perhaps, new efforts are beyond her. I really don't look for that.

INTERVIEWER: You've taken the facts of your biography and shaped them into fictions with universal appeal. When it comes right down to the bottom line, who do you think you write for?

KINCAID: I always assume no one will read the damn thing, you know. Not my mother, the person I really write for, I suspect. My great audience is this one-half Carib Indian woman living in Antigua. I imagine she doesn't read what I write, but I'm quite surprised that people who are the exact opposite of her find anything in it. I'm really quite amazed.

Jim Harrison

Jim Harrison is a poetic experimentalist who brings to his fiction a gift for compression and precision of language. Born in Grayling, Michigan, in 1937, Harrison still makes his home there outside Lake Leelanau, where this interview was conducted in 1984 shortly after publication of his pivotal novel, Sundog. *Despite his reputation for writing "male fiction" full of the love of hunting, fishing, ranching, farming, torrid and often unwise love affairs, and far-ranging adventure, Harrison's vision has grown more quietly spiritual over the years. His books sometimes adopt the conceit of the false memoir or biography.* Wolf *(1971), his first novel, is the story of a midlife crisis that develops into a classic test of man against nature. A similar conflict is revisited years later in the false biography* Sundog, *but the treatment is fundamentally more introspective. His more recent book,* The Woman Lit by Fireflies *(1990), takes another step toward the examination of his characters' internal spiritual lives, and it embodies the abiding respect for women that has become more apparent as his work has matured. In addition to his nine books of fiction, which include* Revenge, Legends of the Fall *(1979),* Farmer *(1976), and* Warlock *(1981), Harrison is the author of ten volumes of poetry.*

INTERVIEWER: Could you tell us about your publishing history? You published a whole book of poems without ever having a single poem published.

HARRISON: I'd heard Denise Levertov read and I never published anything in my life. So I sent her poems and she wrote back that she'd just become the consulting editor at Norton and if I had more poems like this she would publish a book. After I got the book contract, I sent some poems off and they came out about the same time as the book, but that was true. It was an accident.

INTERVIEWER: What happened with *Wolf*? How come you moved from three volumes of poetry to the novel?

HARRISON: I fell off a cliff. I was in the hospital for a month and went into a coma and almost died. I sort of woke up and I couldn't do anything. I had to wear a body corset because I'd torn the muscles away from my lower spine. So Tom McGuane called me up and says, "Now that you're laid up, why don't you write a novel?" I said, "Jeez, I don't want to think about writing a novel." "Write a sort of autobiographical novel," he said and I said, "Okay, good-bye." Then I started writing the novel. I wrote *Wolf* in six weeks or a month. I sent it off the day before the mail strike, years ago, and the only copy of it was lost for a full month. I didn't even think it was important, because I didn't think of myself as a novelist. I wasn't very attached to it. I'd sent it to my brother to make a copy because we were real broke. So he finally went into the New Haven post office and dug it out of the pile of mail there. I don't know how he managed that, but he's authoritative. Then the publisher got it and took it.

INTERVIEWER: You also wrote some novellas . . .

HARRISON: I always loved the work of Isak Dinesen, and Knut Hampson, who wrote three or four short novels, so I thought I would have a try at it. I called the first one *Revenge*—my Sicilian agent gave me a little motto that struck me: "Revenge is a dish better served cold." The second of the novellas is called *The Man Who Gave Up His Name.* I wrote it in a time of extreme mental duress. I envisioned a man getting out of the life he had created with the same intricate carefulness that he'd got into it in the first place. I suppose I was pointing out that if you're ethical you can't just disappear.

INTERVIEWER: You've described yourself as a sensual Calvinist.

HARRISON: Maybe that's true. I wrote a poem in which I said John Calvin's down there under the floorboards telling me I don't get a glass of wine till four o'clock. Not 3:57, but 4:00. I was talking to Kurt Ludkey last night about how if you're a total workaholic and you also drink too much you tend to control it, but that doesn't make you less of an alcoholic. It's just that you never, never have more drinks than you can remember.

INTERVIEWER: Can you really drink like that?

HARRISON: I have done that for years. I had a little trouble in my early thirties with it and then I began tightly controlling it. I went down to a Mexican fat farm in January because I was so exhausted from my novel. And I felt grotesque, I felt about like I do right now. So I didn't drink anything. I expected it would be awful and nothing happened. I didn't feel anything. Reagan's immigration chief was at this fat farm, and I said to him, "Don't you realize that you guys are hassling the greatest writer in the world about getting in and out of the United States?" I was talking about Marquez, who's the only writer on earth that I admire without qualification. He said, "Oh I didn't know that; what's the guy's name, we'll see what we can do."

INTERVIEWER: Have they been denying him a visa?

HARRISON: Yeah, they've been giving him trouble because they know he stops and sees Castro. But you know what he and Castro do all the time? Cook. They cook all night. He gets there and he has fresh stuff he's picked up in Caracas or Mexico City. They cook veal and chicken, everything like that. And drink of course.

INTERVIEWER: Your books are full of great cooks.

HARRISON: What I always liked in Boswell is the idea that if you're obligated to eat two or three times a day, you may as well do a good job of it. I once stopped to see John McDonald and Betty Friedan was there and she asked me why I was so obsessed with cooking. I said, "Why, I cook to avoid adultery." And she says, "My God! are you a mess. To say such a thing." But it's sort of true. When I started cooking frequently, at least three times a week, my wife enjoyed it because it's no fun cooking if you have to cook all the time. And I could also avoid going to the bar when I finished my workday.

INTERVIEWER: A lot of writers seem to have problems with alcohol. Do you think there's anything necessary about the life of the writer that leads to extreme pain?

HARRISON: Well, no. I think it's partly the profession. You're alone most of the time. You're creating other worlds all the time. And it's what Walker Percy talks about in that last book of his—it's the reentry problem. You know how I say, or, I have my narrator say, "It's your return to earth like some kind of burned out satellite." Something like that. Alcohol is the sedative when you finish the day's work—it helps you to reemerge into the world.

INTERVIEWER: Would you say that your personal life has been something of a stabilizing force?

HARRISON: Oh my, yeah. You know I've been married twenty-four and a half years. Not in the clingy sense, it's just the way I prefer to live. Every time I think I'm a mess, a total mess, I sort of look around and find out that I'm not quite a total mess. It's like McGuane said, that alcoholism is a writer's black-lung disease. Which is sort of true. But even that I seem to have under control. I suppose that's a moralistic urge. Just to control. To control it.

INTERVIEWER: You have that passage in *Sundog* where Strang says something about having made up rules when he was a kid. The narrator, Harrison, says, "I love rules." Can you tell me some of the rules?

HARRISON: Do I have any fresh rules? Yeah. I was on page like 197 of that novel manuscript before I realized I was writing about my alter ego, and it blew one writing day. It totally terrified me.

INTERVIEWER: How so?

HARRISON: Strang worked on eleven dams, and I'd written eleven books. I mean it got that bad. And I felt utterly crippled. Just like Strang's been crippled by his work. I said, "Oh my God! Can I go on?" Well the energy of the novel had taken over, so it didn't matter.

INTERVIEWER: The book is, by no means like, but reminds me of, *The Secret Sharer.* You wonder at the end about the secret sharer. Whether or not it's one person or two.

HARRISON: That's giving me goose bumps. James Hillman, who's a Jungian psychiatrist, said that thing I quoted, "The notion that there's a light at the end of the tunnel has mostly been a boon to pharmaceutical companies." I love that.

INTERVIEWER: Would you explain that?

HARRISON: Well, tranquilizers and everything like that. It's because people think they can't bear the nowness of now. They can't bear the present tense. In Zen terms they're either rehearsing something they've already done, to make it come out right. Or they're expecting something to occur in the future. Or trying to change the past. It's like somebody might say, I'm revising my memoirs. I mean something ludicrous like that. A person like Strang is free from dread because he's consented totally to the present. Whereas the narrator, which is another portion of me, can't, can't accept anything.

INTERVIEWER: Where did you get the character Strang?

HARRISON: My brain. I met a few people, in an outward way, that did what he did. And I tried to create the kind of person they would become. On frequent trips all over the world, I would meet these men sometimes in hotels, and I'd ask them what they do. I met one in Costa Rica that was a foreman on a huge construction project, and in charge of thirty-two thousand workers on this dam in the Amazon Basin. He was self-educated, from Tennessee. I became more and more interested in these people and then the character took shape. I wanted to create a hero who was free from dread. Dread and irony have gotten to be literary addictions. And I noticed there are some people that live without it. So I created this character named Strang. When I was thirteen I read about King Strang over here on Beaver Island. He was a Mormon apostate, and he had fifty girlfriends or wives. When you're thirteen you're horny as a toad and you don't even have one girlfriend and here's a guy that's got fifty. So this is what I had in mind. A man free from dread. Maybe that's what I wanted—to be free from dread. I mean besides wanting a drink. I also want to be free from dread.

INTERVIEWER: It has been said that Strang is the metaphor for the artist. How much do you use yourself, in your work?

HARRISON: Strang isn't me though.

INTERVIEWER: What about the subtitle: *As Told to Jim Harrison.*

HARRISON: That was just to have fun. Like Nabokov, I did that to throw people off the track. It is a little bit myself, but I had to have a contrast to Strang. I had to have somebody coming from way outside, coming into this world. And I had to know both people. You could say they're almost extremities of the right and left lobes of the same head.

INTERVIEWER: You wrote this novel as a parajournalistic escapade.

HARRISON: I was just pissed off. Everything is a novelty. Somebody's most utter and terrible grief is a minute and a half of the evening news. That kind of thing. I was thinking of David Kennedy at twelve sitting in that hotel room watching his father die. He didn't ever get over it.

INTERVIEWER: Strang says almost immediately, "Tell me something bad that you've never really gotten over."

HARRISON: I forgot I said that. But that's it. Like his niece can't get over being raped, any better than Karl can get over it. Karl was a strange character. Some people wanted more of him but Karl's effective because there's not more of him. He's the kind of guy that's terribly sensitive but often verges on being the town bully, because he is so eccentric. Karl on a surface level is very attractive to some people for the same reason they like Clint Eastwood. He got back at them. Tom McGuane had a motto over his kitchen door saying "Getting even is the best revenge." And that's okay, but Steve McQueen was out there and he looked at the motto and he said, "Tom, even I'm not that bad. That's really going too far."

INTERVIEWER: In many ways that book is as much the narrator's book as it is Strang's.

HARRISON: Well, it's unpleasant because everything the narrator could say is true to my experience. But you need a contrast. Strang isn't Strang if the whole book is Strang. The narrator comes to Strang. It's almost like that notion of monkey brain. You can't often evaluate yourself because it's your own brain that's evaluating your own brain. Supposedly what removes us from animals is that we can stand back and look. But it's sometimes confusing. My cabin is the cabin that Strang is living in. So I go up there and I say, "Oh, my God, now I'm living in this novel, and I'm not sure which one I am."

INTERVIEWER: And you took a swim like Strang, to test that swim.

HARRISON: Last summer I did. I swam down the river.

INTERVIEWER: Are you that strong a swimmer? Can you swim like Strang swims?

HARRISON: Yeah, I used to swim. I remember when I was ten I swam twelve miles. When I was seven, there was a loon on our lake, and I never could get close to it so I thought, "I'll trick the loon, go out at night and try to catch her." So I snuck out of the cabin, off I went in the dark. When I was getting ready finally to write that novel, I did something similar for that last scene. It's two o'clock in the morning, I've had a few drinks. I locked my dog in the cabin, went down the steps to the river, took off my clothes and swam with the current way down the river, and over two log jams in the middle of the night so I could get that feeling. It's very strange to swim down a river at night alone, naked. But that enabled me to imagine that last scene, say Julian and his son were down there, you'd see those lights off the trees, just the car lights way down.

INTERVIEWER: The narrator and Strang are two sides of one being, together, it seems like. And the telling of the tale is the revelation of the wedding.

HARRISON: What the narrator was finding in Strang is maybe what I found in the left side of my brain. And the tape device amplifies it, which is fun, because you have the more formal narrator, then you have the narrator off-the-wall. And some of the inserts have the narrator wondering what he's going to eat, wondering how he's going to get laid. Textural concretia, the "thinginess" of life. That's an old rule I have on the wall. Make it vivid.

INTERVIEWER: Did you feel like you were taking a chance by letting in the possibility that Strang and the narrator really are brothers?

HARRISON: No, I was flirting with that. No one will ever know. The only one that knew died.

INTERVIEWER: The narrator is flirting with it. He wants to play with it and he doesn't.

HARRISON: It was just an interesting possibility. But of course it's true.

INTERVIEWER: They are brothers?

HARRISON: It doesn't matter if they're blood brothers or what kind of brothers. That was all sort of unconscious. You write and you don't even know what you're writing when you're writing it. It just emerges.

INTERVIEWER: At what point did you start realizing that you had a subject out of writing from what you know?

HARRISON: Well, death did it to me. You can see it in my first book, *Plain Song.* If people die then you better get down to business.

INTERVIEWER: This was your father and sister? They died in a car accident.

HARRISON: That was part of it. That was when I was twenty-two and I'd been writing since I was sixteen. I wanted to write poems like John Keats.

INTERVIEWER: You started out wanting to be a poet?

HARRISON: It was all the same to me. I'd read those romantic novels about artists like Vincent van Gogh and I was thinking that's what I want to be. I wanted to be a wild artist and have lots of love affairs and live in strange places. I have.

INTERVIEWER: But I take it you've found out it's a lot more of a discipline than you thought?

HARRISON: Oh, that's all it is. It's what Stevens said: Technique is the proof of your seriousness.

INTERVIEWER: Are you happy with *Sundog*?

HARRISON: I don't know. It wouldn't occur to me to be happy with something I wrote. It's not healthy to even think about it.

INTERVIEWER: After you've done it?

HARRISON: Nope. It's all gone. I mean you're making me think about it now and it's not unpleasant. It's sort of interesting to get somebody else's point of view.

INTERVIEWER: So you don't worry about judging or assessing your work?

HARRISON: I don't think I'm very competitive about it. I don't see it as a horse race, the way some novelists are always rating each other. You know how in New York every day they take each other's temperature to see who's hot. I don't think that way too much.

INTERVIEWER: You don't look back on a book and say I learned this problem in this novel?

HARRISON: Oh, yeah. You do that to some extent. You write sometimes to find out what you know.

INTERVIEWER: Do you think that the skills you learned in writing poetry transferred into your novels?

HARRISON: Very much. Trying to bear down on the singularity of images. Movement. Those suites were good training for moving from image to mood to mood. It's like Mailer says, "Boy if you're worried about getting people in and out of rooms, you've already blown it." The reader can get anybody they want in and out of rooms. They don't need your help.

INTERVIEWER: You often use animals in your work.

HARRISON: It's the same idea that the Indians had. One is naturally drawn to certain animals more than other animals. Now I like crows and coyotes and pigs for some reason.

INTERVIEWER: Have you ever thought that out?

HARRISON: I could pretend that I don't know what the associations are, but I do. The coyote is a sorcerer amongst animals. He's the trickster, he's the humpbacked flute player. He's an animal of immaculate, precise and varied means. Intense curiosity, but cagey. I think I like that idea. And a crow is a garrulous semipredator, semiscavenger. Sort of foolish, but smarter than other birds. He just likes to fool around. Squawk all the time.

INTERVIEWER: You mentioned pigs . . .

HARRISON: Yeah, I had a pet pig when I was a kid. But you know they're all going to get killed in November. It's a bit of a disappointment. Was it Hugo who said, "All of us are condemned to death with an indefinite reprieve"? A sort of catchy idea. He says that the ultimate that a human leaves is his skull.

INTERVIEWER: You use the animal point of view without it being a pathetic fallacy. To use one of those school terms.

HARRISON: As Strang says, "What's the sense in drawing conclusions about human behavior from animals when you can draw conclusions about human behavior from humans?" There's a danger of extrapolating, but they're our fellow creatures and always have been. What's the sense of ignoring them? I'm writing now about the drama of an English department. Lots of writers are going to start writing about government intervention in the arts. It's quieted literary magazines a great deal, you know.

INTERVIEWER: You want to talk about that?

HARRISON: I've just noticed it. Just like all the writers' schools have created less variety—there's a sameness. I said once that the Iowa Writers School on a yearly basis outproduces the English romantic movement. It's all a delusion. What are you going to do with four thousand M.F.A.'s? It's ludicrous.

INTERVIEWER: You did pay your dues though. You went through and got a master's yourself, didn't you?

HARRISON: In Comparative Literature. I never took a writing course of any sort. In my life.

INTERVIEWER: Do you advise against that across the board?

HARRISON: No. Sometimes they're good. Look at Wallace Stegner's thing out there. I mean, my God, look at the people he got out. Kesey, Robert Stone, McGuane. But you know what he did. They sat around and talked a little and he just sent them off to write.

INTERVIEWER: You have a lot of friends who are writers. And then there are writers who avoid that sort of thing.

HARRISON: Well, I don't see them that much and I think a lot of other writers partly like me because I'm not competitive. I simply don't care. Frankly. I mean I don't ever think about being number one or number seven or number three. Self-publicity or valuation isn't a productive thing for writers. Mailer's *A View from Here* was marvelous because it just totally pissed everybody off. And it was also so on the money. I love novels like his *Barbary Shore* and *The Deer Park*. But the critics were totally unpleasant; those novels weren't part of the nativist tradition. That's why a lot of people hated *A Good Day to Die*. Kazin told me these are simply the nastiest people, they don't exist. I says, "Alfred, they're all over. It's just that people don't write about them." *Sundog* came out of my conviction that the American literary novel as opposed to a more commercial kind of novel tends to ignore about seven-eighths of the people. The literary novel often concentrates itself on people in New York, Los Angeles, academic and scientific communities. People don't write about the Strangs of the world because they don't know any of them. You're not going to meet any in Cambridge or New Haven. People like Strang don't loiter around universities and they don't feed at the public trough.

INTERVIEWER: So you think that the academy has had a negative effect.

HARRISON: I think I would agree with Faulkner when he said, "A writer can't be ruined by having a swimming pool if he's a good writer. If he's a bad writer, it doesn't matter if he has a swimming pool." So I don't think it matters, but it's had a tremendous leveling effect.

INTERVIEWER: On the kinds of books written?

HARRISON: Yeah, they're not as idiosyncratic. They've lost a charm and a self-taught aspect. These people keep track of their credits and that's how they get jobs. They say, "I have been published in *Sewanee, Lust, Spook,* etc., etc." Where I pointedly have no notion of where I published anything, or little memory of it. I've never kept track.

INTERVIEWER: So you'd approve of someone like Wallace Stevens, who sold insurance and wrote.

HARRISON: It's important to know something. Knowing literature is different. Hollywood's always making movies about making movies. Or the movie business. Well, that doesn't play in Kansas. Who gives a shit? It's like making movies about dope. They think everybody does dope. Well, very few people do dope. Why do people in Topeka want to go see a movie about cocaine? They don't know shit from cocaine. Why should they? It's a sense of fungoid self-congratulation that you see in academic communities.

INTERVIEWER: You think it leads to a more narrow vision in literature?

HARRISON: Well, that's true. It's just like academic types who say to me, "Oh Jesse Jackson, yuk, oh he's fascist." "Oh stop," I say, "He got jobs for two hundred thousand blacks in Chicago, what have you ever done? He's a great orator. So he's a little spooky in some areas. But why are you talking about this man this way?"

INTERVIEWER: Henry James said experience is never limited. It's the atmosphere of the mind.

HARRISON: Well, that's true. You make your own environment wherever you go. I don't like to be exclusionary. I don't like art which, I think Williams says, cuts off the horse's legs to get him in the box.

INTERVIEWER: You taught once, didn't you?

HARRISON: [indelicate sound]

INTERVIEWER: You felt like the town clown, is that what you said?

HARRISON: No, it's just that teaching is overrated. It's just not very interesting. You're never done with the job, time's never your own.

INTERVIEWER: As somebody who's worked as a journeyman writer for films in order to survive, what do you think about books being made from films, or movies being made from books?

HARRISON: I don't have any feeling about it; they're different mediums and you're a fool if you don't realize that. Even when I write an adaptation of my own work, I like to feel free to change it as much as possible to adapt it to another medium. My ambition is to write a good movie; I want desperately to write a good movie.

INTERVIEWER: Does it bother you that none of your books have become films?

HARRISON: I only have one regret. John Huston and Jack Nicholson were going to do *Revenge* and Warners backed out because they didn't want John Huston to direct it. I felt badly then because I thought he would do a good job.

INTERVIEWER: They pay you a lot of money, don't they?

HARRISON: For some things they do. One time Sean Connery had read *Revenge* in *Esquire* and wanted me to write something for him. He found I was under contract to Warners and Warners got excited and says, "You gotta come out here." I says, "No, I'm not coming back out there, ever!" They sent a plane all the way from Burbank to Traverse City Airport and I got on it with a bottle of whiskey and a six-pack of beer and some deli sandwiches they'd got me and flew out there on condition they would fly me back the next day at noon. They'll do anything for you. It's curious isn't it, all those years when people were saying, "Poor Faulkner, he had to go to Hollywood." He wasn't nearly as unhappy as he pretended to be, because he had that dancing girl out there all that time. Though Blotner refused to acknowledge it in his biography. Where she said, "Billy liked to take baths together and sometimes we'd buy toys like rubber ducks" and you think, this is William Faulkner. I loved it. Faulkner for a while was getting $3,000 a week during the depression to write screenplays. That's good money now, that was great money then.

INTERVIEWER: Is the writing you do for the movies your substitute for teaching? I mean in the sense of surviving.

HARRISON: Yeah. It is about the same thing and sometimes worse and sometimes better. It's better because it pays better.

INTERVIEWER: Does that mean you can do it less often? Or less frequently?

HARRISON: Maybe, but you get greedy. Somebody gives you $150,000 for a screenplay, you think, well, why not write two. Get more. And then you say, well, why not write three, and get even more. And by then, you're retired.

INTERVIEWER: Does writing for the movies drain you?

HARRISON: No. In the last twelve months I wrote three screenplays and that novel, and I don't think the three screenplays detracted from the novel. Just makes you tired generally. And I'm the most tired I've ever been in my whole life, right now.

INTERVIEWER: You say that when a book comes out you get depressed.

HARRISON: Uh huh, I don't like judgment. I can't stand criticism.

INTERVIEWER: Not even good criticism?

HARRISON: When Bernard Levin of the London *Times* decided I was immortal, I says, "Does that mean I have to take out my laundry in three hundred years?" No, it's okay. If you work very hard, what's wrong with getting admired?

INTERVIEWER: But there's something in you that doesn't think that's right?

HARRISON: Well, it's because people you love died, and they didn't get admired. That's part of it. It's stupid. I mean, you ought to be able to be valedictorian once in a while. It's like pursuing a beautiful model and seducing her and then feeling real bad after you'd literally been thinking about doing it for seven or eight years. Why bother? Why should I kill myself writing a book if I don't want to at least accept one pat on the back for what I'm doing?

INTERVIEWER: What about the sense of place for you? It seems to me that you're a writer that has to be grounded in place.

HARRISON: I think everybody does. I wrote *Locations* partly from that sensibility. But I'm no more a rural writer than Judy Rossner is a New York writer.

INTERVIEWER: And yet, northern Michigan is pervasive in your work.

HARRISON: Yeah, that's because that's where I was born and raised. When I get away from there, I don't think the writing is necessarily weaker as long as I know the other place.

INTERVIEWER: Do you think there's a basic superiority in that "heart of the country" notion?

HARRISON: I think what I believe most is actually, as Rilke said, "It's only in the rat race of the arena that the heart learns to beat." I think you have to do that. It's hard to find more small-minded people than you can find in some areas of Montana, in the most gorgeous part of the United States.

INTERVIEWER: But they're also in New York City.

HARRISON: Well, sure they are, but I mean the country in and of itself isn't going to do anybody any good.

INTERVIEWER: It's what you bring to it.

HARRISON: I was being evasive. I was thinking about an uncapped city water well that I almost fell into in Reed City. Memories are evoked by a location, and I was thinking of San Francisco, the bridge. Six hundred and ninety-three people have jumped off that goddamned bridge. There's something sort of haunted in the air there. Nobody would do that in Missouri, and they don't do it in northern Michigan. But in New Orleans, and San Francisco, these apparently perfect places where everybody's so happy, well that's why there are four hundred thousand homosexuals there. I mean, what the hell's going on? It's a spooky place, but very beautiful. Maybe it attracts them from the Midwest. None of those people ever even want to come to the Midwest, ever.

INTERVIEWER: In *Farmer* the doctor tells Joseph that, yes, Robert's a homosexual and not to worry about it. He'll go to the city and find other people like him.

HARRISON: Homosexuals will gather in one place, for the same reason that the rich all want to be in Palm Beach or Beverly Hills, or Grosse Point, or farmers all go to the Grange. I mean it's natural. And it's not all bad. Think of jazz clubs. If you have three hundred Sonny Rollins nuts and half are black and half are white, then there's no barrier left. It's the same with literature. I'm not a nationalist. I don't want to hear about American literature. It's world literature. And all this sniping about who's good in America is nonsense when you've got Günter Grass, and Gabriel Marquez. Who is good is who is good wherever they are.

INTERVIEWER: You're a wonderful reader. How much do you write for the ear?

HARRISON: I don't consciously, but as a poet you do. Yeats would think of the entire rhythm of the poem before he would fill in the words. You know he says, " 'I am of Ireland and the Holy Land of Ireland and time runs on,' cried she." You say Jesus Christ, I don't know if it makes any sense, but it's beautiful. I think it comes from my early addiction to Stravinsky or Sonny Rollins or Miles Davis or Thelonious Monk. And that's finally the music you hear in your head and you hear word music in that way. I think I was seventeen when I read Joyce's *Finnegans Wake* four or five times. I used to carry it around with me. It was my main sexual reading, I still think it's the sexiest book I've ever read. So *Hustler* magazine doesn't work with me at all. *Vogue* is better than *Hustler.*

INTERVIEWER: Do you think your reputation as a macho writer is the source of the negative criticism your work has gotten?

HARRISON: It's just faddism. When Prescott owned *Newsweek* rather than talking about my book he used me as an object lesson in what's wrong with contemporary writing because, he said, I had none of the new feminine sensibility. He's talking about a public movement, a woman's movement, that I don't think has anything to do with the novel. I mean you write novels. I'm not trying to get out the vote when I write a novel. A novel's a novel. Everybody can't be everything. I don't like to be attacked for reasons anterior to my work.

INTERVIEWER: Do you think it's because you so often seem to use the stuff of yourself in your work?

HARRISON: You are what you are. I'm not going to pretend that I'm a Manhattan restauranteur when I'm not. But it's the illusion, too. I've worked very hard to create the illusion. Wouldn't I be something if I was all the people that people think I am in all these books. God, what a mess.

INTERVIEWER: Does the misunderstanding bother you?

HARRISON: I don't actually care. I pretend to be more upset. *Esquire* offered me a case of whiskey if I would write two paragraphs answering a review. I wrote that it's a misuse of the word. Actually what macho is in Spanish is someone who would fuck a virgin with a swan or throw a rattlesnake into a baby's carriage. Screw his mother. You know, cut his sister. So that's macho. I don't know what it has to do with me. I don't care about being misunderstood. I'm not pretending that I'm right and there's not a lot of my stuff that might be terribly cheap and wrong. That's neither here nor there if that's what they're dealing with. I don't want to be attacked for my failures as a supporter of the woman's movement. Because I'm a novelist.

INTERVIEWER: Where do you find your characters? Do you use people whom you really know?

HARRISON: Just modifications of them. There's such a crazed variety of people that you can take an eighth of this and a third of that and make a human being. In *Legends of the Fall,* I found the character William Ludlow in journals; he's actually my wife's great-grandfather. But I've changed all the details of his life except the initial ones. He did lead an expedition into the Black Hills with Custer as his adjutant; he also did loathe Custer. And in real life he ended up owning some copper mines in northern Michigan, but I'd read his journals and was fascinated by the kind of man he was.

INTERVIEWER: You've complained someplace about the fact that there's so little useful information in novels, nowadays.

HARRISON: I mean useful to, as Robert Duncan would say, your soul. Life information without which we cannot live. Like Pound says, "Poetry is news that stays news."

INTERVIEWER: Larry Woiwode says he's read that most writers are manic-depressive. Have you ever thought that you might be a manic-depressive?

HARRISON: Oh, absolutely, but not to the point where I would need lithium and not so much in recent years. About ten years ago I went through a self-taught Zen training. I had severe colitis from a parasite I got in Leningrad and I thought I was going to go insane with the mood swings combined with physical problems. I got rid of the colitis by sitting. Usually I would go sit on a stump and then on a rock for three or four hours. For some reason that eased all that out, I'm still not sure why. Psychosomatic maybe. For instance I've had a chest cold off and on for a month and a half. I know I have it because I have a novel coming out. No one in the history of my family, including my father, was successful, and I have a lot of questions about whether it's proper to be successful. It's like the craving for anonymity—I've already blown the anonymity shot, but I'm still looking for it. I'm like the kid hiding under the bush or behind the barn. I've gotten so weary or strange about interviews because I've been too trusting on a couple of occasions. The trouble is anything you read about yourself seems to be sort of inaccurate; well, maybe everything that everybody writes about everybody is inaccurate. I've never been really keelhauled, but I read once an article about McGuane in *Village Voice* where they really did a job on him.

INTERVIEWER: That can lead to the "gunfighter syndrome." Whenever a celebrity goes to a party you know that somebody there is going to become an asshole and you never know who it's going to be. I've seen people literally get up in Norman Mailer's face and stand on his feet.

HARRISON: They never do that to McGuane who's 6'4" and weighs 220. It's because Mailer's shorter.

INTERVIEWER: You said someplace that to be an artist you have to be able to hold a thousand different contradictory notions in your head all at once.

HARRISON: I was thinking about that when you brought up that question on *Sundog.* Hillman said, "What have we done with this other who is given us at birth?" Well that's like that *Secret Sharer* idea or Rimbaud talking about my "other" and so on. The unrevealed heart of your personality.

INTERVIEWER: Does that relate to the idea that the essence of all art is the ability to recognize paradox, irony?

HARRISON: Or to be able to accept that good art does not specialize in cheap solutions.

INTERVIEWER: Do you think, at least in the sense that Pound used the words, that all art is didactic?

HARRISON: It's didactic, but boy you better hide it. I can't stand art that's preachy. I think Pound's best poems are free of obvious didacticism. The test is the aesthetic test. If somebody tells me he has things he wants to say, I say, "Well, I don't care, everybody has things they want to say." It's like Philip Roth puts it, anybody on the subway usually has a better story than an artist does. Because they're intensely occupied with life. Whereas we can't see a cow without saying cow. I want to get to the point where I see a cow without saying cow. It's never going to happen in my life. My particular burden is to make sentences. My wife and I saw a man commit suicide in San Francisco last week. We were down under the Golden Gate Bridge and this asshole jumps off. I had a driver that day, sort of an elegant, faggy character, much better dressed than I was. He and my wife and I were standing down under the fort looking over this area, nothing was there. I was watching a man fish. Then I heard a gargle, we looked back and a man had just jumped off the bridge, missed the water by twelve feet and his head was even gone. You know the impact of three hundred feet onto cement, your head vaporizes. My wife and the driver were contorted with horror, and trembling, and I immediately started making sentences. That's my only defense against this world: to build a sentence out of it.

Tom McGuane

Tom McGuane's writing career began in the sixties. This interview catches him at age forty-five, looking back on a rebellious youth and forward toward the issues of middle age. He speaks of his enduring fascination with comic writing. He says that the subject of his early novels was the expression of the American dream in the wild West of the 1960s and 1970s, and the realization that acting on those ideals could not be survived. The author of ten books, McGuane writes about brooding protagonists, displaced people, characters who cannot seem to put down roots or reach out to things beyond themselves. These characters are often ironically connected and shaped by their relationships to landscape and place. Ninety-two in the Shade *(1973) and* Panama *(1978) are set in Key West, Florida.* The Bushwhacked Piano *(1971) tells of an eccentric peregrination through Michigan, Montana, and Florida.* Something to Be Desired *(1984) is set partly in Montana. In many ways his novels are harrowing contemporary novels of manners, about taking drugs, sexual peccadilloes, and chaotic mobility.*

McGuane's personal journey from the drug-taking sixties to the life of a responsible citizen and parent is reflected in his novels. The western stories still retain some of the humor of the Florida novels, but the dilemmas of McGuane's protagonists become increasingly serious: divorces, multiple families, tricky business deals, the desperation to settle down. These themes can be seen especially in his novel Nothing but Blue Skies *(1992). Other acclaimed works include* Nobody's Angel *(1981) and* The Sporting Club *(1968).*

INTERVIEWER: Can you tell us a little about your life and upbringing?

MCGUANE: I was raised in the Middle West, in Michigan, but my parents were both Boston-area Irish. Except when we were in school, we were always back there in Massachusetts in the big kind of noisy, Irish households of the forties and fifties. My parents were upward-striving, lower-middle-class people who had a facility for English. They both were English majors in college. My father was a scholarship student at Harvard; my mother went to a little school called Regis. Books and talk and language in general were a big part of growing up for me. My family was not excited about me wanting to be a writer; they thought that was very unrealistic.

INTERVIEWER: It is difficult to support yourself as a serious writer.

MCGUANE: I think any writer, even an unserious writer, has a bad time of it; a pulp writer or a sold-out writer or a hack has a hard time making a living. To understand the economics of writing is to know that writing and publishing and acquiring some kind of esteem in your community of peers is merely a key to your finances. For example, prestigious writers whose reputations are confined to the literary all live pretty well. They are getting grants and teaching jobs. I would say the people I've seen who teach writing are underworked. Other writers, like me, have been able to find work in film or journalism. There's also a way to get along. I think it's inevitable for writers to sort of feel sorry for themselves and to feel sorrier the more serious they perceive themselves to be.

INTERVIEWER: In the introduction to last year's summer fiction edition of *Esquire,* Rust Hills claimed that the academy has become the patronage system for writers . . . and was defending it, moreover. What did you think of that?

MCGUANE: I thought it was silly. I think patronage, especially homogenous patronage of the kind that academic writers receive, is exceedingly dangerous and leads to trafficking in reputations.

INTERVIEWER: What do you mean by homogenous?

MCGUANE: The colleges are, to a great degree, alike in their form of protection. I think it's good for writers to be in the world, not talking to the converted in English departments day after day—scrambling for survival, having to talk to illiterate neighbors. Obviously mine is a minority voice; this point of view is going to lose. The camp that Rust Hills describes is obviously the camp of sweeping victory.

INTERVIEWER: Because the writers who teach are living pretty well . . . financially?

MCGUANE: When I've been on campus I notice that everybody seems to be getting along better than ranchers in Montana are. There is great security there, the kind of security that the civil service or the post office provides and it goes hand in hand with complacency.

INTERVIEWER: I take it you feel that this situation has a measurable impact on the kind of writing that is being done.

MCGUANE: Well, you get these books like the latest Alison Lurie book that is built around sabbaticals. I think John Barth has suffered from being around colleges. To me the most interesting work that Barth did was the earliest work, before he knew what was going to happen to him—*The Floating Opera* and *The End of the Road*—books which I think he now kind of repudiates. His stuff lately has been less lifelike, less exciting.

INTERVIEWER: So you disagree with Hills's notion.

MCGUANE: I think Rust Hills needed to make a case for the situation now and I think that he felt he needed to overstate it. I think Rust and *Esquire* are excited about making categories, the new realism or the revival of fantasy, the kind of categories they come up with for the purposes of pigeonholing writers.

INTERVIEWER: So you feel that it's the type of writing that working within the academy encourages that has the negative effect; you aren't saying that because somebody teaches he is going to end up just writing about other teachers . . .

MCGUANE: No . . . no . . . I'm not saying that, but I do think that kind of life, that kind of support, is going to limit the access to information and material writers might otherwise have, obviously. I think maybe the best writer we have had in a long time is Saul Bellow and being a chronic teacher hasn't hurt him at all.

INTERVIEWER: So there are obviously exceptions to the rule.

MCGUANE: There are, yes, but there is also a kind of academic writer who meters out his publications, who measures himself and politicizes against other academic writers, and that writer is of no use to readers. I think the kind of thing Hills describes in that article represents a severing of the connection between writers and readers.

INTERVIEWER: To be fair, we should think of some notable exceptions; one thinks of Stanley Elkin.

MCGUANE: He scarcely seems like an academic writer in any way. There are writers in the outside world who are vastly more academic than Elkin. But when I think of Norman Mailer in the outside world, or of Walker Percy, I think of more adventurous spirits reporting to us from the whole world rather than one of its hyperspecific laminates. This is a purely personal reaction, but I am just more interested in people who have not gone to campuses.

INTERVIEWER: Your books are full of work, aren't they? And skills? Useful information?

MCGUANE: Little odds and ends of that sort. Jim Harrison used to needle me because I would hang around the repair bay of a gas station—it really wasn't research. I like to watch people do their thing and I don't care what it is. I like to watch ladies sew, I like to watch people cook, I like to watch people fix cars, I like to watch people commercially fish. I would have to suppress that by some fiat to keep it out of my writing.

INTERVIEWER: At what point did you start thinking of yourself as a writer?

MCGUANE: Very early. It was really all I have ever wanted to do.

INTERVIEWER: Did your parents ultimately support you?

MCGUANE: Well, my father had a nice rule—and it's the same ruling I take with my children, to the degree I can afford to do it—he basically took the position he didn't want to argue with me about what I wanted to do. He would support me educationally. I was a premed major, I was a prelaw major, I went to the Yale Drama School. I was finally an English major, but I waffled around knowing that I was free to do that. Going to school kept me writing. Then I got a grant at Stanford and that extended another year and in fact when I finished there, I was publishing.

INTERVIEWER: Do you value the Stegner experience?

MCGUANE: Not really, no. I value having had the time. I didn't get much out of the Stegner thing; I didn't think he was a good teacher. It was the middle sixties—most of the other writers were thinking that writing was dead and they wanted to march on the electrical engineering building or war contractors; they just weren't interested in literature. I remember

Allen Ginsberg coming up in those years and talking to people and finding they hadn't read Ezra Pound and hadn't read Whitman, didn't care, didn't want to know the names. It was an illiterate age and Stanford was just a place to get out of the weather and work on a book.

INTERVIEWER: Is there some particular break that enabled you to start supporting yourself by writing?

MCGUANE: Well, yes. I had a book on submission to Dial for six or eight months and was working pretty closely with them. I was encouraged to think that we were close to being able to publish the book. Then, suddenly from overhead the book was killed by the then editor-in-chief, E. L. Doctorow. It was just completely out of the blue and it was the most complete devastation I ever received. I remember thinking that I was going to snap. I had been writing daily for ten years and I didn't really think I could go on. And then . . . and then I suddenly realized, God, I didn't know how to do anything else. I had had minor menial jobs, but I just didn't really know what else to do. So I kind of holed up and wrote *The Sporting Club* in about six weeks and sent it to Jim Harrison. Then I lit out for Mexico thinking that I would figure out my life down there. While I was down there a cable came to this little town where I was camped out on the beach in a sleeping bag. This Mexican came out—he had a gun strapped on his waist and he came walking down to my camp and he strode right up and I thought, My God, this guy is going to shoot me. I thought I was going to be placed under arrest or something. I was pretty paranoid. He walked up and thrust out his hand and said in bad English, "Congratulations, your book is accepted." We went hooting and drank beer and had a big celebration. So I came back up and even though the book was accepted there was still work to be done on it. I moved to Montana and worked on the book, and when it came out it did pretty well. Then it was sold to the movies and was made into the worst movie in history.

INTERVIEWER: What was the name of it?

MCGUANE: *The Sporting Club.*

INTERVIEWER: Never saw it.

MCGUANE: If you blinked, it was gone. But I was paid for it. I had been accustomed to living on two to four thousand dollars a year and to suddenly get a movie check, man, I was looking at a decade's writing.

All of a sudden I realized that if I did nothing but fill up scraps of paper I was gonna be a writer for a while.

INTERVIEWER: The only real money in fiction now seems to be movie money. I know several writers who have managed to buy their first house because of their movie options.

MCGUANE: Well, I'm one of those writers for sure . . . I came out and bought a little ranch here and then it quadrupled in value. I resold it and bought another ranch out east of town and resold it. That turned into my land base and that's what my security derives from now. But when I look around I see these kind of writers—I won't name names—who published one exquisite book of short stories twenty years ago, and have had pretty remunerative academic jobs for twenty years on the basis of that one tiny volume. I would say those writers have made a lot of money off their books.

INTERVIEWER: I hadn't really thought about it that way.

MCGUANE: Look what you have to do to get a comparable teaching job on the straight and narrow road: get a doctorate, fight your way through the MLA conventions, hope to get the nod from some backwater school, fight your way for tenure. I think writers have it very easy in colleges. Don't you think so?

INTERVIEWER: In a way, you could say that. And it is unfortunate, because being a good teacher is one skill, being a writer is another. They are not necessarily the same thing at all.

MCGUANE: I spoke to that issue at a writers' conference. I said, teaching ideally requires considerable pedagogical abilities and just because you're not making a living entirely by your writing does not mean you have to become a teacher. I've had some miserable writer teachers; they thought they were purely totemic value sitting at the head of a class monosyllabically reacting to students' questions.

INTERVIEWER: Yet some writers feel that it was extremely beneficial to have that community of other writers. . . .

MCGUANE: Oh, I give you that . . . and the Stanford thing was quite interesting that way, the drama school was great that way, but where that was truest for me was as an undergraduate at Michigan State. I had three or four chums there who were really driven to write. Chief among them was Jim Harrison, of course. But there were others of us there, some of whom were very good and didn't make it. We had a really passionate literary situation. It was really beyond anything that I saw thereafter.

INTERVIEWER: I don't think I have ever talked to a writer who didn't agree that writing is a very lonely profession.

MCGUANE: I don't think loneliness is the word. John Graves said writing is "anti-life." I'm forty-five years old, I've been writing full-time since I was sixteen, I've been writing almost every day for thirty years; and as I look back with a degree of resentment, I realize that I literally lifted chunks of my life out for drafts of things, some of which got published and some didn't. And there is no experience to show for it, there is nothing but sitting in front of a legal pad for what now must amount to a third of my life. It's as though that was a hole in my life.

INTERVIEWER: But you have had this friendship with another writer, Jim Harrison, all these years. Has it had an impact on your work?

MCGUANE: I'm sure we've had an impact on each other's lives and thinking. We've managed to bolster one another in a fairly high view of the mission of writing, so that in lean years and blocked times it still felt that it was kind of a religious commitment. I don't know what writing is seen to be now, but I know that I continue to believe sort of what I believed then; I'm like someone who is intensely and successfully raised as a Catholic or a Lutheran; it just didn't go away from me. And now as I look on a future of freedom from the kinds of worries I used to have, my only vision of excitement is to be able to read and write harder and do what I wanted to do in 1955 or 1956. I am sure that the fact that Harrison and I have been writing back and forth for a quarter of a century almost entirely about writing has been one of the things that keeps that thread intact. Having a handful of writers around the country whose reality is there for you, knowing they are out there, knowing they might get what you are doing, makes you independent a little bit.

INTERVIEWER: Are they the people you write for in a sense of an ideal reader?

MCGUANE: There are some writers whose opinion really matters to me—who could really hurt my feelings if they said the book was terrible, who could make me excited by liking it. The three or four people whom you respect thinking that you're not a complete fool can really keep you going.

INTERVIEWER: Who else do you want your books to be accessible to? In the sense of Virginia Woolf's "common reader"?

MCGUANE: Let me wind back a little bit by saying I think that the sort of burnt-earth successes of modernism have left prestigious writing quite inaccessible to normal readers. There used to be a perennial *New Yorker* cartoon where some yahoo from Iowa was standing in front of a painting at the Museum of Modern Art saying, "All I can say is I know what I like" and I think it was meant to show how stupid the average guy is. I actually think that the average guy is right in saying I know what I like. I'm a little bit dour now when it comes to books which are terribly brilliant by some sort of smart-set consensus, but which nobody I know can read.

INTERVIEWER: How important is the language of a novel to you, the joy of words?

MCGUANE: There is a thrill to be had in language viewed as music, but I think for that tail to wag the dog is a mistake. Obviously there's an infinite mix and there is no right and wrong about it. At this point in my life the writing that I really like has clarity and earned and rendered feeling as its center. Writers who have done that most successfully leave you feeling experientially enlarged, rather than awed or intimidated—those things which have been the basis of the modernist response in writing.

INTERVIEWER: It seems to me that *Nobody's Angel* and *Something to Be Desired* are moving towards a simpler and cleaner style than your earlier work. Do you think anything in the earlier work prepared you for this?

MCGUANE: I think there has inevitably been some kind of an evolution for me in the rise of emotional content. It's also been a moving away from comedy. I set out to be a comic novelist and that's become not clear to me as time has gone on. Things have happened—you can't live forty-five years without things happening to jar and change you. The biggest change for me was a tremendous uproar in my life during the seventies. My mother, father, and sister died in about thirty months flat. I remember very specifically feeling that it was a watershed, that I would never be the same again after that happened. When you have attended that many funerals that fast it's very hard to go back to a typewriter and say, "What is my next comic novel?" You simply don't do that. But reviewers think you do. Reviewers say, "Why isn't he still as funny as he was before all those deaths?" Reviewers are endlessly obtuse. And that makes you shrink away from what they represent; it makes you shrink away from publication in a funny way because you realize there's this dreadful stupor that you are going to have to march through with your latest infant in your arms.

INTERVIEWER: I'm gathering from what you're saying that the "word-drunk" style in your earlier work was tied in with the fact that it was comic.

MCGUANE: Well, yes. I wanted then and will want again to write comic novels. I love comic fiction.

INTERVIEWER: Do you see comic fiction as a tradition and if so, what are some of the elements of it?

MCGUANE: Good comic writing comes from a very nearly irrational center that stays viable because it is unexplainable. It often disports itself in a kind of charged language. That is to say it is not appropriate to use exactly the same prose style for writing an all-out comedy as it is for writing a rural tragedy. Each book demands its own stylistic answers. At the same time, one has the right to expect a writer to have a style. I don't think a writer has to be as transparent as the phone book. I don't want to be that. I think, though, as you perfect your style you should hit the target on the first shot rather than on the fourth, and a good writer should get a little bit cleaner and probably a little bit plainer as life and the oeuvre go on.

INTERVIEWER: But it seems to me that there is a *charged* plainness in your last two books. The simplicity has under it all the skills that went into the others.

MCGUANE: Oh, I sure hope so. You want something that is drawn like a bow and a bow is a simple instrument.

INTERVIEWER: There is a lot of wit in *Something to Be Desired.* It's sad in some ways but it's also got a satirical edge. Was that intended?

MCGUANE: It wasn't intended to be satirical, but it was intended to be comic. I wanted to take a piece of crazy venture capitalism and show how desperate a private business really is. For some people getting their backs to the walls and starting a successful business can be as desperate an action as taking drugs. The guy says, "My God, I don't know what I'm going to do, I think I'll open a pizza parlor. My life is at an end, I'm going to start a dry cleaners." That seems to be a wholly American approach to desperation.

INTERVIEWER: It also is pretty funny.

MCGUANE: It's hilarious. But once you spot it, you can go into a town and all you see is desperation. You see some sad lady with a fashion outlet in downtown Livingston, Montana. You know, the wind is blowing through the town and the town is filled with snow as she is standing behind the plate glass, with a lot of imitation French clothes. What could be more frantic?

INTERVIEWER: Critics talk about you as a comic novelist but always with the implication that this is heavy social comment, social satire and that sort of thing.

MCGUANE: Well, there was an old Broadway producer who said, "Satire is what closes on Saturday night" and I think he is exactly right. I think satire has as its fatal component an element of meanness. It more or less says, look at what those awful people are doing. I'd never do anything like that, but by pointing them out I hope that you people will change them. Comedy, on the other hand, says, look at the awful things those people are doing. I could be doing the same thing, but for this moment I'm just going to describe it.

INTERVIEWER: It strikes me that you have a lot in common with Mark Twain.

MCGUANE: I find that hugely flattering. Nothing could please me more. I see him as immersed in a well-loved American milieu, schizophrenically rural and urban, inclined to bursts of self-pity as the autobiography would suggest and also inclined . . .

INTERVIEWER: In wild and hairy business schemes . . .

MCGUANE: Wild business schemes which I have been guilty of.

INTERVIEWER: That always failed.

MCGUANE: I'm a better businessman than he was.

INTERVIEWER: His always failed.

MCGUANE: And also an element of anger and rage disguised as comedy as in "The Man Who Corrupted Hadleyburg." Some of them are more bitter than anything else and the bad side of Twain is something I identify with, too.

INTERVIEWER: One subject that seems to unify all your books is what happens to people who get hung up on an untested idea.

MCGUANE: One of the great themes of Irish-American literature, if I can pretend to be Irish-American professionally for a moment, is spoiled romance. Scott Fitzgerald was the master of this and while the elements were in balance he was marvelous. But when it became something as ugly and pusillanimous as *The Crack-Up,* which to me is one of the most loathsome pieces of writing in the language, you see the Irish-American stance fall apart. What frustrates me when I think about Fitzgerald is it seems, from the evidence of *The Last Tycoon,* that he was about to go into a thrilling middle phase; having survived drunkenness and shattered romance, he was now going on to be a grown-up writer. We never get to find out about that.

I remember one time meeting Gore Vidal and he sort of stared at me and said, "Funny thing about all you Irish writers, you're all social climbers." And I think that is kind of true, the ease with which the Irish could move in American society once they got going. True of John O'Hara and Scott Fitzgerald for sure.

INTERVIEWER: In many ways, especially in their endings, your last two novels, *Something to Be Desired* and *Nobody's Angel,* remind me of Henry James. They're similar in the sense of the psychological violence, the cross-currents of violence that leave people wiped out. They come to the place where they see too much, they see too clearly.

MCGUANE: I, of course, come to it from a sort of cruder perspective. Partly from being in the horse business, I've spent a lot of time in the Oil Belt and I've gotten to know a lot of petro-chemical zillionaires who breed horses and do things like that. I have also gotten to see a lot of people on what was recently the American frontier who are now living in the world of answered prayers. They go down to the 7-Eleven store in helicopters; they go to Scotland and buy the winner of the dog trials to bring back to keep around the house; they jet around the world and things get very, very accelerated for them. All of a sudden they are up against the accumulated values of the civilization to that point, but they have to deal with them because money, drugs, speed, and airplanes have brought them to a point of exhaustion. Sooner than it ever did before. They are up against the American dream as it's expressed in western America in a way that makes it something that can't really be survived.

INTERVIEWER: But, when you think of the material James dealt with—nouveau riche Americans. The pattern of *Something to Be Desired* reminded me so much of the pattern of John Marcher in *The Beast in the Jungle,* who at the end replaces obsession with obsession on top of obsession.

MCGUANE: It really is a case of a man discovering that a narcissistic crisis is going to bear penalties which are permanent. I think that the nature of the age, say the sixties, the seventies, and the eighties, has been the indulgence of the "me" figure without suitable precautions. People should understand that, yes, it might be marvelous for you to go on a mission of self-discovery, but understand that people will not necessarily be here when you get back. I don't think Timothy Leary ever told anybody that; I don't even think Ken Kesey told anybody that. I think they more or less said that you paint your bus psychedelic colors and you take off, and when you come back the things that you wanted to be there will still be there. That turns out not to be the case. My book is about that. Its implications are not tragic because the narcissist is not a good tragic figure.

INTERVIEWER: You've said a couple of interesting things about your earlier books; I wonder if you would care to comment about them.

MCGUANE: I see the progress of those first three books as technological jumps from each other. The first, *The Sporting Club,* was meant to be a really controlled acid comic novel of the kind that I was then appreciating. Henry Green and Evelyn Waugh . . . Your first two or three books represent all that you wanted to do during the previous twenty-eight years . . . you come out and want to write *Hamlet,* and then you want to write *Don Quixote* and then you want to write *The Divine Comedy.* Then you begin to simmer down a little bit. My second, the *Bushwacker Piano,* reflected my fascination with picaresque novels. The third book really derives from my interest in surrealism, juxtaposition. *Ninety-two in the Shade* has more jagged layering of voices and situations than any book I wrote before or since. When I was writing it I was trying to not write a protagonist-centered novel. I was trying to take a different whack from a different angle and not write a Jamesian novel and not confine the information to what could be seen from a single point of view. And when I look back I realize that I must have gotten so aloft in this project I wonder how I could find the bathroom at the end of the day's work.

INTERVIEWER: That book has been called a giant pun on Hemingway, and your earlier books were compared to Faulkner. Were you in any sense conscious of that element?

MCGUANE: That is just absurd. Hemingway is a figure that casts a tremendous shadow for better or for worse. In the United States, it's a cottage industry to produce books about how terrible Ernest Hemingway was. So when Harry Crews or Jim Harrison or I are called Hemingwayesque, it's merely a way of saying, "We don't like this writer."

INTERVIEWER: The criticism that I've read implied that you were writing the anti-Hemingway novel, turning the Hemingway mystique or code of behavior upside down.

MCGUANE: I would say that the gist of the Hemingway comparison over the years has been by way of belittling my work. But I don't feel singled out. When I talked with Gore Vidal, he said, "I've been rereading Ernest Hemingway, and he is so scriptural and dull," and I said, "Well, I don't know what it is, Gore, but the people of the world go on wanting to read Ernest Hemingway." He said, "Not this people of the world." I think that is a kind of stance. There is a deep, deep hatred of Ernest Hemingway in the American literary community. And they should just admit it.

INTERVIEWER: But you do admire his work?

MCGUANE: I don't like all of his work. Actually, in fact, I don't like maybe more than half of it. But, the thing that is obviously interesting is that Hemingway can acquit himself in prose. Nothing needs to be said in defense of him; his influence will continue to erode his enemies' bastions.

INTERVIEWER: How does a novel come together for you?

MCGUANE: There are two ways a novel can come together for anybody. One is answering to a plan. I've found over the years that that doesn't work very well for me. I'll outline everything and then the outline becomes irrelevant. The writing I like the best is when I don't know what I'm doing. This is another way of saying, if I can foresee the shape of a book and if I can foresee the outcome of things I've set in motion, then that is almost a guarantee of its being too limited. I would rather be a sort of privileged reader in that I get to write what I get to read, and chance having to write six or seven hundred pages to produce a two-hundred-page book. Then there is an element of real, deep-down excitement about the process. It is the harder way to write a book, the wilder way. It's the Indian way to write a book.

INTERVIEWER: Can you identify the place where an identifiable voice, a narrator or protagonist, takes over?

MCGUANE: Yeah, but that comes up from within. It's like metal. You heat it and you heat it and then light comes out of the metal. You can't just go right up to the thing and say, "Happen." It has to arise from some level of your *self* that you don't control.

INTERVIEWER: I'm thinking of what Stanley Elkin has often said, that the first thing he hears is a voice and then the next thing that comes to him is an occupation.

MCGUANE: Sherwood Anderson, who is by way of being my favorite writer these days, always used to try to get the pitch right. He would keep writing and writing on his first sentence until the pitch was right and then he could write it. That sounds very familiar to me. On the other hand, Peter Taylor, who is a superb writer, said one of the wiliest things that I've heard in a long time. He said that when he begins to hear the voices in a story and the story begins to write itself, he tears it up and throws it away. So there you have it. These things are highly personal. I know lots of fine horse trainers who use systems that are diametrically opposite to one another; they would seem to cancel each other, but they all end up making really fine horses.

INTERVIEWER: Do you think people reading your books tend to confuse you with your characters?

MCGUANE: Oh, yes, I'm sure they do, and I'm sure that's partly my doing. I don't think I would have much luck writing a book from a stance or a point of view which I didn't share at all. But you want to separate yourself from your narrow focus in order to broaden the geometry of the book. I used to think in terms of these utterly perverse plans for books. I was once going to write a detective novel in the form of a cookbook. I was hellbent just to shake up the kaleidoscope. I don't feel that way anymore. I find it hard enough to write interestingly and to write well, giving myself all the tools I can handle. I no longer think it is necessary to make it crazy or write a six-hundred-page novel that takes place in two minutes.

INTERVIEWER: A lot of critics and a lot of readers seemed to think *Panama* was autobiographical. When the narrator says, "I'm working without a net, for the first time," is that you giving away yourself?

MCGUANE: First of all, that's a strategy to draw the reader into my web. There is nothing more handy to an author's purposes than to have a reader say, "Aha, now I'm going to find out." Then you can take him anywhere. In fact, it was tonally very much autobiographical; in specific incident, it was partly autobiographical. At the same time I wanted the reader to believe what I was saying, because sometimes one could make up something that would better illustrate an emotional point than the actual thing that happened. All of us have gone into a store and looked at a plastic doll or something that doesn't mean a thing and suddenly been overwhelmingly depressed by it. I can remember when the McDonald people brought out Egg McMuffins and there were Egg McMuffin signs all over Key West. I looked at it and I thought life was not worthwhile anymore if I had to share the planet with Egg McMuffin. Well, that doesn't translate, it's not usable.

INTERVIEWER: But does the experience described in *Panama,* this narrator who's been in the fast lane and gotten totally burned out, at all reflect what happened to you after *Ninety-two in the Shade* and the film?

MCGUANE: Yes, I think I got pretty burned out. . . .

INTERVIEWER: You got in big trouble?

MCGUANE: Yes, I did. It was big trouble, but it was good trouble, in some ways, because I often revert to being a control freak, as they say. And you know, I really had been such a little monk trying to be a writer for so long that I was sick of that. I saw all of these wonderful social revolutions going on around me and I wasn't part of them. Everybody was having such a wonderful time and I was always in the damn library and I was getting tired of it. And so, in 1973 when suddenly I was on the front page of the *New York Times* and movie producers wanted to give me money and people wanted me, I just said, "Yes." I said, "I'm going to go do this for a while," and I did and at the end of it, I was pretty played out. It was a bad time to be at the end of it because that was when my family started dying off. That was not a happy time. At the same time, I could hardly repudiate it; you know I wanted, as the girls used to say in the romantic dramas, to live a little. I wanted to go out and do a lot of things and I certainly did. I got out and I saw just about everything that was going on.

INTERVIEWER: And did a little of it, too?

MCGUANE: I did *all* of it.

INTERVIEWER: And you did it in the seventies instead of the sixties. You were a late bloomer.

MCGUANE: I still am.

INTERVIEWER: You seem to be a person for whom a rich family life and your work out here on the ranch is very important.

MCGUANE: Yes. I'll stick to my guns on that one. You'll find me doing this twenty-five years from now if I'm lucky enough to be alive. I have eliminated a lot of things now, and I really like my family life. I'm married to a wonderful, tough girl who knows what she wants to do. I don't have to prop her up, she's just fine, she fights back. It's great. My kids like me.

INTERVIEWER: How many times have you been married?

MCGUANE: I've been married three times really, but I was married very, very briefly the second time. I was married for fourteen or fifteen years in my first marriage. Then I was married for eight months or something like that. I've been married for eight or nine years now.

INTERVIEWER: Did the burnout you went through in the seventies have anything to do with the breakup of your first marriage?

MCGUANE: I think so . . . I think so. But it also had sort of run its course. It was not an acrimonious conclusion to a first marriage. I very much admire my first wife. She and I continue to be friends. In fact, she and my present wife are great friends.

INTERVIEWER: Your second wife was an actress, wasn't she?

MCGUANE: Margot Kidder. It was just an arbitrary event, has nothing to do with any . . . The record speaks otherwise so I can't say this, but I'm really kind of a monogamist.

INTERVIEWER: What do you do here on the ranch? Can you tell us a little bit about the cutting horses?

MCGUANE: Well, we have a band of broodmares, twenty or twenty-five mares that we use for breeding purposes. Then we run anywhere from 75 to 125 yearling cattle. We raise and sell and break and train cutting horses. Which is actually a bit of a monster; it takes up more time than I want it to.

INTERVIEWER: What is a cutting horse?

MCGUANE: In the West, cattle are sorted horseback, at least they always were. Horses are getting replaced by motorcycles and feedlots and weird things, but still a cutting horse has always been a valuable tool to a cowman for sorting cattle. They take diseased cattle out, or nonproductive cows or injured cattle. To go into a herd and bring a single individual out requires an incredibly smart, skillful, highly trained horse and a very knowledgeable rider. That situation has produced a contest animal, just as range roping has produced rodeo roping, and horse breaking has produced bronco riding. That's what we raise here. We have probably one of the better small breeding programs in the nation. We work hard at it. It's not a hobby. We raised the reserve champion of the Pacific Coast in the cutting-horse futurity, we raised the national futurity reserve champion, and I've been Montana champion three years in a row, and we've had the open champion up here.

INTERVIEWER: What relationship does it bear to your writing life?

MCGUANE: It keeps me thrown among nonliterary people a big part of my life. I spend a lot of time with cattle feeders and horse trainers and breeders and ranchers, and I like that. It also has made me sort of the village freak in their world. When I rode at the national finals at the Astrodome, it was horrifying. As I rode toward the herd, I could hear these blaring loudspeakers: "Novelist, screenwriter," quack, quack, quack. It is as though this geek has come in to ride, you know. That is kind of disturbing. I'm really not one of the boys in that sense. On the other hand, I can compete against them and beat them and they respect our breeding program.

INTERVIEWER: Does it keep you sane?

MCGUANE: Well, it's the outer world. You know you can't go out there and mope around and be narcissistic and artistic in a band of broodmares with colts on their sides who all need shots and worming and trimming and vaccinating.

INTERVIEWER: How do you schedule the two different things?

MCGUANE: It goes up and down seasonally. For example there's not a lot to do in the winter. All we can do is feed. And then about now, as soon as things really get going in the spring, it gets to be too much and sometimes I kind of resent it, because I'm working on a book, and I don't want to be out there doing that all day long.

INTERVIEWER: One thing we haven't talked about is the father-son and son-father element in your work.

MCGUANE: Yes, I would like to say something about that. It seems funny. My father's been dead for almost a decade and I'm forty-five; it seems I should stop thinking about that. But it has never really seemed to quite go away. When I was a little boy, my father and I were very close and as I got older and he got more obsessed with his business and became more of an alcoholic, he kind of drifted away from me. I think I've been inconsolable about that for a big part of my life. Inconsolable. I mean when I look at a blank piece of paper, all of a sudden Dad comes out. It's there and all I've been able to do is write about it. Try to get it down. I think maybe I got it clear in *Panama* and I'm not obsessed with it anymore. I'm more obsessed with my relationship to my children and trying to feel that I've made some progress. If I could write as long as I want to, and I can think of maybe ten books that I want to write right now, I think it will be seen that this is sort of the end of that father-son era in my writing.

INTERVIEWER: What about the business of games people play as an organizing principle in your work?

MCGUANE: Once you leave subsistence, you enter the world of games, whether you move from subsistence to warfare or you move from subsistence to art. They can all be viewed as a situation where people say, "I'll tell you what, you take that position and I'll take this one . . ."

INTERVIEWER: And we'll see what happens . . .

MCGUANE: And we'll see how it turns out. For some reason it is quite automatic for me to see that interpretation of what's going on. I don't mean it in a reductive way. When I see games in life I don't say that life is just a game, that's not what I mean at all.

INTERVIEWER: You do tend to write about people who aren't necessarily against the wall economically. They have the means by which to enter the realm of games.

MCGUANE: In fact, even ranchers, like the people next door here who just barely make it financially every year, have time to do anything they want to do. You talk to people in Livingston, which is kind of a blue-collar town, and they'll often say, "You've got time to ride horses and do all the things you want to; we're really up against it." Yet they'll pay five thousand dollars for a snowmobile and they'll go buy these campers, but they see that as their necessity material. As opposed to silly stuff like horses, they've got serious stuff like campers and snowmobiles.

It's not a valid point, but one of Reagan's henchmen said, "How can we as a government address the problem of poverty when the number one nutritional problem in the United States is overeating?" And it was a real snarky remark, but at the same time I see a lot of people who say "I have a dishwashing job, and you get to be a writer." They don't have to have that job. And it makes it boring for me to write about dishwashers, because I don't see why they do it or why they want to do it.

INTERVIEWER: I take it at some point you've got a character and you say, let's see what happens to him if we put him in this situation. That's in a sense sort of . . .

MCGUANE: . . . a game. In fact it seems to me that life is like that. I mean, that makes the Lewis and Clark expedition a game.

INTERVIEWER: Yes.

MCGUANE: That makes democracy a game. Maybe even first-strike capability is a game. I don't know, I mean I think this game idea gradually moves into meaning nothing. It just means life, charged life versus passive life.

INTERVIEWER: But you do see it as an organizing principle and it certainly shows up in your work.

MCGUANE: I love play. Playfulness is probably the thing that marks our household.

INTERVIEWER: You said something earlier about this Irish family you came from.

MCGUANE: My grandmother was orphaned at thirteen. She was the oldest of the family and she raised all these children, her brothers and sisters. My father came from a small town, and had very little means. He was so astonished he went to Harvard that, to him, life became "before" and "after" Harvard, so we never revisited his origins. But I looked into the stuff. My grandfather's mother died of tuberculosis and malnutrition at twenty-nine with five children. They really didn't have much of a chance. All the girls in the family listed occupation: weaver, address: boardinghouse. You know, all the way down through these records. I just realize how terribly hard they really had it. And then, by the time I knew any of those people, I realized that's why life seemed so exciting to them. They were very optimistic people, and they had had it as tough and as mean as you can have it.

You remember the thing that Galbraith said years ago, "There is a vast difference between not having enough and having enough, but there is very little difference between having enough and having too much"? I think that there are a few sectors of this country that really have too much. Certainly the country has too much. That makes me believe that our burning our candle at both ends, while much of the world has no candle, must represent at least the prospects for decline. I sometimes think I see signs of that, though my view of life is not entirely that dour.

INTERVIEWER: Why not? How do you accommodate the discrepancies?

MCGUANE: Well, for example, I have a five-year-old daughter who is very excited about the orchard and the horses, the new colts. I don't really think I need to beleaguer her with information right now about Biafra, nor do I think that the activities of a Bernard Goetz underline the reality of her pleasure in new colts. All those things aren't necessarily connected. Some people feel they are, and maybe they're right, you know. It's a sort of religious loftiness that I don't have. I think, though, that the people who do have that sensibility don't seem to ever see anything in the foreground.

INTERVIEWER: Do your books stand, in and of themselves, as a defense against what you see around you that's subject for despair?

MCGUANE: Everybody has a responsibility to develop some sort of island theory. I think that life kind of hurtles forward in a massive way for the world, but within it, people invent islands—islands of sanity, islands of family continuity, islands of professional skills and powers, islands of craft, art, and knowledge. Those islands basically are contributors toward a cure for despair, in ways that we probably cannot quite understand.

Louise Erdrich and Michael Dorris

Louise Erdrich, author of Love Medicine *(1984),* The Beet Queen *(1986),* Tracks *(1988), and* Bingo Palace *(1994), was interviewed in 1986 along with her collaborator and husband, the late Michael Dorris, himself the author of* The Broken Cord *(1989), a book about his adopted son who had fetal alcohol syndrome. At that time, Dorris had just completed his first novel,* A Yellow Raft in Blue Water *(1987). Jointly, they are the authors of* The Crown of Columbus *(1991). Erdrich's most recent book is* Tales of Burning Love *(1996). Michael Dorris committed suicide in April 1997. His novel* Cloud Chamber *was published posthumously in 1997.*

It is perhaps the nature of their working relationship at the time of this conversation—Erdrich said they work out of a shared, or joint, vision—that makes this interview so interesting. She and Dorris met in 1972 at Dartmouth College, where he was director of the Native American Studies program and she was his student. Erdrich credits the strength of their relationship to their similar backgrounds. Both are from mixed-blood families and grew up around Native American reservations because their parents worked for the Bureau of Indian Affairs. Louise is Chippewa, and Michael is Modoc. Erdrich grew up near the Turtle Mountain Reservation in Wahpeton, North Dakota. Their shared vision includes an abiding concern with the questions of cultural and personal survival: what remains from the past, both good and bad, and how and why it survives. With honesty and humor, their books deal with the specter of alcohol and suicide in what is left of Native American culture; with murky family situations; and with whether characters will claim an identity even if it contains some defeat, or will lose themselves and become nothing at all.

INTERVIEWER: Can you tell me what word you two would choose to describe the relationship that you have as writers and how what Mr. Dorris does is different from anything that a good editor would do?

ERDRICH: We're collaborators, but also individual writers. Michael and I plunge into each other's work with very little ceremony. We plot together, we dream up our characters together, we do everything together, except write the actual drafts, although even the writing is subject to one another's deepest desires. We go over every manuscript word by word. Then we argue over whatever we feel should be changed and we try to come to some sort of agreement on everything that goes out.

DORRIS: And we succeed. There hasn't been a word from *Love Medicine,* or *The Beet Queen,* or *Yellow Raft* which has not been concurred upon in this process.

ERDRICH: There was one word we didn't agree on in *Love Medicine.* Dopplered. I know it's true that Albertine would never have made that word up right out of her high school science book, but I couldn't get rid of it: I just loved it.

DORRIS: One can have poetic excuses but the other person is the ultimate arbiter as to what this character, given her background, would say. We have been known to look at catalogs and decide what our characters would select, or look at menus and decide what they would eat, so that we get to know them in a very wide-ranging way, not all of which actually appears in the books. I continue to think Albertine wouldn't say "doppler," although as a poetic phrase it works. It was interesting working on the two novels at the same time because there came a moment in which there was a phrase that I really liked in *Yellow Raft* and a phrase that Louise didn't, and a phrase that she really liked in *The Beet Queen* that I didn't and we traded; we got rid of each other's phrases.

INTERVIEWER: How do you decide whose name to use when a piece is published?

DORRIS: It's whoever actually puts the words down on the drafts. *Yellow Raft* will come out under my name, but we plot them together. For instance, in the first draft version of *Yellow Raft,* the main character was a young woman whose mother dies, and we decided to spend our time driving out to Minnesota talking about the plot. By the time we got here it became the story of a young woman whose mother lives. It's an evolving process, this collaboration; it's new to both of us. More and more we feel free to inject phrases, words. I think what has really astounded us is that we totally trust each other's judgment. When you finish a draft and it seems to you very good—it might be a draft of a paragraph, a page, or a whole chapter—and you take it into the other person and that look crosses their face that says "It doesn't cook," you might, or I might, get angry or frustrated, or argue, or whatever, but at this point in our working relationship I think we feel in our heart of hearts that it has to be changed.

ERDRICH: A grim certainty passes within you; you know that no matter how hard you resist it, if the other person truly does not have the reaction you're looking for, then usually it gets changed, and long afterward I've looked back with a sigh of relief and said, "Thank God I didn't hold on to that."

INTERVIEWER: When did you start writing, Louise?

ERDRICH: I was in college and had failed at everything else. I kept journals and diaries when I was a kid, and I started writing when I was nineteen or twenty. After college I decided that that's absolutely what I wanted to do.

Part of it was that I did not prepare myself for anything else in life. I had different kinds of jobs, here and there, and I kicked around until I finally got some extra money from writing a child's textbook, went to a writer's colony, and then to Dartmouth as a visiting writer. That's where I met Michael. I had known Michael before, but we just kind of faded out of each other's lives for a few years, and then when I came back, we Met. Capital *M.*

INTERVIEWER: You had been writing mostly poetry up to that point, is that right?

ERDRICH: At John Hopkins Writing Workshop, and I started writing fiction when I was there because I got encouragement. So I kept doing it, and then I started working on an urban Indian newspaper in Boston—this and that. I didn't really get anywhere until I went to Dartmouth as a visiting writer. Then Michael and I fell in love, married, and started working together. It was like overdrive, or something. I finally began to really get things together.

INTERVIEWER: With this joint vision. I read someplace that you two practice telepathy. Do you, or is that a silly story?

DORRIS: Oh, that was a joke.

ERDRICH: It's true, though; we can read each other's minds. My grandmother said once that you'll know that you're really married when the man, whom she characterizes as the "the king," comes home, and you know what he wants for dinner and he doesn't even have to say anything to you.

ERDRICH: Our telepathy is on . . .

DORRIS: A different plane.

ERDRICH: We like to think it is, although the main telepathic vision we have transmitted is a Big Mac, from one room to the other [laughs].

INTERVIEWER: Do you think you'll ever collaborate completely?

DORRIS: We may, we may, at some point. As I say, it's an evolving process. But the system that now exists works for us emotionally and practically and we have not yet really experimented with sitting down and, I don't even know how we'd do it, writing the words together.

ERDRICH: I think one needs solitude in order to really fall as deeply into a piece of writing as one must. I imagine that when we do do something together we will still write alone, but just put the writing into the books.

INTERVIEWER: Was it for this reason that you chose not to publish *Love Medicine* under both your names, because it's Louise's actual . . .

DORRIS: Words on the page.

INTERVIEWER: Yes, words on the page.

ERDRICH: I think it's coconceiving that differentiates this relationship from an editorial relationship. I can't think of any example of an editor and a writer who sit down and have this swell time imagining into a literary novel this set of characters. I think that's partly why the relationships become so gnarled in the books, because we sit and just imagine.

INTERVIEWER: Can you think of a typical situation that shows this process?

DORRIS: There's a scene in *Love Medicine* where Marie is waiting for Nector to come back from his assignation. He's left a note for her under the sugar jar, and she decides at the last minute, after going through a lot of trauma about how she's going to react, that she's going to put it back and pretend that she has not read the note. But she puts it under the salt instead of the sugar. It was one scene that our conversation really altered, and made a little more complicated, than it was before. Another one, in *Yellow Raft,* is the change of one of the main characters from a male to a female. It was Louise's urging that this happened, and it works a thousand times better in terms of the book.

INTERVIEWER: You brainstorm then. You make up stories about the characters, and you speculate what they might do.

ERDRICH: Yes, yes.

DORRIS: We live out in the country on a farm, far away from most of our friends, and we have five kids. Consequently, the people in the books *become* our friends. They're like real people, although they're *not* real; they're 100 percent fictional.

INTERVIEWER: Writers speak of the different ways that stories come to them; some conceive germs, or seeds, and others know how a book's going to end when they start it, even though sometimes they find out that they were wrong, that the story has to change.

DORRIS: What you're saying is very true of what happens with us, too. I think one of the things that a writer has most to look forward to is finding out what happens to these characters next. I don't think, other than in a very general way, when the first draft is through, we really know quite what to expect. Louise said one time that the criterion for something going well is if it surprises you as you're writing it.

INTERVIEWER: When we think of an artist's conceived and executed piece of work, we think of it as reflecting a vision. Would you say that it is *your* vision, Louise, or is it a joint vision, that you're working out of in *Love Medicine* and *Beet Queen*?

ERDRICH: That is hard to say—I would say now that it is a joint vision. I don't think when I first started I would have been able to say that. We got very close in working on *Love Medicine,* and as the work has gone by, I feel more and more that we're seeing out of the same set of eyes. Part of the reason is that we have similar backgrounds; we think each other's thoughts, truly, so it is very much like having one vision. I think I would probably write about the characters Michael has written about in just the same way. One of the odd things about this kind of relationship is *deeply* wishing, however, that I had written the line that Michael wrote, on a certain day. I'll go back and I'll think, "Oh, no, it's so good." I'll be so happy on one hand that it's us . . . and on the other hand the individual writer says, "Why didn't I think of that?"

INTERVIEWER: What about the first story in *Love Medicine,* "The World's Greatest Fishermen"? Was that your germ, your idea, Louise?

ERDRICH: It was something that had been written in a very rough draft, maybe years before. I always had the idea, but I never had anywhere to put it. The year Michael and I were first married, Michael's aunt gave us a notice about the Nelson Algren competition, which had this five-thousand-dollar prize. We were kind of looking for money, and thought, "Why not just write this?"

DORRIS: This was Christmas, and the deadline was January 15th . . .

ERDRICH: Yes, so it was right at the very last minute. It had been there, but I hadn't really had the guts to do anything with it. Then Michael got ill—he was flat on his back—so it was in this very strange kind of frenzy that that story was written. A very uncomfortable kind of writing, in fact, because I would be writing on the kitchen table with people about to come in at any minute. Michael would read it, make adjustments, and, you know, it was very much the beginning of that kind of process . . .

DORRIS: That story, as it existed when it won the Nelson Algren award, is vastly changed in the first chapter of *Love Medicine.* It's broken down into different parts, and there's a whole section that did not exist in the other story.

When the first story went out, and we heard that people liked it, we took "Scales" and "Red Convertible," which were existing stories, and talked about integrating them, and we recognized that those characters were also related thematically.

ERDRICH: There's a gauze that covers your vision when you try to see the whole of your characters, try and figure out who's related to who. It's very hard to pick out those traits that make a character similar to somebody you've already written about. There's something to be said for that little bit of distance that allows another person to see, to manipulate things with more of a sure hand.

DORRIS: It's almost like we believe these people exist in real life, and we're trying to uncover them, like the sculptor who knocks away marble.

INTERVIEWER: Have you thought about yourself in the context of other couples who write together?

DORRIS: I don't think we think of ourselves as in a category; we're pretty surprised to find ourselves who we are, and doing what we're doing.

ERDRICH: There's this very romantic and often very true notion of the writer's struggling with his or her destiny alone, in some small, painted room . . .

INTERVIEWER: "Out there alone, where nobody can help you."

ERDRICH: We think of that sometimes, as our children are cavorting or careening about. We don't have that kind of life.

DORRIS: But there is one great advantage that we haven't mentioned yet. When writing about both male and female characters, it is a distinct advantage to have an absolutely trusted and equitable input from someone of the other gender who shares the same vision, almost as an opposite-gender version of yourself. *Yellow Raft* is written in the voices of three women, and it would have been impossible to do without this kind of collaboration.

INTERVIEWER: Do you think that your comfort with this kind of relationship is in any way related to your Native American roots?

DORRIS: We both came from specific family traditions, which are probably microcosms of tribal traditions in some respects, of people sitting around and telling stories and embellishing and adding to and participating. It's as though the story evolves out of a set of shared memories.

INTERVIEWER: You, Louise, were the child of a Chippewa mother and a German-American father who worked for the Bureau of Indian Affairs. Was this an unusual "mixed-marriage"?

ERDRICH: Well, it wasn't so unusual in the town where I grew up. It's a town called Wahpeton, on the border between Minnesota and North Dakota. A number of people from different tribes taught or worked somewhere on the campus of the Bureau of Indian Affairs boarding school in Wahpeton, and had either married people in town, or . . . yes or no. It wasn't a big deal when I grew up.

INTERVIEWER: One of the things that I think is especially unique and very interesting about *Love Medicine* is the breaking of stereotypes, the mix, as in both your families, of Anglo and Native American. In other writing by Native Americans it seems like there's often a pejorative connotation to intermarriages.

ERDRICH: I think what you may be saying is that it's a political issue that is almost outside the characters, outside their ethnic background.

DORRIS: When we worked on *Love Medicine* one of the conscious decisions that we made was that it was a book about people in a community and not a book about contact between Indians and non-Indians. Certain political points are implicit in the situation, but it really is about people in a small community who have to get along with each other over time and who know all of each other's stories.

INTERVIEWER: Yet there is some ethnic prejudice in *Love Medicine,* isn't there? Zelda criticizes King Junior's wife, just because she's white, and Aurelia says, "What are you talking about?" There is that back and forth. I grew up in the Southwest where there was virtually no such thing as a full-blooded Indian; everybody was mixed. Yet, as I grew older, I became aware that there were parts of the country where there was prejudice. Do you think it's a regional question?

ERDRICH: Yes, I think it is different in different parts of the country. Where Indian land impinges on valuable non-Indian land, or where non-Indians feel threatened, the prejudice is heightened, definitely. There's antagonism when people aren't safe from each other, when non-Indian people feel that something could be taken away.

INTERVIEWER: In *Love Medicine* there's definitely an ironic element in Gerry Nanapush's becoming an activist. To what extent was the irony deliberate?

ERDRICH: It was deliberate. What else can I say about that? The political parts of the book, I think, are woven into people's lives, but do not completely control their lives. I think our primary concern was to have characters who were like people that really could exist, and whose lives were not taken up in thinking, "I'm an Indian, so I'm in this political situation." Obviously, politics influences people's lives in every conceivable human way in this book, but we hoped it would be more affecting, and more obvious, maybe, to people to have them see it from the human point of view, rather than making political statements every time someone turned around.

DORRIS: By virtue of the fact that we are Indians and we are writing, people are going to inevitably read the books as some sort of a statement; but we don't feel in a position to be spokespersons. What we can do, if we do it well and we do it right, is reflect the reality of our perceptions, and that reality is enmeshed in politics—in a whole history of race relations, and economics, and a whole future, as well—and we're trying to capture a moment of it in time, and make it true, because in our understanding of the world, that truth speaks for itself without us editorializing about it. If it is true, it has meaning.

INTERVIEWER: What about the structure of *Love Medicine*? I understand that the stories were all in a different order, originally, and confusing to your editors, and that Michael stepped in and shaped the book.

ERDRICH: Yes, I did not really think of it as a book. I thought I was writing these disjointed little bits, and at one point I remember we sat down and Michael said, "This is a quartet."

DORRIS: It's hard to look back, and say what was whose. Even on individual words or on things like the structure. I think that probably there was a moment, you know—"Great Moments in Medicine"—in which I said it should be a quartet, and we started fooling around with the arrangement and made it approximately chronological. But they go through so many drafts that unless traced back from draft number one through draft number twelve it would be hard to figure out who had suggested what at any given moment.

ERDRICH: We began thinking of a novella. But as time went on, it became shaped through conversations into a novel that began, and had a certain driving force, I think, that brought it to the conclusion. That was a one-draft conclusion; we never, virtually ever, write out in one draft. But the end of *Love Medicine* was that kind of writing.

INTERVIEWER: How would you respond to the criticism that *Love Medicine* is not a novel, that it's just a set of interrelated short stories?

ERDRICH: I don't know what it matters, I mean, it's a book. I don't really know what it matters at all.

DORRIS: But we think it's a novel. I mean, whether it matters or not, from our point of view, it is a set of themes that culminates in a resolution that ties them all together.

ERDRICH: The shape, really, resembles storytelling in the Native American tradition. Stories that leave something hanging so that the characters can then come back and go onward. Gerry Nanapush as trickster in *Love Medicine* is very much part of this kind of tradition. It's told in a cycle, it does come back; it begins in the same year that it ends, and that is very much part of its structure, as well.

INTERVIEWER: You start with the children and you end with the children. Those last lines are so wonderful, about the water, "but the truth is we live on dry land. . . . So there was nothing to do but cross the water, and bring her home." That's June, isn't it?

ERDRICH: Oh, sure. I mean, she's identified with the car, and that is her car from insurance money. The cars really become sort of repositories for the souls of the dead in this book, and they're also shelter; they're many things. We've lived with cars that are alter egos through the years; that becomes true when you live in the Plains.

INTERVIEWER: It seems that June is the symbol of the beauty and the waste, all at once, of everything that's happened, at least in the context of this particular group of Native Americans. And finally you get the sense that . . .

ERDRICH: That some peaceful plateau is reached. Although there's a lot of anger, too, in the book, and there is, certainly, anger in both of us for what's happened in the past, but more importantly, really, in the present—what's happening under the current [Reagan] administration, the problems that are getting worse. Although there is this moment at the end of the book where one feels, yes, at least there is some sort of homecoming. It's a hard one, and when you really think about it, she's really not coming back. It's a terribly sad moment.

INTERVIEWER: Absolutely, but there is transcendence for Lipsha in finding out who his real grandparents are, who his real parents are. That moment when Marie presses the beads into his hand in the nursing home is one of my favorite moments, because he feels something, but doesn't understand that they're beads that his mother wore as the wild child in the woods when she was an infant. He can't know it, but he feels it.

ERDRICH: It's so nice to hear you say that. I never would have probably thought that up; Michael thought of the beads as coming back to Lipsha.

INTERVIEWER: In *Love Medicine,* you have created a fully realized character, June Kashpaw, who's really not there. That's amazing.

ERDRICH: Yes. But her car's there. I think that really makes a difference. When Henry gets in the red convertible, the red convertible can stand for something like assimilation; it's a very loaded symbol. Then he drives off into the river, and Lipsha crosses the river at the end, crossing the hulks of old cars. He's crossing the old symbols of the people who've not been able to survive. He has, and there's something quite wonderful about that simple fact. He has made it into some sort of resolution; there's a strength that he's found in himself.

INTERVIEWER: The last part of the cycle, the last hundred pages or so of the book, is a retelling of a kind of tale that is heavily characteristic of contemporary Native American literature: the lost child, usually the son, who goes through some kind of a process of initiation, and discovers his roots. Were you conscious of that?

ERDRICH: In a way, yes. We've realized that that is a very important element in a lot of our work. It's discovering parentage, or analyzing your past, trying to come to terms with who you are. Sometimes we think of it as quite predictable. You do look back and you try to pick out the threads to figure out where you're from, and where your tribe is from. Nobody is from where they say they are anymore.

DORRIS: The wild card, too, in this whole thing, is the character of Jude Miller, at the end of *The Beet Queen.* He doesn't know anything, really. The reader knows his whole story, but it is left for the fourth book in the quartet for him to make his discoveries, whatever they may be. We've also thought of each of these four books as having kind of an element central to its symbolism, *Love Medicine* being water, *Beet Queen* being air, *Tracks* being earth, and the last book being fire, because there are missiles in it, for instance.

INTERVIEWER: And you knew sometime toward the ending of *Love Medicine* that it was going to be four books?

ERDRICH: Yes, when Michael said, "This is going to be part of four books," which surprised me. I didn't know this.

INTERVIEWER: Can you talk about the publishing history of *Love Medicine*?

DORRIS: It really surprised us that *Love Medicine* received the reaction it did. It surprised the publisher, too. It started out as a very small first novel and a small first printing, and it's now been translated into fourteen languages. It's amazing to us that people all over the world have responded to this little book that came out of our living room.

ERDRICH: Let's start with the agent's history of *Love Medicine.* The agent is part and parcel of the publishing history, because Michael and our first editor just threw themselves into trying to get attention for the book. And we really were afraid that it was simply not going to happen.

DORRIS: We had an agent, a very prominent agent, in New York who agreed to represent the book and the draft of *Tracks* that existed at the time. And it didn't go anywhere; nothing happened for almost a year. Finally we said, "Let's give it a whirl ourselves." So I went and had stationery printed up with my name on it and claimed to be an agent and sent it out, and two major houses bid on it. Not extraordinary contracts or anything, but they were willing to publish. Then through luck and the efforts of a lot of people at Holt who really believed in the book, the wonderful reviewers, and other writers, like Philip Roth, who read the story in *Atlantic* and wrote us a letter, the book began to get attention.

ERDRICH: It was also a word-of-mouth book. That's how it's been characterized in the publishing world. People began to tell other people about it, and get it for other people, and that's how it began to show up on their computers, because one person would say, "I've got three friends, and I want them to read this book."

INTERVIEWER: This is a very crass question. Have you done okay, financially, by it?

DORRIS: We don't really know, because it has sold more overseas than it has sold in the United States, and foreign royalties take years to appear.

INTERVIEWER: How many copies has it sold here, so far?

DORRIS: In the United States, in cloth, it sold about forty thousand and in paper it sold over one hundred thousand. It was on a lot of best-seller lists. But those are hard to understand. I think from the point of view of the publisher, it was successful beyond their wildest expectations.

INTERVIEWER: Who do you see as your reader?

ERDRICH: I don't see one person. I see a real spectrum of people, and it's hard to say now what an ideal reader would be. We've been very lucky in that *Love Medicine* prompted many people to write. We got an enormous amount of mail from people who told stories on themselves, "This is what my life is like," you know. When I see our ideal readers I really see those people. We've had one letter that's pinned up on the wall because it's so beautiful; it's just a beautiful letter, but it wasn't signed. It said "You should be writing, and I'm not going to sign this, because you might take the time to write back."

DORRIS: And if that person is listening, thank you!

INTERVIEWER: Was this person a Native American?

ERDRICH: Are you asking whether our ideal reader is Native American?

INTERVIEWER: I am wondering about that. Do you see yourselves as Native American writers?

ERDRICH: Well, I think it's simply a fact, but I don't think it's right to put everything off in a separate category. All of the ethnic writing done in the United States is American writing, and should be called American writing.

INTERVIEWER: There is an impulse out of which some writers do write, which is to say, "I'm writing for a black audience, I'm writing for a Native American audience, I'm writing for a Chicano audience." I gather that in your case this really could not be true.

DORRIS: I think we are writing because the stories are interesting to us. We try and tell them as real as we can. We'd be terribly worried if Indians hated the books; it would tell us that we were doing something very wrong.

INTERVIEWER: How has it been?

ERDRICH: It's been terrific. There is a very special kind of encouragement that comes from being well received by . . .

DORRIS: Grassroots people who don't read much fiction, normally, and who are proud of it. I mean, that's the only way of saying it.

INTERVIEWER: How do you get your characters? Are they a composite of people that you've both known in your families?

ERDRICH: It's very mysterious in some ways. There are traits we can say, "Ah, that might remind you of someone," but most of the characters have kind of developed themselves into real people, and real characters, by being talked about, and thought about this whole process. I don't know where Lulu, our favorite one, came from; she just began to gather details, and steam, and there was just no stopping her. But she was certainly no one I ever knew.

INTERVIEWER: It strikes me that humor plays an important role, ritually, in every aspect of Native America.

ERDRICH: I'd say everything tries to get humorous. But it's survival humor.

DORRIS: If there is one generalization that you can make in terms of the difference in reaction to *Love Medicine* between Indian and non-Indian audiences, it is that the Native American people who have talked to us about the book absolutely and unanimously pick up on the humor, right from the very beginning. I think many times that non-Indians who read the book feel almost guilty about laughing or finding things that are funny in the book, and we hope that they get over that. Because it's supposed to be there.

INTERVIEWER: What humor would you say is characteristic of Native American culture?

DORRIS: Self-deprecating, I think.

ERDRICH: But also deprecating of the dominant culture, I think.

INTERVIEWER: What about before the fall, before the circle was broken? What was humor like then?

DORRIS: It's really the same. You hear the stories about Trickster, for instance, and it's about the foibles of being human, about the silliness of situations in which people find themselves, and that the way out of a situation is to laugh at it, basically. I don't know whether it's that uncomplicated in real life, but as a metaphor, I think that it probably works.

ERDRICH: I think some of the humor is also spawned by the years of being dominated by another culture in many ways. Nector talks about the life he's led—he's been in the movies, all he gets to do is die over and over. Fall off his horse and die; that's the extent of his acting. And then he talks about the books he's read—he's talking to his mother about *Moby Dick,* tells her it's about a great white whale and she says, "All those whites, what do they got to wail about?" It's taking bits and pieces of another culture and working them into the fabric of your culture.

DORRIS: There's also a great deal of play on words. In nonliterate cultures there's a larger active vocabulary than in literate cultures because the entire lexicon has to pass from one generation to the next; there are no libraries and dictionaries. Consequently people have at their disposal this great number of words to use, and to play off of, in both humor and expression. It's a total misrepresentation to presume, as people sometimes do, that tribal cultures are inarticulate. They sometimes are inarticulate in English, but within a native language there is a tremendous resource. I think that is the oral tradition.

INTERVIEWER: There are those who say that the outsider has a better vision of the culture as a whole and consequently Native American writers, black writers, Chicano writers are some of the most powerful writers in American culture. Do you think there's anything to that?

DORRIS: That's an anthropological truism; the whole theory behind anthropology is that as an outsider you can see more clearly.

It's hard to talk about Native American literature because there really are three hundred different traditions and many different languages. It's like saying "non-Indian literature." Indian literature is as inclusive a term as non-Indian literature. Ultimately, it comes down to writing out of our collective experience and understanding.

INTERVIEWER: Louise, what parts of those elements do you think reverberate in the work you've done so far under your name?

ERDRICH: Well, to me, storytelling is having an audience waiting for the next word. In writing you get this sense because as you're trying a piece over and over, you get pretty tired of it. If it can keep you slightly interested by the time it finally goes away, I think you know that you're at least going to have some of your audience involved. I don't know how that fits, traditionally, into a traditional culture. I do know that Native American oral and literary tradition is a changing, ongoing, vital tradition. Not only a Native American tradition, but more particularly, it is a Chippewa tradition, that forms the work. So I suppose the most knowledgeable people who read this book are going to be Chippewas, but it's for everybody, of every background.

INTERVIEWER: In the *New York Times* you mentioned that Native Americans have to write after the fact about the broken circle, the holocaust, the loss. I wonder how this applies here.

ERDRICH: I think both of us feel, in writing from our background, that we're really spurred by this feeling that we have to tell the story. When both of us look backward we see not only the happiness of immigrants coming to this country, which is part of our background, but we see and are devoted to telling about the lines of people that we see stretching back, breaking, surviving, somehow, somehow, and incredibly, culminating in somebody who can tell a story. I think all Native Americans living today probably look back and think, "How, out of the millions and millions of people who were here in the beginning, the very few who survived into the 1920s, and the people who are alive today with some sense of their own tradition, how did it get to be me, and why?" And I think that quest and that impossibility really drives us in a lot of ways. It's central to the work, and so as we go about telling these stories, we feel compelled. We're, in a way, survivors of that tradition; there aren't a lot of people who are going to tell these stories, or who are going to look at the world in this particular way.

John Edgar Wideman

John Edgar Wideman, a Rhodes scholar and author of more than a dozen books, is known for writing about the area in Pittsburgh where he grew up, especially in his Homewood Trilogy *(1985), which includes* Damballah *(1981),* Hiding Place *(1981), and* Sent for You Yesterday *(1983). He writes about the alienating effects of race and the ways in which his characters attempt to overcome it in order to join some sort of community, in the sense both of the larger American community and of the family. Wideman has shown himself to be one of the most adept American authors writing about the destructive effects of black rage and anger. His characters are often violent and alienated. He is admired by readers for his ability to vividly represent personalities distorted by rage against white society, and for showing the destructive effects of that rage, and their struggle, without sentimentality or facile answers.*

His life and writings have been haunted by issues of violence. His brother was involved in a murder similar to that described in Hiding Place. *His own son was sentenced to life in prison for murdering another teenager on a camping trip. Yet Wideman is always most fascinated by those characters who try to reconnect themselves rather than give in to despair. This interview was conducted in the spring of 1985, shortly after publication of* Brothers and Keepers *(1984), one of his most critically acclaimed works. His most recent novel is* The Cattle Killing *(1996).*

INTERVIEWER: Mr. Wideman, we know a lot about your biography from both the *Homewood Trilogy* and *Brothers and Keepers,* in which you try to come to terms with your brother Robby's imprisonment for first-degree murder. But I wonder about your life as a writer. Can you tell us at what point you began to know that's what you wanted to do?

WIDEMAN: I liked to get up and tell stories in grade school and I was pretty good at it. Most of my stories were bits and pieces of the reading I'd been doing, which would vary from the kids' fiction in the Carnegie Library to comic books. I loved comic books. I guess I began to identify myself as a writer even that early. Not as a writer with a capital W; I just liked to write and I had a lot of encouragement all the way through high school. But I don't think it was until probably my senior year in college that I actually began to make life decisions based on the idea that maybe I wanted to write.

INTERVIEWER: Were your parents supportive in that?

WIDEMAN: My parents have always been enormously supportive. Anything I've wanted to do was okay. I was told, do it well and work hard and make sure it's something you really like. That kind of support. But for my parents and really for the whole extended family I was a test case. Nobody else had gone all the way through school. Almost everybody in my parents' generation had a high school education, but nobody had gone on to college, so I was the flagship; I was out there doing things that no one else had done. My parents were smart not to try to monitor that, except by being supportive. The reasons that I went to college were basically mine. I thought I wanted to play pro basketball, and I knew in order to play pro basketball you had to play college basketball and to play college basketball you had to get a scholarship, so things sort of dovetailed and it was a lockstep kind of future that I had figured out for myself.

INTERVIEWER: You were on an athletic scholarship at the University of Pennsylvania?

WIDEMAN: Well, not exactly, because the Ivy League schools claim that they don't give athletic scholarships. That means that I had to qualify for an academic scholarship. In reality if you were a good athlete they gave you a certain number of points so that if I were competing against some kid from Illinois who had the same grades and the same sort of test scores as I did, I would get the scholarship.

INTERVIEWER: You went on to become a Rhodes scholar. Were you the first black Rhodes scholar?

WIDEMAN: There had been one black Rhodes scholar, Alaine Locke, in 1905, I believe it was. And then the same year I was elected, 1963, another man, Stan Sanders, from the West Coast was elected. So we were the first three. And Stan and I were the first two in about sixty years.

INTERVIEWER: Do you have a political attitude toward the Rhodes Scholarship program? Do the origins of the money bother you?

WIDEMAN: I'm not trying to hedge, but there's very clean money. Whose money do you take these days if you look at it very hard? To tell the truth, when I won a Rhodes Scholarship, I didn't know a thing about South Africa, or Rhodes. I just knew it was a chance to go to England and study. So I went into it ignorant, and ignorance is bliss. I had a grand old time. Subsequently, I've been part of the Rhodes selection process, and I've served on the board of directors of the Rhodes Trust in America. Not very actively I'll admit, but I've had an opportunity to try to change things from inside. That has its advantages. I've made it my business to look for qualified black applicants and also talked to other members of the committee in a political way. But for me it was not so much political as it was an attempt to explain why certain black applicants should be looked at very seriously. In any selection process, whether you're talking about Rhodes Scholarships or Marshalls or Churchills, there's an old boys' network and it ain't all bad. Once you get blacks into that kind of process—blacks, women, anybody who hasn't been in that process before—then I think you can work to change the process and educate people within a particular system. In the past few years many large questions have come up before the Rhodes trustees, among them the admission of women, the question of whether to say no more scholarships to South Africa, the question of isn't it ironic that Rhodes' money came from Africa but there are only a handful of black African scholars. I've tried to vote and use my weight to move the trust in the directions I think are right.

INTERVIEWER: When you went to Pennsylvania, what did you study?

WIDEMAN: I started out as a psych major, found out that meant mostly counting the number of times a rat went down a particular tunnel and got tired of that pretty quickly. I wanted to learn about Freud and Jung and all that fancy stuff about the unconscious and be able to look in somebody's eyes and tell what they were going to do and who they were going to be. That wasn't what psychology meant at the University of Pennsylvania at that time, so I flirted with anthropology for about a half semester and then I eventually became an English major. I took some creative writing classes there—one with a man named Christopher Davis, who is a very good novelist. Also I had a chance to meet Archibald MacLeish, who came in for a three-day stint at the university. He met with the writing class and looked at samples of writing from Penn students. I was very encouraged by having someone whose name I'd seen in the lights actually look at my writing, pat me on the back and say, "Son, you're doing pretty well and keep at it." The climate at Penn at that time was even freer than when I was a teacher at Penn in encouraging the arts and encouraging writers to come and spend time on the campus. All that helped me make up my mind.

INTERVIEWER: Did you write while you were at Oxford?

WIDEMAN: By the time I got to England I was fairly serious. I began to see myself as a writer and I saw the whole experience of getting out of the country as something that would forward a career in writing. I thought that was one way to get the kind of seriousness that I needed in my work. All of us grow up very confused and I thought writing was something that was connected with Europe. The matter of Europe. I didn't want to be a good American writer, let alone a good black writer. I wanted to be world-class, man, and to be world-class you had to be Thomas Mann and you had to be Marcel Proust and you had to walk along the Champs-Èlysées and you had to know about bullfights. Those were the things that were kind of stirring around in my head. I wanted to go where the action was. So going to Europe was a very conscious attempt to become part of that tradition.

INTERVIEWER: Was James Baldwin much of a model for you when you were young?

WIDEMAN: Not at all. I came through school with a standard English-lit education. I knew that there was a man named James Baldwin, because he made the newspapers, but he was not taught in my classes and I didn't know his work. I'm not sure whether or not I read any Ralph Ellison in college but if I did, it would have been probably the only piece of writing by a black writer.

INTERVIEWER: Did you read Langston Hughes and Richard Wright in the public schools?

WIDEMAN: They may have been in my high school anthology—"The Negro Speaks of Rivers" maybe for Hughes. But he certainly wouldn't have been picked out as a black writer and he probably was skipped because most teachers didn't know how to deal with it.

INTERVIEWER: You went through mainly a white school system in Pittsburgh. In fact, didn't your parents move so you could go to a better school?

WIDEMAN: Yes, but the race of the clientele didn't matter. Westinghouse High School at that time would have probably had 70 percent or 80 percent black kids.

INTERVIEWER: And the teachers were white?

WIDEMAN: There were schools that had predominantly black students, but the system was white. I remember in my senior year a black man came to teach and that was a real shock, a pleasant shock, but I didn't quite know how to deal with it.

INTERVIEWER: Had you read Baldwin when you wrote *Hurry Home*?

WIDEMAN: I had educated myself a little bit about black literature. I had taught Baldwin by that time, I believe, so I was much more familiar with black writers.

INTERVIEWER: There are some similarities: the sensitive, alienated black intellectual going to Europe, taking up with some kind of strange guilt-ridden white man, looking for a black son that he's never seen, who may or may not be real.

WIDEMAN: When I wrote *Hurry Home,* I was certainly trying to deal with that need to get out of the United States which Baldwin writes about quite explicitly. So sure, that was an influence and he was—as a black man wandering around in Europe trying to gain a purchase on his identity, trying to find out what he needed to write about—he was an archetype in the back of my mind, but by then I also knew about other people who had to go through the same kind of thing. Sculptors, actors, musicians. It was go to Europe, be appreciated, and then maybe they'll pay some attention back in the U.S. of A.

INTERVIEWER: You said that you had started educating yourself about black literature. What made you start doing that?

WIDEMAN: One way I got involved was my own curiosity. I had begun to read a few things. The sixties brought that whole necessity to examine one's own race and one's own background. I was part of that. By 1968 I was teaching at the University of Pennsylvania, and a group of black students asked me to start a course in Afro-American literature. I hemmed and hawed because I didn't know anything and I had my own writing to worry about and I didn't want to get involved in the work to put together a decent class and I didn't want to do it in an offhand manner either. So there they sat in front of me and I suddenly heard myself giving them all the excuses, "That's not my field, and I don't know it, and I have my own work." I sounded like such a punk; I sounded like the very voice that had turned so many people back that I stopped short in the middle of all my excuses and said, "Yes, I'll do it, sure." It was the eye contact, it was the sense of myself sitting out there listening to me, that did it. That was a very important moment and I think my reading began to be quite serious at that point. I spent the next summer in the Schomburg Library. I got a little research grant from the University of Pennsylvania and some money from a publisher who wanted to do an anthology of black literature. They were shopping around for people to put that together and asked me, which was really kind of a joke because I was a neophyte, I didn't know anything, but I was kind of safe because I had an Ivy League credential. I'm sure they were thinking about marketing. The upshot is that I was given both the time and a little bit of money to put an Afro-American lit class together. I worked for about a year and familiarized myself, as much as I could, with a black tradition.

INTERVIEWER: Had *A Glance Away* already been written?

WIDEMAN: It was published, yes.

INTERVIEWER: In *A Glance Away* you use different versions of the trio in *Sent for You Yesterday.* Is there anything in *Sent for You Yesterday* that's an attempt to go back and redo *A Glance Away,* or is it just that the threesome has been ringing in your head all these years?

WIDEMAN: Oh, it's probably a little of everything, except certainly no conscious attempt to rewrite *A Glance Away.* But on the other hand, as you say, that trio may be reverberating in my imagination. The three main characters in *A Glance Away* and the characters in *Sent for You Yesterday* were based on actual people, so in that sense a prolonged meditation on what they meant to me and who they were would explain the similarities between the two groups of characters. But I had to write a lot and think a lot and grow a lot before I could visualize Tate and Alice and Carl in *Sent for You Yesterday.* In a simplistic sense I guess all the writing in between is a way of processing that initial material, a way of learning to transform it. I frankly had not thought of matching the groups of characters in the way you have put it, but part of the correspondence is the simplest thing in the world—the actual, real-life models were the same.

INTERVIEWER: I'm fascinated by the chronology in the beginning of *Homewood,* the story of Sybela Owens and her husband, Charlie. Is all that true?

WIDEMAN: Not exactly, which isn't going to help a lot, I know, but that's fine, because it shouldn't. For me any kind of writing is invention, selection. The more I write the more I'm sure that some generic discriminations we make don't really hold up. The most important matter is the author's intention and the degree to which the author shares that intention with the reader. The tables were simply to orient the reader. They are not accurate family trees. They're very close, but only somebody privy to our family history would be able to make the few little changes that actually would make them documentary.

INTERVIEWER: Were the slave woman, Sybela, and her white husband, Charlie, based on real-life models?

WIDEMAN: As real as the Bible, as real as most things. I heard those stories from ladies in my family who were seventy and eighty years old, and they had heard those stories from their mothers and aunts and grandmothers. They have the truth of oral history, which for me is a probably more reliable kind of truth than written history.

INTERVIEWER: In the preface to the *Homewood Trilogy* you write, "By 1973 I'd published three critically acclaimed novels. It was hard to admit to myself that I'd just begun learning how to write, that whole regions of my experience, the core of the language and culture that nurtured me had been barely touched by my writing up to that point. If a writer's lucky, the learning process never stops, and writing continues to be a tool for discovery." What happened?

WIDEMAN: Well, lots of things happened. To begin with, I was moving, I was learning about things, trying to understand things and I had a body of work to stand on. It brought me to a certain place. And then, what do you do next? A simple question. "What do you do?" Well, you can not write at all, you can write a book about basketball. While some of this was going on in my mind I moved out to Wyoming. We came out here for what seemed like good reasons at the time but it was another semiconscious break. Unfortunately that first year out here two very important people died. My editor died, and then my grandmother died. I went back East both times, very upset and very emotional. The journeys took on a kind of archetypal shape because once more I was separated from the places and people that were familiar to me. I had to get on a plane and go back and become involved in the rituals that surround death and talk to people and share some things that all of us share at those junctions in our lives. The night after we buried my grandmother her house was full and my Aunt May was there drinking a lot of Wild Turkey—she's a little old lady and she sits in a chair and her feet don't touch the floor—and she began to tell stories. Everybody was telling stories but sooner or later she just took center stage and told the stories like the story of Sybela Owens and how our family came to Pittsburgh—and I listened.

INTERVIEWER: Was it the first time you'd heard these stories?

WIDEMAN: Probably not the first time I literally heard them, but the first time I paid the kind of attention which made them special. As I listened to the stories and heard about the past, it was a way of trying to capture some of the things that I believed were gone forever, because my grandmother was gone forever. I was hearing her life. That was what was done at these wakes. You talk about the person who died, you talk about their friends, you talk about the time you saw them with ice cream on their chin and the crazy situations that person had been in; it's almost like a voodoo ritual where you talk down a departed spirit. A communal, a collective will forces the spirit of the departed person to return, and you draw strength and direction from that spirit. And that's what was happening. As May talked about the old days I saw my grandmother as a little girl and courting, and I saw John French coming to steal her away from Aunt Aida and Uncle Bill. And I saw Uncle Bill sitting there with a shotgun waiting for John French. It was a way of recapturing some of my grandmother's spirit. It seems to me as I look back that was one of the first times that I was fully accepted as an adult—I must have been at least in my thirties—I was a full dues-paid member. I had my own children and now my grandmother was gone, so I had a place to fill. I came all the way back here to Laramie and I suddenly knew that I couldn't let all these things just wither away. Maybe I couldn't tell them the way the women in my family had told the stories, but maybe if I wrote them down. And this part was literary, but also it was a way of healing. It was a way of dealing with my own sense of loss.

INTERVIEWER: So it was one of those times in your life when things just start coming together?

WIDEMAN: Yeah, I think it was, but there are always two movements. Things were coming apart, too. I had moved far away from Homewood, far away from Pittsburgh, far away from these people. I was an academic, I was out here teaching English lit in Wyoming and people were dying back in Pittsburgh, people who were very important to me. So there was that sense of the world losing the shape that had been familiar and important to me.

INTERVIEWER: In the preface to the *Homewood Trilogy* you write, "It became dear to me on that night in Pittsburgh in 1973 that I needn't look any further than the place I was born and the people who'd loved me to find what was significant and lasting in literature. My university training had both thwarted and prepared me for this understanding." How do you think the university had prepared you?

WIDEMAN: It kept me out of trouble for one thing, out of certain kinds of trouble. I had read lots of books and through reading these books and writing I was learning to take the language that I heard and give it a twist and get it down on paper. And through reading Joyce and reading Eliot, I was learning the language, learning how to write, learning technique. I think that was the piece that had to go together with my own background.

INTERVIEWER: How did the university thwart you?

WIDEMAN: It gave me the crazy sense that I had to write about the same things that the writers I read in my English classes wrote about, that I had to go to school and learn their environment and learn their quirks and learn their social system and the religions that supported them.

INTERVIEWER: This wasn't altogether easy for you, was it? They even made you change the way you played basketball when you went to Penn.

WIDEMAN: I learned to play kind of freelance, spontaneous, improvisational basketball. But for college basketball you had to learn systems, you had to put yourself within this kind of disciplined, coach-centered style. What I did was playground basketball and they erased that from the kids who came in.

INTERVIEWER: That was funky.

WIDEMAN: Yeah, that was bad. Not baad, but bad. So I learned to go along with that program and now, ten years later, the style of the game has changed and the very best ball being played is the style that originated on the playground. Of course, it's been renamed now; it's the passing game and coaches get the credit, but what in fact happened is that the players remade the game according to their skills and the coaches tried to catch up. As in most things in this country, if it comes from the street, if it comes from the underclass, it doesn't exist until it's given a name, until it's patented. Then the credit goes to somebody who's very late in the field.

INTERVIEWER: You have written that you see your vocation as a writer to be that of authenticating your background, authenticating black life.

WIDEMAN: Not so much a planned campaign but the inevitable direction that my writings turned. For me writing is more and more a tool of self-expression and as I understand better who I am, I understand more about the culture of which I'm part. That's what I'm trying to get into my writing. The possibility of individual growth, coupled with the idea that a given culture can help you select or select for you a framework in which it's most natural to work and from which you draw your range of choice. In any matter, whether it's playing basketball or dancing or speaking.

INTERVIEWER: And in your case it's language. "Language is power," you say at one place. Beginning with the *Homewood Trilogy* it seems that you are trying to authenticate that language.

WIDEMAN: It started even earlier than that; it just wasn't a central concern. I had to work my way through it. *Hurry Home* is all about mastering one's own culture and the kind of paranoia and craziness that comes when you can't make those decisions or when people keep making the decisions for you.

INTERVIEWER: What do you value about the first three books?

WIDEMAN: I don't look back that often. The work that's past is gone. Some of my books are going to be reprinted and I'll be curious to see what the reaction to them is. When the books were published they were always published in small editions and had readers who were very appreciative, but not many in number. Yet through it all I knew I was doing some things the other writers weren't doing and I knew that I was doing some things that might be valuable if somebody would listen, if somebody would pay attention.

INTERVIEWER: Can you name any of those things?

WIDEMAN: They're the same things we've been talking about. Experiments with language, experiments with form, bringing to the fore black cultural material, history, archetypes, myths, the language itself, the language that black people actually speak and trying to connect that with the so-called mainstream.

INTERVIEWER: And yet you have said that what you felt like you were doing was translating one language into another language.

WIDEMAN: I think I had my priorities a little bit mixed up. I felt that I had to prove something about black speech for instance, and about black culture, and that they needed to be imbedded within the larger literary frame. In other words, a quote from T. S. Eliot would authenticate a quote from my grandmother. Or the quote from my grandmother wasn't enough, I had to have a Joycean allusion to buttress it, to keep an awareness that "Hey, this is serious writing and this guy's not just a solitary black voice, but he knows the things that you know, he's part of the shared culture." I felt you had to leave a signpost to make that clear. Sometimes it works and sometimes it doesn't. But the urge to do that, the urge to make my work a blend of all the different cultures that have filtered through me is still there. It's tough, it's very tough because if you really do bridge two cultures it probably happens not because that's what you want to do but because you are so thoroughly part of both those worlds that what you do comes out being a true blend.

INTERVIEWER: In our classes they teach us to distinguish between the local color writer and the genre writer and the regional writer. And in every case the local color writer is the outsider trying to write about something and his outsiderness both moves and somehow lessens the work.

WIDEMAN: There's that and there's also simply the politics of writing in this country. And the politics of our national psyche which tends to see things in cartoons and tends to try to grab things without really touching them. We look for either/ors: things are either black or white, up or down, you're either rich or poor, you're a winner or a loser. Who knows where that fault in our imagination comes from: maybe it's because Americans have felt so alienated from the land, their past, that the notion of cleavage, the notion of either/or is fundamental. I personally think it comes from racial politics. In order to define yourself as an American you had to define yourself over and against something. And to define yourself over and against Europe actually meant always to put America in the derogatory light.

INTERVIEWER: Toni Morrison has said that she is working for a black audience. She uses the analogy that if Dostoyevsky were writing *Crime and Punishment* for an American audience it would be a totally different book. I think she was getting at the universality that comes from focusing on the particular, focusing on one place from the inside. Do you think that in focusing on Homewood you have managed to move someplace that you didn't go in the first three books?

WIDEMAN: The notion of being grounded is a very important notion in all traditional cultures. I'm using the word "grounded" metaphorically: the forefathers entered this land and it was dangerous and nobody ever lived here before. But they spoke to the spirits of this land and those spirits gave them information and knowledge that they needed to start a village. The village could grow and would be sustained because the people kept alive that knowledge of the original contract, a knowledge of the rootedness. Everything flows from that ancestral bargain. And I believe that in order for my art, anybody's art, to flourish it has to be rooted, it has to be grounded, in that sense. So, yes, particularity, yes, the very unique and real ground that you fought for and bled in and created as a people. In my case that's Homewood.

INTERVIEWER: Does the epigraph to *Hiding Place*—"I went to the rock to hide my face, and the rock said, 'There is no hiding place.' "—represent a recurring theme in your work? Is the work that you've done since the *Homewood Trilogy* an acknowledgment that there is no hiding place?

WIDEMAN: Oh, there is no hiding place, but that will not stop us from running like hell and trying to find it every chance we get. That's part of the irony.

INTERVIEWER: And perhaps the guilt you felt about Robby—the sense that in your attempts to hide or to run, you were somehow bearing witness to the wrong priorities.

WIDEMAN: Yeah, I think that was true. When you write a book you schematize things and you write for effect, so the whole motif of running was also rhetorical. There was never a stage in my life when I was not very worried about both the direction in which I was running and what I was running from. That was part of my culture, if you will: those warnings that you receive very early in life and those walls that you keep bumping into if you don't keep your eyes very alert. I was never simply somebody who bought the American dream, the Horatio Alger myth. I was always somebody who had ghosts, who had demons. The hellhound was on my trail. It was a question really of degree, and I'm sure that somebody who's smarter than I am, somebody who's standing on the outside, could point out at this very moment ways in which I'm going to the rock and hiding my face. The irony is, it's impossible to do that without endangering the very thing you're trying to protect. You put your head in the sand, your butt shows. You put your butt in the sand, your head shows. There's not enough sand to cover the whole thing.

INTERVIEWER: It seems like that since the *Homewood Trilogy* you've been hurrying back home. How have you been received in Homewood?

WIDEMAN: One of the most heartwarming experiences I've had in the last couple of years was just a few months ago when I went back to Pittsburgh to receive an award and speak at the seventy-fifth anniversary of the Carnegie Library in Homewood. They'd brought the kids from Peabody, my former high school and our rival, Westinghouse. The privilege of being able to share with that group of young people the kinds of things that have been happening to me and at the same time have in the back of my mind, "Well, now this—my life, what I've written, what I've said, what I've felt—is now part of the record; it's accessible to them." I felt a great sense of completion in the same way I felt during the best moments with my brother as we were working on *Brothers and Keepers.* I'd been writing about Homewood and black people for a long time but Pittsburgh never paid any attention. But now if you live in Pittsburgh, you have to know about Homewood and you have to know that there's somebody who's talking about Homewood in a very special way. You have to take that into account and so yeah, that's important.

On a different level there's my family and our story. I've gone public with lots of things but luckily, for the most part, people have been delighted. They've been delighted in the same way that they're delighted in hearing stories about themselves at a wake or a wedding or on a picnic. I'm very careful, I don't spill any beans or tell tales on folks. In fact I change names if there's any kind of intimidating thing. For instance, if it was really Ernie who drove to the ballpark on the wrong day for the game, then I'll say it was Charles and everybody who reads it in my family will know who in fact did that and they'll all get a laugh out of it but Ernie won't be teased by guys at work. It's almost like "in" jokes. The information is coded, so that people close enough to know what it's about can have fun with it.

INTERVIEWER: Do you have any feelings about the issue of the writer as a plunderer of other people's experience?

WIDEMAN: I remember once in college reading a story by Henry Miller. It was a story about coming home from Europe and going back to a family gathering, and he used his own name and I assumed the names of the people in his family. I was shocked. I was absolutely shocked by the candor and the frankness and even the fact that he said his father had a wart, or his mother was a crabby old bitch, that his father burped at the table, that somebody's ears weren't clean. That seemed to be telling tales, seemed to be betraying mother and father and home. I just couldn't believe that as a writer he would trespass that way and reveal that kind of information, be that intimate. So I started with a very conservative idea about what was okay to reveal and what wasn't okay to reveal, combined with the very powerful cultural imperative that you don't tell most of what you know. It would just get you in trouble.

INTERVIEWER: Baldwin writes about that.

WIDEMAN: It's crucial. You can find the same proverbs among the Russian serfs.

INTERVIEWER: It's the underclass, whatever that class is.

WIDEMAN: Exactly. You can't speak what's on your mind, you can't be frank with people because it will be used against you. Your language and your customs, etc., revolve around the hard, cold facts of your servitude, of the oppressed state that you live in. I couldn't ever see myself writing about my family at all. So when I wrote my first novel, I didn't name the city, the people were disguised very carefully, I didn't use things—I sort of made up most of the book. I brought in major characters from my life as a student, from my life in Europe and put them into this sort of vaguely big city atmosphere. But it wasn't until the *Homewood* books that I actually began to try to deal with that primal ground. It was a question of getting enough confidence in myself and knowing enough about my people so that I knew that I wasn't embarrassing myself and I wasn't embarrassing them but that the truth about them, if I could ever write the truth about them, would be powerful and it would be beautiful and it would be true.

INTERVIEWER: You have written, "One of the earliest lessons I learned as a child was that if you looked away from something, it might not be there when you look back. I feared loss, feared turning to speak to someone and finding no one there. Being black and poor reinforced the wisdom of a tentative purchase on experience. . . . If you let your eyes touch lightly, rely on an impressionistic touch—then you may achieve the emotional economy of faint gains, faint losses. Writing," and this is the remark that is so important, "forces me to risk ignoring the logic of this lesson." Could you expand on that a little bit?

WIDEMAN: From the writer's point of view writing is a laying on of hands. I feel that if I'm going to write well, I have to take the risk. I have to take lots of risks, risks of finding out something about something I've done or something I haven't done and having that knowledge hurt me or hurt somebody else or disorient me. All those risks are involved if you want to write well. So I had to start taking some chances that go against the grain of that wisdom. I also learned that the people who loved me and whom I cared about most were people who flew in the face of that initial wisdom of touching lightly. The people I love most and who loved me most were folks who did expose themselves, who did make themselves vulnerable, went the whole nine yards, if you will. I reacted in a personal way to the examples of my mother, and my aunts and uncles, and my grandfather and the people who, as I wrote about and thought about and learned about them, came to be the most important people in my life again. I had kind of lost touch with them and lost touch with their importance. I was looking in other places for the nurturing and the wisdom and models. But coming back to them I found that they had taken the most dramatic kinds of chances. They had united their fate with mine. And as I looked around more carefully I found that that had occurred in no other arena of my life.

INTERVIEWER: Then you would agree with Lucy's assessment of those people in the closing section of *Sent for You Yesterday.*

WIDEMAN: Oh, yes. The people stood for things, they were their own people. The community was a projection of what was inside of them.

INTERVIEWER: Do you agree with her assessment of Carl that he gave up too easy?

WIDEMAN: Yeah, he should have taken some chances, there should have been some blood spilled, he should be marked by resistance. He should have taken his stand here and there and the other place.

INTERVIEWER: Am I overreading when I say Brother is the central figure in that book? He's everyone's alter ego.

WIDEMAN: In a funny way he's a mirror, but you can't see through him. He's not a glass. He's solid. But he has the qualities of a spirit; he's immaterial. He doesn't have blood but everybody's afraid that when they look in there they'll see through his skin. And of course if they see through his skin what they'll see is their own mortality, their creaturehood, their own blood.

INTERVIEWER: He's music; he's the force of art in this world.

WIDEMAN: He does contain or express the kind of background music that I sense is part of life. I do believe that music's there. When I'm going good, when I'm playing basketball, I get attuned to some rhythm and become much more than myself. Two people are hanging on you and you're twenty feet from the basket and you go up in the air and as soon as the ball leaves your hand—you don't even see the basket, you may be falling down on the side of the court—but you know that the darn thing's going in. I wanted Brother to be somebody who had access to that in himself and could put people in touch with, to be a vehicle for, making that music real.

INTERVIEWER: Is it correct to say that Brother is the muse, the embodiment of everything that becomes the tale and the telling of the tale?

WIDEMAN: He's the quicksilver that the narrator's trying to catch in his net. But I don't want him to be an idea, I don't want him to be the protestant God, I don't want him to be an African spirit who's transcendent, who's immortal. I want him to be flesh and blood, I want him to suffer, I want him to go through a lifetime, which in one sense is just the blink of an eye, but that's all any of us ever gets so it's also pretty important, pretty significant. If he had been some kind of transcendent supernatural being, then the whole novel would have fallen apart because that has nothing to do with the lives of most human beings. We suffer, we bleed, we lose people, we grow, we decay, we're gone. But we take part in that sensual music and Brother embodies both what is transcendent and what is very earthbound. That's why he can be such a powerful personage to the people in Homewood. If he just walked all through it, through fire and earth and water and it didn't hurt him, didn't touch him, then what would he mean? But if he was really your brother, if you drank wine with him, if you saw him cry because he lost his son, if you were hurt because you learned that he died suddenly, then the music has a human scale.

INTERVIEWER: The three central figures in *Sent for You Yesterday* seem to be displaced. Is that a theme in the novel?

WIDEMAN: I hate to schematize, but you can see John French's generation as hardy pioneers. They came from the South and made a world. It was a world that was very tenuous, but they prevailed and had their children—the generation of my father and of Carl and of Alice. They are the ones who were wiped out because they didn't have the pioneers' struggle to survive. They tried to move out from what the generation before had done, but society said no, there's no place for you to go, we don't want you here, you are no good, you are wasted. So that generation became sacrificial; they were just ground up. That's why the marriages didn't work, the children were stillborn. The animosity was so strong that as a generation they could not overcome it. Then my generation followed, and in looking back over this space, I think there is strength to be gathered from the experience of a Carl and an Alice and a Brother but also from that other generation, the John French generation, and Brother is the bridge over the lost generation. That is the scheme of the novel that eventually came to me. Significantly, Doot has children, so the future is open. The ones in the middle turn out to be not so stillborn because in a symbolic and a metaphorical sense they become brothers to Brother.

INTERVIEWER: It's as though the interconnectedness of family is enhanced by the stripping away of literal blood ties. Lucy and Brother, who are in fact not brother and sister at all, have been raised by foster parents.

WIDEMAN: Another way of looking at it is connected to statistics about broken homes, a definition of family codified in the Moynihan report. If you look at black culture, the black culture is deviant and delinquent because it does not have a family structure which reproduces the Moynihan model. But of course that is just a stipulative, narrow, and arbitrary definition of what a family might be. I think one of the powerful things that's happening, not only in black writing, but in contemporary writing, is a reexamination of bonding, male-female, older generation–younger generation. We're mixing it up and trying to see what it actually means. We're redefining what brotherhood and sisterhood mean.

INTERVIEWER: There are people who think that writing being done in the black American tradition during the last generation is in many ways the very best writing that's being done, that being a member of an oppressed group in society gives you an insight that leads to the creation of novels that are beautiful and socially responsible at the same time, as Toni Morrison would say.

WIDEMAN: I think that you might look at black writing and say that this is some of the best that the culture is producing and it's a splendid time for black writing. A judgment like that suggests that what's happening is new, that what's happening is rare, and that what's happening has no history; but there have always been powerful black voices. Ellison between 1940 and 1960, and before him Richard Wright and Zora Neale Hurston. They've been at the forefront of fiction; we just didn't know it, we just didn't know where or how to look. The other reason I don't like to endorse that kind of Golden Epoch of Black Literature notion is that the same conditions, economic and social, that made so many black writers invisible before, could happen again. A force of circumstances could quiet the black voice, but would that mean that there weren't any good black writers anymore? That people could nostalgically look back at the 1960s, 1970s, and 1980s and say, "Boy, there were some good black writers then, but there are none now." No. It would probably mean that publishing had decided that blacks are not in vogue this year, and so all those good black voices would just be quieted. Same thing as John Thompson winning the NCAA. Yeah, he's a talented man and a great coach, but the reason he's the first black coach is not because of his unique and individual talent; it's because he was allowed to be. He was allowed to be. We always have to keep that in mind when we look at firsts, and bests, among black people in any endeavor.

INTERVIEWER: Many people point to Native American writing—work by Scott Momaday and James Welch and Leslie Silko—and argue that being in the underclass somehow gives you a better eye for creating these very beautiful and very big novels.

WIDEMAN: When it works. Yes.

INTERVIEWER: But you don't think there's anything magic about it?

WIDEMAN: It's hard work and it's discipline. The writers you're talking about are—first of all their art and genius should not be connected to the sociology of their lives because you could point to a hundred people who went through the same kinds of experiences and didn't write novels. So what's the difference? When you talk about cultures and styles even, you can't have it both ways; either you're ethnocentric or not. You're not ethnocentric if you believe that all cultures have values and you have to get inside and understand them and look at them in their own terms. You can't go around praising exotic people for being exotic, or outsiders for being outside. It's like lots of Americans will—I've noticed this, it's not original with me—but if there's an Indian woman, East Indian woman, at a party inevitably someone will come and tell me, "Did you see that beautiful woman over there, isn't she beautiful?" A white person will say that to me. That overcompensation is pigeonholing, is cataloging, is talking about the otherness of the person, and I think we have to resist that.

INTERVIEWER: James Baldwin felt that there was no way to tell the truth about the American culture without trying to get white culture to see its relationship to black culture.

WIDEMAN: Well, that's not quite clear to me, I'm not exactly sure what he was getting at or what you're getting at. I think you have to be very cautious. I believe that I have a very definite advantage in being black in America. Both insider and outsider, that's the archetypal artistic stance. Whether or not that stance becomes a discipline, produces art, has to do with countless other factors. It may be a flying start, but there are a whole lot of winos and junkies who have been alienated from their society and stand on the outside—who have the perfect angle for writing novels—but they're killing themselves, not producing art.

INTERVIEWER: You've said that the best stories are those written for a specific person to read.

WIDEMAN: Yes, in a funny way I don't think a writer has a choice. How shall we write a universal story, how shall we write a story that's appealing to everyone? You might as well go to the Propp fairy-tale index and pick out one or two of those recurring myths and just put in characters and write them over and over again. No. You have to be aware of the particular. You have to be aware of the specific people, the specific words, the specific locales and then something grows out of that. It doesn't work the other way around. At least I've never seen it work the other way around.

INTERVIEWER: Are the stories in the two novels in the *Homewood Trilogy* letters from home to your brother, Robby, as you say in the beginning?

WIDEMAN: They didn't all start that way, but once I had enough of them done I did feel that was a fair way to describe them and some very consciously were that. What I look for when I write is a kind of register, an emotional weight, and I get that by thinking of particular people who would understand or at least care about what I'm talking about. It's best for me as a writer to think not of a group of people but of one person who serves as a fully sort of mirror. I create that person in the mirror. I mean I'm writing to Robby but as I write I'm also creating him as audience.

INTERVIEWER: Is there a sense in which the work in the *Homewood Trilogy* is an attempt somehow to expiate—to somehow marry your brother, Robby, back to what had seemed to become lost in Homewood between your growing-up years and Robby's?

WIDEMAN: I've thought about that a lot and find myself losing sharpness of response because I've gone beyond the simple answers, the answers that somebody could write down and figure, "Yeah, now I understand what this guy's doing." So when you ask that question, yes, the answer is I love my brother and I was terribly hurt and frightened by what happened to him, and I feel a little bit responsible and guilty, as all of us should; therefore I want to do what I can with writing. But if it were only a question of somehow making this crazy instrument that could document the past in the way that videotape can document the present, I think writing would not have all that much interest for me. What's more important is the possibility of having an influence on my life now and on the lives of the people who are important to me. Writing is power. On one level I am wielding that power to the best of my ability to get my brother out of jail. If that happens then the effort is more than rewarded, and I'd be very happy. But I'm greedy; I'm hoping other things are also happening, I'm hoping I'm preparing a place for both my brother and me to live. I hope I'm growing, and I hope I'm connected with his growth.

INTERVIEWER: Is there any chance that Robby can get a parole?

WIDEMAN: There is hope and work is going on daily. I've dedicated myself to that; I'm determined, he is determined and we'll find a way.

INTERVIEWER: Do you think the books have had a measurable impact?

WIDEMAN: I hope so. Whatever public impact they've had, privately they've become a vehicle for us to get closer. The books have reconnected him to the world outside the prison walls. He has groupies, people who write him. People are aware that he's there. He draws strength and energy from those folks who are supportive of him.

INTERVIEWER: And what about your community of readers?

WIDEMAN: They're welcome to enter at any stage, whether it's learning something about a person like Robby or a person like me or even learning something about themselves. Writing is, after all, an enterprise of the imagination. If you look too hard for the way that it impacts our real world, then you either get phony answers or half-assed answers or maybe just confused. It's a very subjective and internal process and the rewards and benefits act themselves out in a realm that most people can't understand. What actually happens when you write fiction is still extremely mysterious.

INTERVIEWER: In *Brothers and Keepers* you ask, "Is what happened to Robby the price that had to be paid for my success?" Why do you feel that way?

WIDEMAN: As I get older, it's become clear that there's the individual way of looking at things, the microscale, but on top of that there is the macroscale, which any individual behavior has to be balanced over and against. Those two worlds often contradict one another. It's perfectly understandable why I might buy a fancy new car for me and for my family, but it's not understandable when you look at it in terms of the fact that people are starving. I don't go around feeling guilty all the time for my good fortune and I don't cry all the time when I think about Ethiopia. But that inevitable clash is something that bothers me. I do believe that the idea of connecting oneself to a literal brother or to other people on the earth is probably about the only notion that's going to have any chance of saving us all. I've tried to do that with Robby. Working through a nonfiction book about him, a sort of made-up book about him, and a long story about him, I've been asking myself questions that have to do with how people are connected and what's at stake in these connections. And what, after all, do they mean? That's the meat of the fiction I've been writing. That's the meat of all of it.

Robb Forman Dew

Robb Forman Dew grew up in Baton Rouge and lived with her grandfather, John Crowe Ransom, in Kentucky and Ohio. She writes about the intricacies of family life, in connection with southern or pseudosouthern culture. Her novels are filled with the small mysteries and delicate complications of families. Her characters are sensitive, comfortable, middle-class people, although they are often emotionally and psychologically hanging on by their toes. The Time of Her Life *(1984) explores the effects of alcoholic but charismatic parents on the life of their child. It is a novel that she admits was inspired by the real-life domestic dramas of F. Scott and Zelda Fitzgerald. Dew's subtle and precise prose evokes dramatic tension in the rich inner worlds of her characters with an alertness to the small tremors that presage large changes in peoples' lives. Her novels bring a dash of either the mystery novel or the gothic to the domestic crises of her characters, not unlike the work of Jane Austen.* The Family Heart *(1994) is a memoir about a crisis within her own family when one of her sons reveals that he is gay.*

This interview was conducted in 1984 after her first novel, Dale Loves Sophie to Death *(1981), had won the National Book Award. The interview originally appeared in* The Missouri Review *in 1991.*

INTERVIEWER: Miss Dew, you've said that your southern background is the source of your interest in the intricacies of family life. Could you elaborate on that?

DEW: Southern families tend to be extraordinarily involved with each other, not always in a good way. The influence of family, I think, is what makes a story. When you're a child you try to piece together where did that aunt come from, what uncle was that, how did this happen. I think I began to realize I was going to write when my family started to disintegrate. In realizing that it was an internal combustion rather than an outside force that broke the family to pieces, I began to have to tell a story about it.

INTERVIEWER: You seem to have avoided southern settings, although Avery and Claudia Parks, Jane's parents in *The Time of Her Life,* are from Natchez.

DEW: That's right. Claudia and Avery grew up together. They can't break away from each other; they're almost like siblings. It seems to me that the South's incredible heat bonds people together. It's a very sexual, sensual place. There's such luxuriant growth—the heavy scented air and decay all around. There's something dangerous in the atmosphere.

INTERVIEWER: Is it also a glamorous place?

DEW: I think glamour and decadence go hand in hand. Glamour is right on the edge of failure. That's where Claudia and Avery are just skimming right along. They're intelligent and irreverent—interesting, I think, to other people. I would like to know them, but I wouldn't like to know them too well.

INTERVIEWER: I was curious about why *The Time of Her Life* is set in Missouri.

DEW: I lived in Missouri for ten years during a very crucial time in my life. I had my two children there. To me it is my home, really more than the Deep South, and I wanted to write about it because I care about it.

INTERVIEWER: It's obvious that Lunsbury is Columbia. Why did you change the name?

DEW: The *New Yorker* asked me to. I had to change the name of the town in *Dale Loves Sophie to Death,* too.

INTERVIEWER: Is that a *New Yorker* policy?

DEW: That's what they told me. But as a matter of fact, I didn't want to name the town Columbia for various reasons. I sort of invented the weather, for example. It's amazing—letters arrive that say, "But we never had that ice storm . . . it never rains like that . . . we never have winds from the west." On a subconscious level, too, if I name an exact town, I am locked into the exact facts. And that stops invention.

INTERVIEWER: The weather rang pretty true, for me.

DEW: I was in Columbia during an amazing ice storm and the river froze over a long period of time. I have telescoped that into three days. I don't believe a river can freeze that quickly, but I decided it had to for the sake of my book. That's what I mean about inventing the weather.

INTERVIEWER: An interesting tension between the political consciousness and the purely private sensibility runs through both your novels. There's a funny scene where Avery has Claudia down on the floor, practically strangling her and saying, "Who is the chancellor of West Germany?" And she says she doesn't care. What does this tell us about your worldview?

DEW: I'm still battling it out in my mind. We moved to Baton Rouge in 1950 when I was four years old, and my high school was integrated during my junior year. Before that I didn't realize that my high school was not integrated. I never thought about it. I worked hard in the Civil Rights movement, as did my parents. We were considered rather eccentric. My father was shot at. They were perilous times, and yet those are not the events that shudder through my life in memory. Those things all interest me, but they aren't my subject for fiction.

INTERVIEWER: Yet they're in your fiction.

DEW: But not the main thrust of my fiction. I had a very sketchy education, which was my own fault; I simply didn't pay any attention. I was much more interested in running for homecoming queen and being popular. It wasn't until I was about nineteen or twenty that I even realized that the Holocaust had taken place. I don't think anything has shaken me as much as realizing how inhumane humans can be. Every child has seen another child torture an animal or dissolve a snail in salt or something, and that's a horror in its own way. But I thought that there really was such a thing as grown-ups. And when I discovered that grown-ups were just as dreadful as children, and just as good, I remember thinking, "My God, the president is only a grown-up," and being terrified at that idea. I still am.

INTERVIEWER: Are you saying that because political and social consciousness came to you late, they are not central to your concerns as a writer?

DEW: Yes. And also I didn't feel especially oppressed in any way. I didn't have to work out any sort of political reaction in my writing. My parents wanted me to be a neurosurgeon; I wanted to be a housewife.

INTERVIEWER: Do you think it's true that the stuff of early childhood—family relationships, the psychological interplay between parents and child—is the bedrock of most writers' material?

DEW: It's probably the stuff of their best material. I remember being terribly disappointed when I realized I would not be Tolstoy. I might write about peace, but I wouldn't write about war.

INTERVIEWER: Even though the germ of *The Time of Her Life* was a community, a town, it becomes Jane's story. Do your characters "take off" for you? Do they take on their own life?

DEW: I always hesitate when I answer that question. When I first began writing, I read interviews and writers would say, "My characters then became themselves." I thought, "That's ridiculous." But in fact it happens. You cannot write the truth about a person you really know.

INTERVIEWER: How would you describe your vision? From the world of the family as we see it dramatized so thoroughly in these two novels, would you say it's a negative vision, a pessimistic vision, or a tragic vision?

DEW: I think it's an ambiguous vision. There are people for whom life is utterly tragic, but for the people I know who don't have great, terrible burdens in the world that they will have to shoulder, I think ambiguous is as close as I can come to naming my idea of their lives.

INTERVIEWER: It seems to me that in your two books the picture of family structure rings true. It also reflects the dark side of the family in our culture.

DEW: I think that there's no escaping family. That may be a particularly southern view—family as destiny. No matter how much you may like to be separate from how you grew up, I believe it shapes you forever. I don't think that that means necessarily that one is "doomed" by a bad family, but I think it does shape one's empathy, ability to be compassionate, all those things. In fact, Jane will be a kinder person, for instance, than her friend Diana, who has an easier life.

INTERVIEWER: Toward the end of the book, after Jane's overdose, the narrator says that Jane will become "a person who will never be able to throw herself into anything in this world."

DEW: She won't dare take the risk that Avery and Claudia take to be glamorous, to try exciting things. She's going to be cautious.

INTERVIEWER: What will become of her?

DEW: I sold the book with a coda that summarized what happened to Jane. Then I took it out because it was a lie. It seemed like cheating. I certainly don't know if Jane will be a staff writer for the *New Yorker,* which is what I had her become. She changes, but she survives. She's a very strong child. I don't know how damaged she will be, I don't know if she will recover. But the one thing she does know, in spite of everything, is that her parents really do love her. They just don't love her well.

INTERVIEWER: Does Jane have a real-life model?

DEW: I was watching a program one afternoon and Jane Pauley, I think, was interviewing Scotty Fitzgerald. They were walking around the room looking at Fitzgerald memorabilia: letters and dresses and books, and Jane Pauley was saying, "You must have had a terrible childhood. It must have been terrible for you." Because we all know Zelda died in a fire and Scott died early. And Scotty said, "Oh, no. I had a wonderful childhood. It was a wonderful time. I met exciting people. It was the time of my life." That astounded me. I knew she was lying; I imagine she's a very careful person. I liked her on this show. She clearly loved her parents; she was going to protect them. She wouldn't for the world have said, "They destroyed me." Well, they didn't destroy her. She's all right. In fact, I hope Jane will be just like Scotty Fitzgerald. I'm sure there were wonderful times with her mother and father. They were fascinating people, as I intend Claudia and Avery to be.

INTERVIEWER: As Nick Carraway says about Daisy and her husband, "They are careless, careless people."

DEW: And that's what Avery and Claudia are. Literally. They don't take responsibility, nor do they understand that their actions have consequences.

INTERVIEWER: Was Fitzgerald in fact an influence?

DEW: A tremendous influence, although I cannot, unfortunately, write the way Fitzgerald writes. Perhaps his life as much as his writing influenced me. But it was when I began reading Fitzgerald that I realized I really wanted to write. I read *Tender Is the Night* first, so it will probably always be my favorite. Then I learned more about Fitzgerald—he fascinates me and so does Zelda. They're both tragic, and yet, they're both brilliant, too. I wanted Avery and Claudia to have some of that, although I certainly didn't want to set them in Paris or the Riviera or wherever. I didn't want to give them those trappings. I wanted them to be accessible.

INTERVIEWER: It's perfect to set that kind of domestic drama in the Midwest.

DEW: If I had set it in an exotic place I would have owed the place some part of the book. And I didn't want to do that because I wanted their personalities to be what drove the book, to be the momentum, the tension of the book.

INTERVIEWER: You lived with your grandfather, the poet and critic John Crowe Ransom, for a portion of your adolescence. How does that bear on your work?

DEW: I lived with him my senior year in high school and my grandfather was an incredibly kind man. He would read my English themes, which must have bored him terribly, and I would take it upon myself to give him critiques of his essays on Blake which I knew nothing about. He allowed me that vanity. I wrote a very awful piece of fiction—it was sort of gothic southern with watermelon and maggots and everything possible in it. He finally said, "Robb, don't embarrass your reader." He said that's the most important thing to remember. And of course it is. None of us succeed at that all the time, but you don't want your reader to cringe for the writer. You don't mind if they cringe for the character but for a reader to feel embarrassment on your behalf—that's awful.

INTERVIEWER: I should think that one reason some people have placed you with Virginia Woolf and Henry James is because those writers are known for the idea that metaphor and symbolism have to grow out of the particularity of the characters and their circumstance—that's the direction Scott Fitzgerald worked in, too. *The Great Gatsby* is packed with imagery and metaphor.

DEW: And actually it's my least favorite of his books because of that. I really do resent conscious or contrived symbolism and metaphor. When I was living with my grandfather, during exams students from all over the country would telephone him and ask, "Mr. Ransom, what did you mean in the poem such and such?" And he would say, "What did you think I meant?" I don't know what they said. But he would say, "That sounds just right." I thought he was tricking them, but he wasn't. If a reader discovers symbolism or metaphor that the author didn't, perhaps, intend, the reader's interpretation is still legitimate.

INTERVIEWER: It wasn't a southern caginess on his part?

DEW: Well, he was pretty cagey, and he didn't like students to cheat. I think he thought of it as a form of cheating for them to go to the source.

INTERVIEWER: We've all heard about Eudora Welty saying that she didn't mean anything at all. She just wants to hear those people talk. Do you believe that?

DEW: I do. Although I think she meant more than she knows she meant. The same is true of almost every writer. If the intention isn't too clear in the writer's mind then there's often nothing exciting in the work. Most writers discover things as they write; maybe they don't intend to, but in spite of themselves something happens as they're working.

INTERVIEWER: Is there a discernible germ behind *Dale Loves Sophie to Death*?

DEW: I thought that book was going to be about a woman who thought she could not live a life as full as the lives of the people whose house she rented. That picture of the girl jogging started the whole thing moving along and I then had to figure out what I was writing about. You aim towards something and as you approach your intention you often realize it was not what you were heading for. So you have to change gears.

INTERVIEWER: That seems to reflect your comments about character. You ask yourself if the character would act this way in this instance. Is that how you plot?

DEW: My plots always disintegrate in front of me. As I write I have to adjust the plot to encompass the characters. What I would love to do more than anything is to write a mystery. But I'm incapable of plotting that absolutely.

INTERVIEWER: *The Time of Her Life* is beautifully structured. Many of the chapters are self-contained, with their own rising action, falling action. How do scenes shape the structure of your novels?

DEW: At my house no one can throw away a Kleenex box because I have scribbled scenes on the sides of them. Once I have just a little bit of a picture, then the characters move outward from that picture. That's the kernel of each chapter, and I tend to work in chapters. Yet they have to build. I think in *The Time of Her Life* they build more than they did in *Dale Loves Sophie.*

INTERVIEWER: When you plot a novel, then, although the plots tend to disappear from in front of you and the story insists on going its own way, do you have benchmarks in mind?

DEW: Absolutely, and in fact it may be those moments as much as the characters' personalities that insist that I shape the book a certain way. If I realize that I'm getting away from catching those scenes that I know are crucial, then I alter the way the book is going.

INTERVIEWER: In *Dale Loves Sophie* you allow the characters to explain themselves more than you do in *The Time of Her Life.* Have you moved toward a definition of the novel that says if the meaning isn't implicit in what everybody does and says to each other then . . .

DEW: . . . the novel has failed.

INTERVIEWER: That takes me back to the John Crowe Ransom influence. You mentioned that the piece has to stand on its own, and that southern caginess: "I'm not here to explain my work to you," and, "If you see it, then it's true." But while most writers in the twentieth century tend to take the very small, the seemingly insignificant, and invest it with significance, Ransom's gift was to take a situation that was loaded with the possibilities of melodrama and to undercut it. You seem to do the same thing.

DEW: I think if you don't undercut real drama, it loses its power. It doesn't hold. Perhaps that's why I hear my grandfather's voice reading my passages. Eudora Welty once said that she always hears a voice, not her own, but a voice when she writes. I hear my grandfather's voice, and also Peter Taylor's. He has a wonderful voice.

INTERVIEWER: Did you feel an anxiety of influence because of your relationship to John Crowe Ransom?

DEW: Oh. Terrible anxiety. And it was not his fault. It had nothing to do with him. He would wish me nothing but well, he would wish me Godspeed. It's the terror of failing. I couldn't even admit I wrote until I was sure I could do it.

INTERVIEWER: Did your grandfather know you were writing?

DEW: No. He died before I had finished a book or published a story. He wanted me to write. He was very encouraging. I didn't want to embarrass him either. Not only did I not want to embarrass my reader, I didn't want to embarrass anyone at all, particularly myself.

INTERVIEWER: What about the form your work has taken? The fact that it's prose instead of poetry?

DEW: I can't write poetry. I wish I could. I've tried and the efforts are so dismal that they will never see the light of day. When I began writing I wanted to have the reader see what I see and feel it without ever saying, "This is how you should feel, this is what you should see." I think Fitzgerald does that better than anyone. He writes portraits, practically. Little, vivid pictures all strung together. When *Tender Is the Night* opens, you see the people right away and yet he doesn't walk up and give them to you. You gather an impression of them, of the place, the ambiance, bit by bit, which is how real perception happens.

INTERVIEWER: Do you write for the ear? That's often said of southern writers particularly, and most writers say they do to some extent.

DEW: With dialogue I definitely try to write for the ear because one reads it as something heard. Otherwise, I think I write more for the eye, if that makes sense. I write for a visual sense. Something on a page is quite different from something said. It requires the sight of the word to make it record in the reader's imagination.

INTERVIEWER: You've mentioned the influence of Fitzgerald, and you grew up around John Crowe Ransom; Robert Penn Warren was your godfather. Did these experiences give you a perspective on the writer and the writer's life? You don't strike me as someone who buys into the Scott Fitzgerald myth of the writer.

DEW: I don't. I think that's terribly destructive and the women's movement is responsible in part for my not buying into that. Male writers destroyed themselves with the help of women who believed that they were serving genius or who were forced to pretend they believed this by society.

INTERVIEWER: It seems like most of the writers that you were surrounded with in your growing-up years were male writers. Did this have any effect on your self-identity as a woman and a writer?

DEW: No, because their wives were also writers. For instance, Cal Lowell's wife was Jean Stafford; Red Warren's wife is Eleanor Clark. Peter Taylor's wife, Eleanor Ross Taylor, is a short story writer and a poet. I just never did feel any hesitation because I was a woman. That was partly because my parents really did think I could do anything, as did my grandfather. He was not sexist, although the tradition of the time was that one's wife did certain things.

INTERVIEWER: Anne Tyler wrote a very favorable review of *Dale Loves Sophie to Death.* And she made a comment that I don't agree with, describing it as a woman's novel, "delicate, vibrating with hidden meanings, so personal that when Dinah dusts her sirloin cubes with powdered ginger I reach for a pencil to write down her shish kebab recipe." Then she goes on to say that Martin's chapter sets us straight. Do you buy into that?

DEW: No. I don't really think she does, either. After I saw that review, I sent her the recipe for the shish kebabs. I think she was trying to say that in spite of the fact that this is a domestic novel it could be and should be read by both men and women. I don't think there is a stereotype of women's fiction anymore. In my case, there was a time when writing about anything that didn't address the feminist issue was almost like betraying one's sex. I think it held some of us back a little. I'm not sure of that, and I would never speak for other women that way.

INTERVIEWER: What effect, if any, did marrying young and having children young have on your development as a writer?

DEW: I think that was what made me develop as a writer. When I was in college I wrote really terrible stuff. I look back at it and cringe. I didn't have a subject—I tried for very large subjects, the whole Civil Rights movement. But the thing that I think I do best is character examination. I didn't have any characters to examine. I didn't have any distance, either, from the emotions that had shaped my vision. Well, I didn't really even have a vision. I had my first child four years after I was married, and my second child was born twenty months later. About two years after that I simply had to write. I certainly didn't have children so I would be a writer, but I think it made me a writer.

INTERVIEWER: How long did it take to write *Dale Loves Sophie to Death*?

DEW: It took about three years. The *New Yorker* took the first chapter, then Bob Giroux took the novel right away so I didn't suffer what many first novelists suffer.

INTERVIEWER: Did you ever worry that being John Crowe Ransom's granddaughter helped you to get published?

DEW: No. Anything that would get me published would have been a relief. By the time I had finished the first stories, I thought I was a good writer. So I thought I deserved to be published. I would have pulled any strings I could have. However, no one will publish you unless they like your work.

INTERVIEWER: Did the connection influence the reviews?

DEW: I don't know. Probably. It interested people. On the other hand, Red Warren wanted to give the book a quote and couldn't because he was my godfather and thought that would hardly be right. It can hurt as much as help. If I had lived in the South when I wrote, I would never have mentioned my grandfather, because it would have endangered my perception of myself. It would have made me anxious, it would have made me think, "Well this is because I am . . ." In fact, it's almost the opposite. My grandfather is quite disliked by a great many people in the Northeast. He's perceived as a sort of apologist for the agrarian South, a wrongheaded southerner.

INTERVIEWER: What did you write before *Dale Loves Sophie to Death*?

DEW: In five years I did five short stories published in various places—*Southern Review* and the *Virginia Quarterly Review*—all of which I liked, but I slowly began to realize that I don't have a short story voice. I didn't know such a thing existed until I discovered that I didn't have it. Two of those stories are just stories, but the other three probably will be novels. One of them already has become *The Time of Her Life* to a degree. In both of my stories that are just stories, the reader may not feel it, but I have a sense that I know yet more. So I'm dissatisfied and edgy. To take a year to write a short story is quite a long time. I'm not a tale-teller.

INTERVIEWER: How would you describe the tale-teller?

DEW: The tale-teller begins with the story and then peoples it. The character examiner—that's a terrible-sounding category—begins with the people. I don't think one is better than the other, just different. Even when I intend to come at it as a story, it never happens. That's why I end up writing a novel.

INTERVIEWER: The kind of novel you write seems to be associated with the new criticism, which is sometimes criticized as the religion of art. Do you buy into the notion that art justifies everything?

DEW: I believe it was Faulkner who said that a good book is worth a dozen little old ladies. I don't agree with that for a second. Luckily, I'm not forced to choose. I would be bereft without literature, without music, paintings, all those things. My life would be a sad thing, but we don't exist in that vacuum. I don't think that art justifies anything. I think art just exists.

INTERVIEWER: You said that your goal as a writer was to make people see the way you see, to try to help them see. In that sense would you go along with Pound's view that all art is didactic?

DEW: I suppose that's true because I was going to say it's not even wanting to help them see, it's wanting to "make" them see. I don't mean to instruct. I don't imagine that my book will make anyone's life particularly better except for the moment they're reading the book. I have no moral in mind. In that case, I don't think "didactic" is the word I would use—perhaps "arrogant" would be an accurate description, though. I don't know anyone who doesn't want to be the one who's right and if I can write a whole book that someone will read, then they're listening to me while they're reading that book. It's not consciously arrogant, but it's something I simply seem to have to do.

INTERVIEWER: Did your circumstance as a wife and mother make it more difficult to find time to write?

DEW: Oh, certainly. On the other hand it gives you a good excuse when things aren't going well. It did give me some legitimate time to find out what I could do. I almost needed those limitations.

INTERVIEWER: So the lack of time determined both your sense and your pace?

DEW: It's not just actual time, it's emotional time. If you have small children, you're emotionally involved with them. They take up great amounts of energy. They've taken up as much of my husband's emotional energy as mine so at least we're not in conflict about that. While I was writing *Dale Loves Sophie,* I was amazed that we lived so serenely or happily together. It was amazing to me to see how a family that was content worked, because for various reasons my own family when I was growing up was not content. We were in a place that was not particularly tolerant of our views; we weren't religious. We were prointegration. It was a difficult time. My parents were not happy. They finally were divorced. They weren't always miserable either. Childhood is a mixture of being happy and sad—no one is miserable all the time. Or perhaps some are; I was not. Discovering that I had become part of a happy family, I think, gave me my first subject.

INTERVIEWER: It would seem to me that what you're saying is that what we call happiness is really rather beside the point. We carve out truces; we make adjustments.

DEW: It's compromise, perhaps. It's as much as one can hope for, a comfortable compromise. Being happy is very nice, but it only happens now and then. One can aim for contentment, a sort of slow pleasure that's quite different from that burst of spontaneity that is real joy. I think serenity and contentment is what I would aim for in my life. Joy is almost hard to handle all the time. It would hinder contemplation. You couldn't cope.

Rosellen Brown

Rosellen Brown may be best known for her novels, but she is also a well-respected poet and essayist. She often writes about domestic and family matters, though her approach is almost the opposite of Robb Forman Dew's, with her characters often being caught up in quite dramatic events. She is a heavy-lifting novelist, with her prose filled with facts and details.

The Autobiography of My Mother *(1976) chronicles a mother and daughter living together in New York. It is a sixties, generation-gap novel about differing manners, morals, and standards.* Tender Mercies *(1978) is the masterful, ambitious tale of a marriage from hell. A well-bred eastern girl marries an idiotic adventurer-outdoorsman and becomes the victim of his carelessness when he runs over her with a boat, leaving her paralyzed.* Civil Wars *(1984) tackles the life of a white idealist living in a black housing development in Jackson, Mississippi, during the sixties. He faces hostility in the form of theft, vandalism, and phone calls, but his life is truly changed when his sister and her husband die in an auto accident and he must care for their children. This story retells much of the recent history of the South, a subject that Brown grasps naturally because she grew up in Texas and Mississippi during the Civil Rights movement. Brown is adept at continuing to bring up the issues of the sixties while avoiding sentimentality.*

This interview was conducted by correspondence over a number of months through January 1994.

INTERVIEWER: Can you tell us about your background, your family, and early influences?

BROWN: I think my beginnings as a writer were not unlike those of a good many others. I was feeling particularly cast out at a certain point. I was nine, and the writing was a comfort. We had just moved from one coast to the other and I was very lonely in a new school, so I started taking along a secretarial notebook in which I didn't so much confide as create friends for myself, and play with language, right out there on the playground where I thought at the time I was being ignored by the real kids. I'll bet that endeared me to them, this girl sitting under a tree writing conspicuously in her little notebook. Interestingly this was the same year I felt it necessary to rename myself. I was being called Rose Brown by a teacher too inattentive to notice that my name was actually Rose Ellen. So I began writing it as Rosellen, which has led, instead, to a lifetime of mispronunciation—but that's another story. My sense of who I was or wanted to be was up for grabs, clearly, in this new place, and I can see now that I did an unprecedented, and unrepeated, job of self-creation. A thorough makeover.

INTERVIEWER: Would you subscribe to the "writer-as-outsider" theory?

BROWN: It's always been pretty clear to me that most writers are slightly mismatched to their surroundings. Nothing original in that; it's the sand-in-the-oyster theory. Whether the discomfort is that of personality, class, family situation, sexuality, whatever, very few seem a perfect fit. So writing begins, very often, defensively. It fills a void. I was a pretty decent artist when I was a kid, and a good musician, with an older brother who became a jazz drummer. Why the writing stuck I can't say. To be honest, I often wish I'd become a musician. I'd rather be doing something nonverbal, something for which you didn't have to be *smart* so much of the time. My intuition is better than my intellect.

INTERVIEWER: But in the end you chose writing over music.

BROWN: The thing that fascinates me about writing in my own life is that I don't tend to think of myself as very daring or aggressive or even ambitious about anything else. Yet obviously it takes not only a sort of public boldness but a private, deeply held conviction of one's talent and of the world's need or desire to hear your particular voice to make you persevere against so many odds and so much silence. It is my single anomaly, this conviction that I must and would write, and that I would make myself heard. Just think of—oh, I don't know, choose anybody—Flannery O'Connor, Philip Roth, Virginia Woolf, Muriel Spark, Donald

Barthelme—I'm intentionally naming very mixed company. It isn't hard to account for the certainty of their calling and the endlessly opinionated vigor of their writing—those are all people full of convictions. But my own fascination with the voices of others, and the pleasure I take in making them up and delivering them before live audiences, are mysteries. I sometimes think it's just that I so enjoyed reading, early on. Although you don't exhaust a book by consuming it, I still thought I needed to try to replenish the well a little with my own words. I'll never understand this uncharacteristic self-assertion any better than that.

INTERVIEWER: What kind of reception did your first books receive?

BROWN: I remember that the editor for my book of stories sent me some yellow tulips on publication day. As a friend said recently, I didn't know enough to realize they were the book's funeral flowers! I had a two-book contract. My first advance was five thousand dollars for the two, and I was delighted with it. I had been a poet and it never occurred to me that I'd make any money at all.

INTERVIEWER: What was the process that brought your first novel, *The Autobiography of My Mother,* into print?

BROWN: It was a pretty typical deal: Doubleday would do my collection of stories, *Street Games,* if I'd commit myself to write a novel. It happened that I wanted to write one, so this was not an unwelcome form of coercion. If anything it got me organized and kept me going when I felt like throwing in the towel. I suppose I could have reneged on the novel. It never occurred to me.

INTERVIEWER: Were you surprised at the good critical response to that novel?

BROWN: I'll never forget receiving a telegram from my editor saying, "Congratulations! This is a wonderful book." People think I'm exaggerating but believe me, I can hardly reconstruct my utter amazement. If I'd actually been aware of how little I knew, I'd have been even more astonished and grateful! Then the critics went on to educate me about what the book was about. It was beautifully reviewed by everyone but Anatole Broyard, who had also disliked my stories. But he was the only one who went into print about it. It won the Great Lakes Colleges Association prize for the best first novel of the year. Of everything I've ever written, this was the book I knew least about and was most in need of help with, but the help came after the fact. It restored my faith, in a funny way. It assured me that I could write even on automatic pilot. True, pure writing in the dark. Such innocence! It will never happen that way for me again.

INTERVIEWER: You say the help you needed with *Autobiography* came after the fact. Did you have help before that, with your poems and stories?

BROWN: I had a couple of mentors. In college, the poet Robert Pack taught me a lot of things, the most important of which was to sit back down and write it again. And again. And again. When I finally found the right word, I knew I'd never have done that on my own. And the late George Elliott, a very dear man and an undervalued writer, had a good deal to say about compassion, about not judging one's characters, about treasuring patience and neutrality. It's cause for concern that, gender politics having become the abiding preoccupation it has, many women these days will only value instruction they get from other women. Yet the two men I've just mentioned, and another who was my journalism teacher in high school, took me and my talent very seriously and taught me lessons that transcended gender. Of the three teachers who most affected me in my hope to be a writer, only one was a woman, my freshman English teacher. What she did was simply to ask me if I intended to teach college. Since neither of my parents had gone to high school, it had never crossed my mind that such a thing might be possible for me, so that was an extraordinary encouragement.

INTERVIEWER: You've worked in a variety of genres—fiction poetry, essays. Have you ever written drama?

BROWN: I've actually had a little experience with drama. The first theater piece I did was in 1983. A children's theater in New Hampshire, where we lived for eleven years, until '82, commissioned a musical, and a composer friend and I adapted that beloved classic *The Secret Garden.* We couldn't market the play because of some unexpected copyright problems, and in the meantime Marsha Norman came up with her $6 million Broadway version. Ours cost something like $250 to stage, and we did get our money's worth! I've never had such a good time. Having collaborators—especially, I suspect, if you're not working on your own book but on an adaptation of someone else's—is an extraordinary experience for a writer who's lived in that terrible isolation of her own mind for so long. To have set builders, costumers, a director and earnest, hard-working actors all putting their art into what you're used to thinking of as your own fantasy is sheer pleasure. After *The Secret Garden,* my husband and I collaborated on a sort of documentary drama, featuring Isaac Babel as narrator, which gathered together testimony about anti-Semitism in Russia starting in the tenth century. The play, *Dear Irina,* was produced in Houston, where I live. I learned a few things about theater from it, but it was more agitprop than art, and intended to be so.

INTERVIEWER: Not all fiction writers can write drama. Henry James is the classic example of a great novelist whose plays flopped. In your mind, how different are the two genres?

BROWN: My most recent novel, *Before and After,* actually began as a play. I had an idea that felt too easy, too familiar, to render as a novel, and that coincided with my curiosity about whether I could write a decent original script. So I wrote an act of it, just enough to get into the meat of the story but not out the other end. I'd sent it to a director friend to ask if it had any promise and he entered it in his theater's works-in-progress competition and it won! So more or less by accident I got to see my one act, my half play, in a semistaged reading and get a sense of how it worked as theater. There I discovered, as I had even with the children's play, that the popular idea that writing good conversation has anything to do with creating viable theater is resoundingly wrong. Making visible equivalencies to what's on the page—finding dramatic climaxes, tangible symbols—all that makes theater very different from fiction.

INTERVIEWER: How did the play metamorphose into *Before and After*?

BROWN: It happened that I had just put a failing novel away so that I could get a little perspective on it, and I was hungry to have another large project going. So I took the play and sort of wrote around it—transformed it into narrative. To be honest, I think the novel begins much more cleanly than it would have had I begun it in my usual wordy way; you might say it "cuts to the chase" a lot faster than it would have. A few reviewers called the book "cinematic," some as a compliment, some to give voice to their suspicion that, since the galley-copy advertising had given out the word that the movie rights were already assured, I must have been thinking of it as a film all along. Not true, but I was seeing it as a play initially, so things move cleanly early on, uncluttered by too much authorial expansion.

INTERVIEWER: What are you working on now?

BROWN: I've gone back to writing poetry, not only to clear my head but to announce, to anyone who cares to notice, that I'm going about my business doing whatever presents itself as needing to be done. My favorite of all my books is a sort of novel-in-the-form-of-eighty-four-poems called *Cora Fry* that I published in 1977. I wrote that after *The Autobiography of My Mother,* literally to restore silence in my mind. Now I've gone back to visit Cora fifteen years later, to see how she's doing in middle age.

INTERVIEWER: How did the first book of poems about Cora "restore silence" for you?

BROWN: Actually, silence was only half of it. In fact, I saw it spatially. After the very gray pages of the long mother/daughter argument that constitutes *Autobiography,* I needed spare, laconic, controlled speech, with a lot of empty white space around tiny little utterances. And that's what I gave myself. The poems in *Cora Fry* are syllabic, tightly measured out. Cora is New Hampshire born and bred. I wanted a kind of analog to the rigorous speech of a native New Englander.

INTERVIEWER: How does the sequel differ from the first book?

BROWN: This time, having established Cora's personality and her family and situation way back then, the challenge is in finding a new voice that's still recognizably hers, yet shows the inevitable changes that have taken place. The problems and their solutions are as much technical as they are spiritual or emotional—no more syllabics, a looser, more variable line, a more expansive kind of prosody. I'm having a fine time doing these poems, which I hope will succeed because I love the character and many readers have been wonderfully devoted to her over the years. Farrar, Straus, and Giroux is publishing the two books together next year.

INTERVIEWER: You just called *Cora Fry* a "novel-in-the-form-of-eighty-four-poems." Even when you work in other genres, you seem to have a novelistic sensibility. Is it a natural form for you?

BROWN: I may or may not have begun with a "novelistic sensibility," but I'll say that in my experience, after you've written a couple of them you develop a novelist's muscles—by which I don't mean strong, I mean stretched! It's gotten very hard for me to go back to small forms, which now tend to feel puny to me. As a reader I really prefer the short story to the novel, and a good story or poem already achieved doesn't feel at all slight. I'm only talking about what it feels like to embark on the writing of one. The long forms are so spacious and the speed with which details accrete is so leisurely compared to the story, that it takes real discipline, and more flexibility than I think I have, to meet the demands of both genres simultaneously. Yet, I love the outcome of that discipline far more than the novel, which can and must accommodate so many imperfect choices. I appreciate the compression of stories and poems. A good story is like a jack-in-the-box: open it and be prepared for something surprising to leap out!

INTERVIEWER: Your story collection, *Street Games,* could also be described as "novelistic." The stories are linked through setting and characters.

BROWN: The suite—the collection of interrelated stories or poems—is one of the wonderful compromises available to us. You can be the architect of something larger than its parts: The cumulative effect makes the payoff far more satisfying than the individual small work. I think a lot of short story writers who'd like to write a novel but haven't much interest in, or skill at, the creation of plot have found that the way to make their work cast a larger shadow is to build it in small increments that, taken together, weigh more than they would individually. There needn't be a long, intricate arc of plot, only the kind of path you can make out of modest mosaics. This is, to overstate it a bit, Chekhov's answer to Tolstoy—a very contemporary pleasure.

INTERVIEWER: How deliberate was the decision to link the stories in *Street Games*?

BROWN: I had already written about half the stories when it occurred to me to join them into a kind of confederation. This was at a time when there weren't a lot of those linked story collections out there. By virtue of my concentration on the neighborhood I was living in, I had been unintentionally painting a kind of portrait of the place. Once I had the concept, I was able to fiddle around the edges of a few stories to make those people seem like plausible neighbors, and then I generated such an endless list of other characters and emotional and sociological situations that I could have written a book twice as long before I exhausted it. The same is happening to me now with the "update" to *Cora Fry.* Every day I sit down to my notebook wondering what Cora has to tell me today. I have a list of possible—what should I call them?—complications.

INTERVIEWER: What kind of complications?

BROWN: Complications with implications. Wrinkles in the fabric of her life. At the rate they've been leading from one into another, I can see that I could probably write a poem every day forever. The momentum is thrillingly liberating. Out of it certain directions take shape, just as they do in fiction. To create a character we can understand and sympathize with, I have to find actions to elicit her reactions, and that's essentially a fiction writer's strategy; this is a hybrid form. I can indulge my desire to make large gestures at the same time that I have the pleasures of extreme condensation, the pressure I can put on the word, the line, the stanza.

INTERVIEWER: Do you have a sense of message, of purpose, as you write?

BROWN: A lot of my fiction, and my poetry too, has been fueled by a sort of displaced political energy. My first book of poems, *Some Deaths in the Delta,* and my novel *Civil Wars* concern themselves with Civil Rights–era Mississippi. *Street Games,* my short story collection, is about the diverse group of people who live on one block of Brooklyn, a very mixed block racially and economically. That, too, engages political questions, some head-on, some obliquely. *Cora Fry* is the voice of a woman very tentatively finding herself. And my most recent novel, *Before and After,* turns out to be far more political in its implications than I had originally expected it to be. A "safely" middle-class boy murders his small-town, working-class girlfriend, and many questions inevitably follow, not only about morality in general but about class and small-town chauvinism.

INTERVIEWER: Where did the political energy originally come from?

BROWN: I grew up in a somewhat Left-leaning family, though no one had done much besides vote for Henry Wallace back when he seemed a wild radical to many, and send angry telegrams against the execution of the Rosenbergs. My mother used to tell us proudly that she was what was called a YPSL back in the twenties—that's the Young People's Socialist League. But I suspect hers was more idealistic, and social, than active participation. We were a rather typical family of a sort that included a majority of Jewish New Yorkers who were always liberal and committed to what we'd have called "progressive" political ideals. Voting Republican would have been as foreign as interterrestrial travel.

INTERVIEWER: *Civil Wars* is probably your most political novel. Where did the material for that book come from?

BROWN: In 1964, just at the point when my husband was finishing his graduate degree, I received an invitation from the Woodrow Wilson Fellowship people who had paid my way through my master's degree, to teach in a "disadvantaged" college in a program they had just begun. The colleges were mostly in the South, mostly, though not solely, black. I remember we looked at each other and said, "How can we not?" This was just before the summer of '64 and there was an urgency to the call that we couldn't ignore. We were eager to do our bit in what we thought was the relatively protected setting of a college rather than a Freedom House; we hadn't really intended to walk right into the heart of the action. But when we were given a choice of postings, we ended up in Mississippi and, there in our first jobs, at the college and in the early poverty program, we had our lives turned around. My husband, who had just gotten his Ph.D. in clinical psychology, never became a practicing psychologist, but pursued more community-related work. And I found not only the subject matter for two of my books, but got what I think of as an initiation into the realities of American political life. People are lucky, sometimes, to be swept up by interesting times—though under a cruel star they can be ruined by them. We didn't have to go looking hard for an experience that gave us heroes and heroines, ideals and some of the means of addressing them.

INTERVIEWER: Do you consider yourself an activist?

BROWN: I've spent a lot of time wishing I were of the turn of mind that makes for activism. I admire Grace Paley and Tillie Olsen and dozens of others tremendously, but I have no talent for public life, either organizationally or emotionally. So I've resigned myself, not without a searing sense of guilt, to chronicling some of the inner landscape that's shaped by political realities. I felt at least momentarily exonerated when an anonymous reviewer in the *New Republic* took me to task for saying somewhat defensively on the back of my first book of poems, *Some Deaths in the Delta,* that "poems are not action nor action's substitute." Someone told me the writer was Robert Coles, whom I unabashedly admire. Whoever it was, he or she said that good poems are events, and that their utility perhaps lasts longer than many of the acts that could be done by any one of a thousand soldiers for change. I know what the reviewer meant, but I still wish I were a more flexible and efficient person so that I didn't feel I continually have to make a choice between a life in the world and a life at my desk.

INTERVIEWER: How deliberate is your choice of political themes?

BROWN: Much of what I've written has more than incidental political implications, and all the way back to the time when I lived in Mississippi in the mid-1960s I've felt that the activism I wasn't very competent at could be sublimated in my writing. But I have to search for those subjects; they don't seize me and demand to be given voice. I work at figuring out how to embody other people's voices, not all of them aggrieved. I find myself wishing I didn't have to feel defensive about starting, not with an agenda, but with that elite-sounding motivation, a love of words; or, pardon the expression, "art."

INTERVIEWER: Would it be fair to say, though, that political themes contribute to the success of your work?

BROWN: I think they do. I don't know if people read me as political with the possible exception of *Civil Wars.* But I'll tell you that from the Mississippi and Brooklyn poems in my first book, to questions about history and about personal versus public duty in *The Autobiography of My Mother,* to many of the stories in *Street Games,* and on into the present so-called family novel, I've thought my work political, though not with any didactic intention. I don't have a particular constituency—race, gender, whatever—on whose behalf I write. I also tend to raise more questions than I want to answer, so I think it wouldn't occur to some to think of me that way.

INTERVIEWER: Would you agree with the notion that all art is political?

BROWN: Yes, all art is political. Thinking it's not is a political stance in itself. It was very strange and disquieting that one of the approaches taken by a lot of interviewers when *Before and After* came out last year was to invoke "family values" as a background against which to talk about my book. At best, after I'd disposed of the right of any political party to appropriate such values and to assume it represented the only "truly American" ones, it gave me a chance to talk about the question that lies somewhere near the heart of that novel. Are we obligated to love, that is, to protect, other people's children as well as our own? The family is a tribe, and if we are ever going to get beyond the most primitive concern only for "our own," then we need to see our responses as political even if they don't seem on the surface to have any ramifications beyond the "home and hearth." This of course can be extended to neighborhood, to ethnic group, to nationality and race.

INTERVIEWER: While we're still on the subject of politics, you sometimes come down hard on a certain kind of liberal. Sarah and Michael Rappaport, for example, indulge in "fashionable mercies" and "knee-jerk charity." Do you see such characters as symptomatic of a larger impulse?

BROWN: I suppose I find attractive—I wouldn't call them "targets" exactly, but "tokens" of certain kinds of contemporary earnestness in characters like Sarah and Michael, though I tried not to caricature them. They are decent, concerned, the "best kind" of liberals out there, doing the best they can from their comfortable place in the scheme of things. I'm not unsympathetic; in fact I'm similar in some respects, except that I may see myself more clearly, and thus more harshly, than they do. At the far distant end of the same spectrum I have made characters like Gerda Stein in *The Autobiography of My Mother* and Teddy in *Civil Wars,* who are so passionately involved in their political and ideological pursuits that they lack many "merely human" and domestic virtues—common sense for one. That's clearly a stance I don't recommend, either, so I don't know that I challenge the pious simplifications of my "liberal" characters so much as I try to show that, viewed from the perspective of anyone who's radically troubled, their pleasant solutions are simply inadequate—wishful thinking.

INTERVIEWER: One of your more impressive characterizations is Jacob Reiser in *Before and After.* Can you talk a little bit about how that character developed?

BROWN: Readers are always curious about how characters develop. I have to admit that I display the same somewhat naive curiosity about the books I like. But how does anything in a book develop? How do we combine the things we "know" with the things we "guess" or "intuit," and how do the demands of a particular work shape our knowing? The answers are all extremely specific. In *Before and After,* for example, I had to make Jacob into what I needed for the circumstances. Disappointingly mechanical as this might sound, he was a "what" before he was a "who." The situation was simple at the outset. What stimulated me to write the book was a murder case, an intriguing component of a case, here in Houston. A seventeen-year-old boy was accused of a terrible murder and when it came time for his parents to give their testimony to the grand jury, they refused, on the grounds that the same privilege should extend to parents that protects spouses from having to bear witness. They went to jail rather than give evidence against their son.

INTERVIEWER: How close is your story to the actual case?

BROWN: The details bear no relation to the ones I ultimately invented. I began with the absolutely un-fleshed-out premise that if a boy were accused of murder, his whole household would be thrown into wretched disarray. This is a family crisis—the catastrophe would befall all of them. Period. The first thing I thought of was to move the action to a small town. Someone else might have seen this as a quintessential big-city story but I knew that I didn't want to write that story. Here I was driven by my own obsessions, which in this case include not only my knowledge and love of small-town New England life, but also the sense that the effects of such a crime would cast a firmer shadow, full of social and psychological implications, across a village of five thousand than a city the size of Houston. Then I started building backwards, in a sense. What kind of family might this be, to precipitate the greatest dramatic conflict?

INTERVIEWER: Jacob, the teenage murderer, is amazingly convincing—especially considering you're the mother of two girls. Would you say he's a normal kid?

BROWN: I wanted him to seem a more or less regular kid with a few kinky, inexplicable habits. I have two older brothers but I can't say they were really my models. After all, they were teenagers in a different generation. Living in the world, you sop up a lot of things you don't even realize you've taken in. My husband teaches high school kids; some of our friends have boys—teenagers—who slouch and mumble and terrify their parents into wondering if they're pathological or normal. I remember Anne Tyler saying once that she was grateful for all the pop culture her daughters dragged in across the doormat. A lot of those details aren't as gender-bound as you might think. So the little fragments of Jacob's life were cobbled together without much difficulty. As for his soul, his offstage inner life—it's kind of up for grabs, isn't it? I don't see him as terribly disturbed. I wanted him to live on a continuum not too far from where boys live, with better luck, who don't fall into the pit of their own worst possibilities. Where my real concentration lay was in the construction of the parents' sense of loss as their children grew up and began their hidden lives. Any parent could write those scenes, provide his or her own sad and happy little details. Really, all I wanted to do was try to build a more or less ordinary family life and then make it run askew, but not so askew that my readers wouldn't see themselves watching their children's lives as they recede into privacy and mystery.

INTERVIEWER: You say you don't see Jacob as terribly disturbed, yet you make a lot of his "kinky inexplicable habits," and of his temper.

BROWN: Jacob's temper is his father's, visited upon him out of Ben's unresolved problems. But even Carolyn is finally compassionate about Ben's anger. She says to their lawyer, what is a person to do with problems he's tried his best to solve? Ben's had therapy, he's done as well as he could. But, she says, "Children taste what their parents swallow." Try though one might, children will feel those effects, but what is to be done? Should we give our children up? Should we be prevented from having them until we're perfect?

INTERVIEWER: The scene in which Jacob stones a dog is especially disturbing. Why did you choose that action?

BROWN: I'm not sure I should have chosen anything quite so alarming as the stoning of that dog. I've given it a lot of thought since I've published the book and heard how many readers are practically ready to have Jacob committed for this act of random cruelty. What I was really trying to do—and it might not have been calibrated quite perfectly—was to show a boy still unformed, trying out his capacity to give pain. At one point his mother thinks of how she's watched him trying to look a little sinister in his black and red and yellow parka. He's a boy on the edge of manhood, uncertain of what constitutes masculinity. In fact, though it turns out that she suffers violence at his hands—an act of passion, not of intention—he has been very decent to his girlfriend, Martha. He has not been brutal. He's even been careful and thoughtful in their sexual relationship, about making sure she doesn't get pregnant. And she accuses him of being a wimp, because she has another boyfriend, the one who has made her pregnant, who wasn't as controlled and mature. She uses this against Jacob.

INTERVIEWER: A fair amount of *Before and After* revolves around the workings of the criminal justice system. What role does research play in your work?

BROWN: Most books take some kind of research. Even when you're in an arena you know well, there are always specifics you need to learn. That's one of the pleasures of trying to go far afield from your personal experience. Most writers don't know enough about other kinds of work. It does us good to turn our attention outward, away from the subjectivity we invest in our characters. The major danger of research is that you don't want to stop to begin the writing. I did a lot of talking to lawyers to help me straighten out procedures, not to mention legal attitudes, for *Before and After.* One of my terrors was that somebody like Scott Turow would embarrass me in public—in a *Times* review, say—for making some egregious legal error. It was a great relief to get a note from him telling me that he envied me my book! I also got a note from Perri Klass, who's a pediatrician and a writer. She seemed to find my pediatrician sufficiently convincing. You breathe a real sigh of relief when you hear that from the horse's mouth, so to speak, especially because, unlike Tom Clancy who learns all about tanks, or Michener who has a staff of researchers, you want your research to be discreet. You want to keep it in perspective and not let it get the upper hand.

INTERVIEWER: What about *Tender Mercies*? What research about quadriplegics did you do to create Laura?

BROWN: For *Tender Mercies* I had some wonderful cooperation from a woman I realized, when I was about a third of the way through the book, I'd read about in an old *Ms.* magazine. She sounded very much like my character. Both were quadriplegics, and their similarity sprang from their particular brand of irony that's not surprising under the circumstances. I searched her out, and she talked with me quite candidly and let me watch certain procedures when the "handlers" in her nursing home came to take care of her. She was able to do that without embarrassment because people whose bodies have become objects have buried their sense of self. Watching her helped me locate what was left to my character, Laura, and her husband, Dan. As the body becomes a burden, no longer a pleasure, one seeks elsewhere for the soul.

INTERVIEWER: Would you recommend a writing career to your children?

BROWN: I do happen to have a daughter who's pursuing the writing life, but she never asked me what I thought of the idea. I don't think anybody can give useful advice about becoming a writer. It's one of those things, like dancing or acting or any number of chancy, expressive things about which vocational counseling will not avail. If you're not passionate about it, the question will soon enough answer itself. The one thing I do say to people who think they want to do this is that they probably ought to major in something other than English in college. Even now, with a very congenial teaching schedule, I wish I were doing something else besides the endless dissection of other people's headwork. But by now I'm stuck with it—though this isn't to say I don't enjoy it a lot of the time.

INTERVIEWER: What would you tell a young writer about the financial unpredictability of the profession?

BROWN: It's gotten hard for this generation to live with the uncertain financial situation that writers have put up with in the past. There are too many well-worn paths to fellowships, teaching jobs. If others have them, why not themselves? Understandable enough: it's hard to go barefoot when everybody else is wearing good shoes. I'm saddened, often, to see our students graduate and stop writing because they think they need to maintain a certain standard of living that might be more negotiable than they dare imagine. They've grown up without much patience for penury. For the children of the middle class, it feels outdated. I hate to sound self-righteous about this, but the fact is that early on, my husband and I lived mighty close to the bone because I didn't have a paying job. I was home writing; that was my apprenticeship. Would-be writers need to recognize how many of what they think are rock-bottom needs are really choices, within their control.

INTERVIEWER: What effect have the opinions of others and the pressures of the marketplace had on your choices of subjects and genres?

BROWN: I don't think I've been much influenced by others' expectations in choosing, or letting myself be chosen by, genres, subjects, level of accessibility. Partly this comes of starting out as a poet, with no expectations of commercial success. And of being a poet, and then a fledgling short story writer, at a much more innocent time. Though I didn't write in a vacuum, I was pretty isolated from any group of knowledgeable writers. For a little while in New York I used to get together with Erica Jong and Norma Klein, old college friends, to look at each other's work—we were quite near the beginnings of our publishing careers—and talk about this cottage industry of ours. Then I moved to New Hampshire, where I didn't really know many writers. What I remember is that I had pretty modest ambitions: I wanted to publish in the little magazines. Of course I wanted a book, but unlike my graduate students these days I had no idea what any of that actually meant or what I might dare demand. They are jealous very early of other people's publications, advances, reviews, visibility. In my innocence, I truly didn't have a clue that any of that might be mine—I just wrote, sort of dumbly. Now I work with students who've taken the pulse of every writer out there. The poets, especially, are avid analysts of career, reputation, rising and falling stars. I'm not sure I could have withstood this competitiveness—this sense of writing as a profession with a job description and salary demands, and a timetable.

INTERVIEWER: You've made it in the profession now—you've written a best-seller. What demands are made on the author of a commercial success like *Before and After*?

BROWN: Well, I have to say I think of it as a pretty stingy success: lots of praise, a place on the best-seller list, a dream set of reviews, many other fantastic, unimaginable commercial things happening to it, but none of it enough to make me exactly a household name. Before this, no one had much bothered to market anything of mine as far as I could see. In the case of *Before and After,* I finally had an invitation to the dance—the exhausting, exhilarating, frequently preposterous business of the book tour, the endless readings, the tedious, earnest questions—for which I'm not ungrateful. That's what you get, or rather give, when you finally have an audience.

INTERVIEWER: Would you say it was a valuable experience?

BROWN: I learned a lot about marketing this year. It's very interesting, but it's in the hands of the publicity department at your publisher and you're pretty passive if you're willing to play the game. I will say that being available for all the self-promotion takes a lot of time. I don't know how people manage to rise to it book after book. It's a great way to keep you from writing for months at a time. But once in a lifetime—it was a terrific ride!

INTERVIEWER: Now that you have gone back to poetry, do you worry about losing your new audience?

BROWN: I'm sure that the next thing I publish, which will be as uncommercial as my other seven books, will disappoint my new readers, but I consider the "marketability" of *Before and After* a happy coincidence of subject, marketing and luck. I don't expect to repeat it, nor do I even want to try. The only reason you keep your audience in mind when you write is to help your work make the best possible sense it can make, on its own terms. The charge you give yourself is self-fulfilling, self-delighting. You are shaping the best story or novel or poem possible. Part of that imperative might demand a certain lucidity, or a certain mood, or a certain playfulness. Sometimes you add details that make something manifest, or you struggle to fulfill a certain form. The point is that the command comes from within the work. Hack writers aren't writing for themselves; they're cutting their fabric to a preexistent pattern that they know is selling well that season. All serious writers are their own audiences, with all the books of the past looking over their shoulders. If our readers' pleasure coincides with our own, that's all the better.

Peter Matthiessen

Born in 1927, Peter Matthiessen was a New Yorker *writer who founded the* Paris Review, *which he turned over to George Plimpton in 1955. An avid adventurer, he became a chronicler of wild places and people, traveling to rain forests, the mountains of Nepal, and Tortuga. Matthiessen is considered by many to be more accomplished in nonfiction, although his* At Play in the Fields of the Lord *(1965) is a favorite novel of all time for many. His other best known novel is* Far Tortuga *(1975). Among his well-known nonfiction books are* Nine-Headed Dragon River *(1985),* The Snow Leopard *(1978), and* In the Spirit of Crazy Horse *(1983). This last was the subject of a highly publicized lawsuit for slander, which caused the book to be pulled from the stores and shredded. He finally prevailed against the suit, and the book was reissued in 1989. An engaged Zen Buddhist, Matthiessen regards his nonfiction as work in the service of certain issues and groups. He often gives the money from his books to causes, like trying to get Leonard Peltier—subject of* In the Spirit of Crazy Horse*—out of jail.*

In this interview, conducted in 1987, after a decade of writing nonfiction, he has just returned to fiction, having begun the "Mister Watson" trilogy, the first of which is Killing Mister Watson *(1990), a quirky novel about a place as much as a character, the Ten Thousand Island area of southwestern Florida near the turn of the century, a zone he sees as inhabited by outlaws and losers, as well as by decent people trying to make a way in the world.*

INTERVIEWER: Can you tell us a little about your early life? You're a veteran, I understand.

MATTHIESSEN: Yes, I served in World War II and then I went to Yale. I took my junior year abroad at the Sorbonne.

INTERVIEWER: Did you grow up in the city?

MATTHIESSEN: I was born right here in New York City, Madison Avenue and Sixty-fifth Street, I think it was, at a little lying-in hospital. I went to school in New York City and then we lived up on the Hudson for a while, then moved to Connecticut. So I've been around the New England coast all my life.

INTERVIEWER: What did your father do?

MATTHIESSEN: He was an architect. Then he went in the navy and helped design various gunnery-training devices used during World War II. He didn't really want to go back to architecture. After the war, he became a fund-raiser and spokesman for conservation groups, the Audubon Society and Nature Conservancy, that kind of thing.

INTERVIEWER: So you would credit your family life then, with your interest in nature, the environment?

MATTHIESSEN: We had a wonderful piece of property in Connecticut, back up in the hills, and my brother and I were both very interested in snakes and birds. We had a big copperhead den on our property. Until my mother put a stop to it, we had a lot of copperheads in cages. I went on to birds—starting with my mother's feeder—and my brother became a marine biologist. I think we kind of taught my father—it was the other way around.

INTERVIEWER: What did you study in school?

MATTHIESSEN: I was an English major, but I took courses in biology and ornithology. I began writing in boarding school, smart-aleck articles about this and that. Then, with a friend, I did a column for the *Yale Daily News* on hunting and fishing.

I started writing short stories while I was at Yale, and I was still there when my first short story, "Sadie"—it's in *On the River Styx*—won the *Atlantic* prize, which was very useful because I came back there to teach writing my first year out of college. I didn't last very long as a teacher, just one term, but the publication was a big help. The *Atlantic* took a second story, and I got an agent. Then I started my first novel and sent off about four chapters and waited by the post office for praise to roll in, calls from

Hollywood, everything. Finally my agent sent me a letter that said, "Dear Peter, James Fenimore Cooper wrote this a hundred and fifty years ago, only he wrote it better. Yours, Bernice." I probably needed that; it was very healthy.

INTERVIEWER: Did that novel become *Race Rock*?

MATTHIESSEN: No. That was, I think, the only novel I ever junked. *Race Rock* was the second one I started, the first one I finished.

INTERVIEWER: Tell me about the *Paris Review.*

MATTHIESSEN: I started it in Paris in late '51 with a guy called Harold Humes, who was an absolutely brilliant fellow but rather erratic. People had trouble working with Doc Humes, so I got hold of George Plimpton, who was at Cambridge then. I'd gone to school with him in New York and I've known him since I was little. Why he accepted the editor's job I've no idea, but he did. I came back to the States in '53, and after 1954, the editorial office was mostly in New York, and Plimpton was the one who held it together.

There were a lot of good young writers around Paris. Bill Styron was there, Terry Southern, Jimmy Baldwin, Irwin Shaw. A lot of people were coming in and out. Years ago, E. P. Dutton did a collection of *Paris Review* fiction in the early years. You should see it. Beckett's first appearance in an English-speaking magazine, Kerouac—about the first appearance under his own name—and Phillip Roth's first appearance, too.

INTERVIEWER: When did you know you were a writer?

MATTHIESSEN: I always knew. I can't remember even considering doing anything else after I was about fifteen or sixteen. I wrote only fiction for a long time. But then I got married, and I wasn't making a living. I became a bayman and haul seiner and I ran a charter boat out of Montauk Island for a few years, deep-sea fishing, but it wasn't enough. While I was in Paris I had written a nonfiction piece for the *New Yorker,* one of their "Annals of Crime," together with Ben Bradlee, who now runs the *Washington Post* and was also in Paris at that time. I decided I'd better try some more nonfiction.

I had this idea about wild places—everybody was writing about civilized places, but the wild places were being destroyed in many parts of the world, and indeed still are. I went to the *New Yorker*'s Mr. Shawn and asked him what the *New Yorker* would think of sending me around the world to look at some of these places and write about them. To my amazement, he agreed. I took a freighter from New York, all the way up the Amazon into Peru; I went all the way down to Tierra del Fuego. That began a long series of travels that lies at the heart of my nonfiction, some for *Audubon Magazine,* but mainly for the *New Yorker.* Some of it's anthropological in tone, like *Under the Mountain Wall,* the New Guinea book, and some is almost purely natural history like *The Shore Birds of North America.* Then I got into social advocacy, like the book on Cesar Chavez and the farm workers—that became a *New Yorker* profile.

INTERVIEWER: Did these books and articles put groceries on the table?

MATTHIESSEN: The *New Yorker* is very generous, and I was writing fiction at the same time, making a little bit of money, and I was commercial fishing. I wasn't getting rich, but . . . The first real money came with a novel called *At Play in the Fields of the Lord,* which had a movie sale.

INTERVIEWER: Was that ever made into a movie?

MATTHIESSEN: Oh, they're still talking about it, and it now seems that Hector Babenco *(Ironweed, Kiss of the Spider Woman)* might be doing it. Virtually every star and director you can name has been involved in that book at one time or another. About five different scripts have been done.

INTERVIEWER: Aesthetically, in terms of the vision in your head, what is the relationship between the fiction and the nonfiction?

MATTHIESSEN: I've always thought that my real writing was the fiction, which seems odd, since I've done over twice as many nonfiction books as fiction books. Yet I really haven't changed my view. Nonfiction usually involves research. One has to stick to the facts, piecing together a construction; it's more like cabinetwork or carpentry. Fiction is totally different, much more natural, more fun. Yet somebody told me that I mustn't repudiate my nonfiction, because it's saying very much what the fiction is saying. They work together well because the underlying themes are the same. That's probably true. *In the Spirit of Crazy Horse* would make a marvelous novel—I could turn that into a novel in a few months.

INTERVIEWER: My sense is that *Raditzer* and the other two early novels were apprentice books, the sort of books that young men were supposed to write.

MATTHIESSEN: I had a very interesting letter from Styron about *Partisans.* We shared a place in Italy the summer I was working on it. He said,

"This isn't a novel; it's a short story that goes on too long." I think that's absolutely true—it's too pared down, too cut away. A novel should have some sense of shambling looseness, unpredictability; it shouldn't be taut. A lot of modern novels are, I know, and Styron's remark applies. *Raditzer* has the same feeling; it's a little bit too tight, too neat.

INTERVIEWER: Do you feel like you hit your stride, in terms of fiction, with *At Play in the Fields of the Lord*?

MATTHIESSEN: I haven't hit my stride yet. I hope to hit it with the one I'm working on now.

INTERVIEWER: You went to the Amazon for six months. Was that where you found Lewis Moon?

MATTHIESSEN: Lewis Moon is, as far as I can piece it together, an amalgam of three people. When I was doing the research for *Wildlife in America,* traveling through the West, I picked up this hostile Navajo kid who wouldn't answer a single question, and any attempt to be friendly was rebuffed. We eat, we drive, but we don't talk. Then somewhere in the middle of the desert—about six hundred miles later—I didn't see a connection with anything—he bangs on the side of the car and I let him out. Now I know Indian people better, and I know that the guy probably didn't speak English, or if he did, he was ashamed of it. He was unsophisticated. Also hostile, but not as hostile as I thought. It seemed to me at the time that it was alienation, tremendous alienation from the white culture, though I've probably romanticized that all over the place.

The second one was a guy I ran into in a bar in Brazil, at the mouth of the Amazon River. Absolute loner of a man, pursuing some dream of exploration in the jungles. He had a little kit— maps, a spare shirt, spare underpants. Everything was cut down so that he carried all his gear in a little packet. He'd had a successful business in Canada and got sick of it. He ran out on his wife and children, became a merchant seaman, was washed off a deck of a cargo ship and miraculously picked up, not by his own ship but another one, way out in the middle of nowhere. He said that gave him real pause about his life, knowing how close he had come, and he wanted to see things.

Those two guys, with a little of me thrown in, came together as Lewis Moon.

INTERVIEWER: One theme that unites your work seems to be the impossibility of purity in the ultimate corruption of civilization, and the impossibility of finding one's way back. In light of that, how do you assess the ending of *At Play in the Fields of the Lord,* where Moon is the one man under the sun?

MATTHIESSEN: I don't know. One great thing about fiction is that you don't have to have a wrap-up. I always sort of loosely thought that Moon didn't survive, but I don't know. I may bring him back for another novel.

INTERVIEWER: Where did you get that image of the moth that reverberates through the book? The moths fly off into the moon, and finally, in that last scene, he builds the bonfire. The idea of the sparks flying off brings the reader's mind back to the opening lines of the novel.

MATTHIESSEN: Some Amazonian Indian myth, the moths trying to reach the moon. Or I may have made it up, who knows? I may as well claim it.

INTERVIEWER: *Far Tortuga* was such a change in terms of style. What happened?

MATTHIESSEN: It was a purposeful change. I just got sick of all the metaphor. Originally, *Far Tortuga* began as a nonfiction piece for the *New Yorker.* I'd heard about a man who was still running a schooner from Grand Cayman down to Nicaragua, fishing sea turtles. I got the *New Yorker* to send me on the schooner, and I was stunned by the men and their attitudes toward the sea, the way they handled themselves with no life-preserving equipment, dangerous reefs, and everything so worn out, so bare and spare.

I was drawn by that spareness. *At Play* is in the jungle and it's lush, but in the Miskito Cays, everything was worn out by the sun and the salt and the sea, and despair and poverty. I came back to Mr. Shawn and said, "Listen, I can do the article, but I'm going to hold back the best material. I don't want to tell you that I'm giving you everything I saw, because I'm not. I want to do a novel about it."

The magazine had spent a lot on expenses, but without any hesitation—he's a great editor—he said, "Do what's best for the work, Mr. Matthiessen." I did an article for the *New Yorker* and then I went ahead with what I really wanted to do.

INTERVIEWER: How long did *Far Tortuga* take you to do? One has the feeling that doing a spare novel takes more time than the other kind.

MATTHIESSEN: Off and on, it took about twelve years, and I could've put in another twelve years. I enjoyed it so much I didn't want to stop working on it. I think it's my best book. But I was doing a lot of nonfiction, too.

INTERVIEWER: Was Captain Raib based on a real person?

MATTHIESSEN: There was a very colorful captain of that turtle boat I was on, it's true. I can't possibly admit that Captain Raib was based on him, because if I ever do go to Grand Cayman, he'd put me in jail.

INTERVIEWER: Robert Stone wrote: "From its opening moment with daybreak over the windward passage, the reader of *Far Tortuga* senses that the narrative itself is the recapitulation of a cosmic process, as though the author had sought to link his storytelling with the eye of creation." And he goes on to say: "In a way, there is only a single insight: the unity of things beneath an ever-changing multiplicity of form." Are you comfortable with that?

MATTHIESSEN: Certainly in terms of the cycles and the time, the tides, and the hour—I use those funny spaces and marks, you know—yes, I did have some idea of universal time, but I think Bob Stone was giving me a little bit more credit than I deserve. Sometimes you do things that aren't consciously worked out in your mind. At the very, very beginning of the book, when the sun rises, coming hard around the world—yes, in a sense, that's an expression of what he's saying there.

INTERVIEWER: That seems to be another of your recurring themes—the unity with the multiplicity.

MATTHIESSEN: That's very much a Zen theme.

INTERVIEWER: At the beginning of your *Nine-Headed Dragon River* you describe an encounter with Soenroshi. You were just in from Africa—from travels that became *The Tree Where Man Was Born*—burned-out, haggard, exhausted, whatever, angry, nervous, all those things. And your second wife, Deborah Love, was already involved in Zen—you hadn't gotten interested yet—

MATTHIESSEN: No. We were both interested in LSD, we were doing a lot of drugs. Then she went over to Zen—this was in the late sixties—and she and I weren't getting along very well. I left and was away for about seven months and I just showed up without warning in the driveway. She was there with three Zen masters, but I didn't know that—they were just three guys in my driveway in weird costumes. She introduced me, and then they went away. "Oh, poor Debbo-lah," they said.

INTERVIEWER: You've written about the historical tension between Zen practice and art.

MATTHIESSEN: When Zen first came to Japan, and especially the Rinzai school of Zen, many so-called Zen monks and teachers became poets and translators, painters, and so forth, and their insights infused the whole culture in a marvelous way. Japanese culture is grounded in Zen, but as far as pure Zen practice goes, it was fatal. These people spent all their energy in the arts, being aesthetic and hobnobbing with the courtiers at the palace. The real Zen spirit was dying. So writers were harshly criticized because most of the monks at that time were writers and poets.

INTERVIEWER: How do you reconcile art and Zen? Or is it necessary?

MATTHIESSEN: It's difficult for me because I am a Zen monk—in fact, I'm a Zen priest—I can marry you or bury you or whatever. I don't talk much about Zen in my public life, but I've been a Zen student for a long, long time, and I probably should be giving more of my time to it than I do. But I have this idea that American writers, by and large, do weak work in their later years. I'd like to have the character to quit writing sooner rather than later, and maybe at that time I'd go over more fully into Zen practice.

INTERVIEWER: You mentioned that the composition of *The Snow Leopard* was your Zen practice for several years, and I wonder if you'd explain what that means?

MATTHIESSEN: I'd parted with the Zen master I was working with originally, as had most of his senior students, so I was without a teacher. I was in touch with another Zen teacher only intermittently, so I made the writing and composition of *The Snow Leopard* my practice. I did a lot of study—a lot of sitting and meditation with it—and I think that gave the book a meditative quality that it might not otherwise have had.

INTERVIEWER: To what extent is *The Snow Leopard* a shaped creation?

MATTHIESSEN: Fortunately I had that natural, built-in structure of the dates themselves; the book is faithful to the time in which it took place. It has a symbolic shape as well. We literally—and in Zen this is an important symbol—we literally walked up across the Himalayas to the Tibetan plateau and then walked down again. The wonderful thing was that, in late autumn, when you're coming down the mountain, you're walking against the season. Even though winter is coming, you're walking back towards summer because of the altitude difference. So this yin/yang inversion of things was built-in and very helpful.

INTERVIEWER: And literally true?

MATTHIESSEN: And the nefarious Tupten, suspected of being a thief and a drunk, and foul-mouthed and so forth. Yet he was my teacher in the book, throughout.

INTERVIEWER: Did you rewrite to emphasize that for the structure?

MATTHIESSEN: I rewrote a lot but the basic book is in my original journals. I'm a terrific rewriter, I polish and polish and polish and polish. I rewrote the last chapter, the river descent, in *At Play in the Fields of the Lord*—I'm sure I rewrote that thirty times. Even then I didn't get it the way I wanted it. I had started to wreck it, as you do—you go stale, and become stiff and literary and useless. That's when you have to quit. That's the only reason I quit with *Far Tortuga.* I started to do it damage. If you find yourself coming back the next day and erasing more of the so-called improvements than you keep, you'd better get the hell out of that book.

INTERVIEWER: After I read about jaguar shamans in *At Play in the Fields of the Lord,* I couldn't help thinking of Tukten as a snow leopard.

MATTHIESSEN: I saw him that way, too. I did kind of push things that way, because he had yellowy eyes. It was nice to interpret him that way. Tukten was amazing, a beautiful person.

INTERVIEWER: Did you ever meet him again?

MATTHIESSEN: No. An odd thing happened after I'd been back about a year and a half, two years. A woman called up one evening and I think she'd had a drink or two, maybe getting her nerve up to call me because she thought she was being a fool. She said, "You're not going to believe this, but I was in Nepal with my daughter and we took a trek to Manang. One night in camp this rude sherpa, who was a friend of our sherpa, came over to me and said in very, very bad English, 'You America?' " She said, "Yes, I America." He shoves this dirty-looking packet at her, and says "Give Massin." She says, "America's a very big place, I just don't know." He just shakes his head and shoves it at her again and says, "Give Massin," as if he knew there'd be no problem at all. So she has this little dirty packet with her, comes home to New York and doesn't know what to do. But she has another daughter, and that daughter calls up and says, "Oh, Mum, isn't this an amazing coincidence, you're just back from Nepal and there's a wonderful series of articles in the *New Yorker* about Nepal, by Peter Matthiessen." And she says, "Holy Mackerel," or something. That was too much, you know, the coincidence, the timing—you see, Tukten really is a shaman. So she calls up this stranger and says, "Does that sherpa sound like anybody you know?" I said, "It sounds like Tukten." And she says, "Great," and fired off this thing. It was exactly what Tukten would've sent to me. It was—quite a nice one—a lama's delusion-cutting knife; it's for cutting your delusions. It's kind of a half-moon crescent blade with what is called a dorje or bell handle on it. Bong! I have to assume that was Tukten. It just felt right, it felt exactly right.

INTERVIEWER: The two big books you've done since then, if I've got the chronology right, are *In the Spirit of Crazy Horse,* which deals with American Indian issues, and *Men's Lives,* which deals with your friends, the commercial fishermen, at home. Do you think you've learned, to quote Thoreau, "to travel much in Concord"?

MATTHIESSEN: Stay on my own cushion and not go seeking dusty lands? Yes, I think so. Certainly, my lust to travel has moderated. Still, I get itchy. Someone comes along with a great idea for an expedition—for example, I did a book called *Sand Rivers,* just before the Indian books, and it was a safari into a very remote part of Africa. I didn't want to write that book at all, but I wanted to go to that place. I had to sing for my supper, that was the deal.

The *New Yorker* took it, and it worked out okay, but I have a queer feeling about books that don't originate in my own oyster, so to speak, that little sand grit in the oyster that goes on and on and becomes a book. You can feel it, and then suddenly it's ready to write. I think sometimes it's like a line of eggs in a hen; it begins with a tiny seed up in the ovary, then a progression, egg after egg, getting bigger and bigger, until finally one's ready to lay. Well, books are like that, too. If a book begins with some outside purpose or support system, it's always a frail child. You don't give birth to it; you construct it. *Sand Rivers* was one of those books and *Blue Meridian* another—I wanted to see white sharks so badly that it was worth it. To a certain extent the Indian books are the same way. They're all written for a cause.

My English publisher wants me to do *In the Spirit of Crazy Horse* again, cutting out all the special pleading, the legal argument aimed at getting Leonard Peltier a new trial, and doing the book again from a literary point of view, because it's a wonderful story. I think he's right. But I had to push it toward a certain end; that was the reason I wrote it.

INTERVIEWER: Do you think that aesthetically and spiritually you've perhaps come home?

MATTHIESSEN: No, I think perhaps the opposite. These last four books before the novel—two books about Indian problems, one about the commercial fishermen and their problems, and one about Zen—were all written to help out certain groups. I don't regret it, but I don't have any illusions about the literary quality of those books. Those books are not as good as *The Snow Leopard,* or *The Tree Where Man Was Born.* They're not. And they could have been. I knew how to make them good. But I couldn't make them good from a literary point of view and accomplish my purposes. It's very difficult to do.

INTERVIEWER: A critic, I think his name is Robert Sherrill, sees a change in your work since *The Snow Leopard.* He wrote: "Unless I've been misled by the internal evidence"—and he's speaking of *In the Spirit of Crazy Horse*—"there has also been a profound change in Matthiessen. He is losing confidence in mankind, and perhaps in himself." I wondered if you shared Sherrill's assessment, that you seem to have lost your hope, or your confidence?

MATTHIESSEN: I'm a little more skeptical about social action and what can be done. You don't have to be much of a reader to recognize the human tendency throughout civilization's long, long history to blood and gore, rapine, greed, and the worst kind of misery. You can make a little betterment here, a little solace there, but it's not very much. Nonetheless you have to do it. You have to do it. I passionately think that. We all must make an effort for the betterment of mankind, even though we know it won't do any good.

INTERVIEWER: To what extent do you buy into the belief that if the individual becomes enlightened, that adds to the betterment of the universe in and of itself?

MATTHIESSEN: When Shakyamuni the Buddha was enlightened, he said, "Above heaven and below earth, I alone am." He said at the same time, "How wonderful, how wonderful, all creatures are enlightened." So there's the unity and the multiplicity both. "I alone" signifies the One, not one single ego. So when you are enlightened, the world is enlightened, but that isn't a lasting condition. In the next moment, everything must be renewed again. It's a very subtle teaching.

INTERVIEWER: So it's a continual process?

MATTHIESSEN: A continual process.

Scott Turow

Like Dickens, Scott Turow seeks to be both a popular and a serious writer. He was among the first contemporary blockbuster lawyer novelists, which has now become a genre all in itself. As a young writer at Stanford University, Turow accepted the art model for fiction and tried unsuccessfully to write "literary" knockoffs. He eventually gave that up for Harvard Law School, where he wrote One L *(1977), a highly successful book about the first year of law school. He became a criminal prosecutor in Chicago before going into private practice. Turow claims to love being a lawyer and finds that the literary models he got in school are of less use than his experience. He does not believe that the law is value neutral, but rather that it defends "a certain concept of humanity." Questions of honesty, loyalty, trust, and concealment—between people and between people and society—are the issues he explores in his fiction. "Nothing is as ambiguous as the actual world, the different kinds of truths we recognize," Turow says.*

Conducted in 1989, this was one of the first, if not the only, in-depth literary interviews of Turow. It took place after Presumed Innocent *(1987) became a huge best-seller and after he had completed work on* Burden of Proof *(1990), but before it was published. He is also the author of* Pleading Guilty *(1993) and most recently* The Laws of Our Fathers *(1996).*

INTERVIEWER: Mr. Turow, can you tell us just a little bit about yourself? As I understand it, you live in Chicago now and you're a hometown boy.

TUROW: I was born in Chicago, grew up on the north side of the city. I was thirteen when my parents moved to Winnetka, which is one of the most affluent areas outside Chicago. I went to New Trier High School, sometimes described as a public prep school, and from there to Amherst College as an undergraduate, then Stanford for grad school. At Stanford I was a writing fellow for two years, and then a lecturer in the English department for three. I went to law school in 1975, and began practicing law in 1978, which I'm still doing while attempting to write.

INTERVIEWER: I understand that you studied writing at Amherst under Tillie Olsen?

TUROW: I studied with a number of people. There was no formal writing program at Amherst and so I tried to cadge whatever advice I could from anybody I could find, and Tillie was enormously influential, the first person who really took me seriously as a writer. I also owe a substantial debt of gratitude to Leo Marx, who's a great scholar of American Studies, and David Sofield, whose poetry appears now and then in the *New Yorker.* He was not writing publicly at that time, but was kind enough to encourage me.

INTERVIEWER: Is that the Leo Marx of *The Machine and the Garden*?

TUROW: It's the Leo Marx of *The Machine and the Garden.* He's a great teacher and a good friend.

INTERVIEWER: At what point did you know you wanted to write?

TUROW: To some extent, most of my life. My mother has always harbored ambitions to be a writer, and the first recollection I have of writing anything was when I was in about the seventh grade. I pretended to write a novel, but the novel I was pretending to write was virtually plagiarized from something that I had read at school. In my junior year in high school, I became involved with the school newspaper, and ultimately became editor. That rekindled my interest in writing, but when I went to Amherst I decided that I wasn't going to be a mere journalist. I wanted to be an artiste and a writer of fiction, and I began writing seriously then. I finished my first novel by the end of my first year in college. I talk, you know, with a humorous kind of pejorativeness about it. The book was not terrible. It was called *Dithyramb,* which is a Greek word, the meaning of which I don't really fully recall. It was about two young men from the north side of Chicago who run away from home and, like Huck and Jim, go down the Mississippi to New Orleans where they witness the murder of a black prostitute in those "bad old days" in the South, this being set in the mid-1960s. The novel had certain problems, however, one of which was that I had never been to New Orleans, and so the book, to say the least, was somewhat lacking in atmosphere.

INTERVIEWER: This is the novel you worked on at Amherst?

TUROW: It was roundly rejected by publishers while I was at Amherst. I went on to other things.

INTERVIEWER: Did your teachers see it?

TUROW: Nobody saw it. I think the only serious and appreciative reader that *Dithyramb* had was my girlfriend at the time.

INTERVIEWER: You did publish a short story in the *Transatlantic Review* back then, didn't you?

TUROW: I think I had two stories accepted by *Transatlantic,* one of which came out while I was in college, which was of course a great coup to be a college senior and publishing anything. It was greeted with tremendous jealousy by the other young people who wanted to be writers and even astonishment by the faculty, Amherst being one of those places where most of the scholars, frankly, were somewhat constipated, and seldom got anything together to publish themselves, at least around the English department. They were truly stunned by the thought that I had published something. I was not regarded as one of the stars of the English department, certainly not from a scholarly perspective, and certainly never so regarded myself. It was an unusual event, but I was just delighted to be published. It was the kind of confirmation that all young people in the arts are always looking for.

INTERVIEWER: How did that story compare with what you're doing now?

TUROW: Oh, it was a story essentially about my grandparents. My grandfather had gone out one day and somebody had given him a fish, and he came home and put the fish in the sink. It turned out the fish was still alive. My grandmother, who passed away only a couple of months ago, was a remarkable, gentle soul, and she refused to kill the fish. Instead, she put it in the bath tub, and the fish lived with them for a while. It was a very naturalistic kind of low-keyed story about these two old people and this fish. It's certainly nothing like what I write now. The next story I sold to *Transatlantic* was much more in what I consider to be my main vein, which is trying to make sense out of fairly unusual events. This was a story about a young exhibitionist, who was both adored and rejected in his high school community. You know, worshiped as a renegade and also as a star athlete, but from a kind of lower-class home and not well accepted and certainly didn't have a happy home life. All of that strikes me now, looking backward, as more typical Turow.

INTERVIEWER: Were you a Stegner fellow at Stanford?

TUROW: Along with a writer in New York named Ann West, I was the first of Stanford's Mirrielees fellows, which was a two-year fellowship that was given to degree candidates. It was an extraordinary experience. I was around people who had a lot to teach me, both fellow students and instructors, and I came to believe that I was a writer, which is one of the fundamental hurdles that everybody who wants to be in the arts must get over.

INTERVIEWER: You worked on a novel titled *The Way Things Are.* And what happened?

TUROW: As I'm often apt to joke, I learned about the way things are. I worked on the novel for four years and couldn't find a publisher for it. And it wasn't bad, folks. It wasn't great, but it wasn't bad. It was a novel of my early twenties and I will probably never write sentences as good in my life. *The Way Things Are* now sits under my computer monitor. It supports my literary endeavors both metaphorically and in fact [laughs].

INTERVIEWER: You turned away from writing and went to Harvard Law School. What happened?

TUROW: Writing *The Way Things Are* was one of the more painful experiences of my life. I wanted desperately to be a great writer, and was, in some parts of *The Way Things Are,* not even a remotely good one. I found that terribly painful. I couldn't get used to the idea that mere will would not produce a creative work that I was satisfied with. I tore at myself in the kind of obsessive-compulsive way of people who have a scab and are always picking at it. I just wanted to drag great literature out of myself and I couldn't do it. I began saying to myself, "I gotta get myself another job, I gotta get something else to do, I'm gonna drive myself crazy being a writer." I had developed this totally, to me, surprising interest in law. *The Way Things Are* was about a rent strike on the north side of Chicago, and perhaps one of the problems with *The Way Things Are* is signaled by the fact that the implied covenant of habitability was one of the major premises of the plot. As boring as that may have been for the readers of *The Way Things Are,* it was fascinating to me. The courts had suddenly decided that in landlord-tenant contracts, so-called leases, there was implied a condition that the premises would be habitable, something that somehow courts hadn't recognized for centuries before. That notion of recognizing the legal implications in ordinary social relationships seemed like a fascinating undertaking to me, so I decided to go to law school.

A lot of this is involved with the process of becoming an adult. You suddenly confront the fact that you have to buy a car and rent an apartment and get married. You begin to realize that, "Hey, a lot of what I'm doing as a grown-up is entering into legal relationships." I saw the law as sort of the armor of the adult world. I wanted to understand it, perhaps to come to grips with my own emergence as an adult. I view my decision to go to law school as being, in part, a reluctance to accept the fact that I had grown up.

INTERVIEWER: So your decision to enter law school really was a decision to do something else besides writing; you didn't go to law school with the idea of . . .

TUROW: Of writing about the law? Absolutely not. When I went to law school, I went with a contract to write a book about it, but that was purely after the fact. I had no idea of combining law and writing, even though I claimed that was my intention, to soften the blow for my friends in the Stanford literary community who couldn't believe I was making this U-turn. I told them, "Well, I'm just going off to learn some mumbo jumbo, so I can have something to write about."

INTERVIEWER: You say you had a contract to write *One L* when you went to law school?

TUROW: In the spring of my last year at Stanford, I was accepted at law school. *The Way Things Are* was then complete and being rejected, roundly, by publisher after publisher, and I wrote a letter to my agent, and I said, "You know, I'm going to law school. Sorry to tell you that. I know you've worked hard for me. I appreciate it. So to sort of return the favor, let me tell you that at some point you ought to find some young writer—not of course an artiste like me—but a writer of nonfiction who could write a book about law school from a student's perspective." One of the difficulties with my agent was that we never quite managed to understand each other. I went to my mailbox one day, with literally no further communication, and found a contract to write a book. Now, since I was about twenty rejections along on *The Way Things Are* this struck me as a somewhat unanticipated and ironic development. But all my scruples about being an artiste were quickly put aside. I signed the contract and went off to law school, where some of my best friends knew what I was doing and most of the others did not. But all of the central figures in *One L* knew that I was writing that book.

INTERVIEWER: You describe in detail your study schedule in *One L* and I don't see any time for writing.

TUROW: I have worked very hard at many points in my life, but I never worked harder than I did during that first year, when I was both writing that book and going to law school. There wasn't a lot of time for writing, and what little time that probably would have gone to spend with my wife, Annette, or to have a more sane life, was lost. I had the opportunity in writing *One L* to reflect on this very stressful and emotionally charged experience that I was undergoing. I enjoyed the writing. It wasn't without benefit, but my bet is that without the discipline of a book contract, I wouldn't have done it.

INTERVIEWER: In the preface to *One L,* you make it clear that your characters are composites. Yet it seems that Perini must be based on somebody real because he turned up in a novel called *The Paper Chase.* What's the chronology?

TUROW: *The Paper Chase* came out prior to *One L.* When I got the contract, my initial response was, "Well, you don't want a book about the first year of law school because that's already been done in *Paper Chase.*" "No, no. Do it again. *Paper Chase* was fiction, we want nonfiction."

Perini is something of a composite of a couple of professors who were around Harvard while I was there. One of them, Arthur Miller, has laid claim to being Perini. I've never been drawn into the game of commenting on who was who, but certainly he was not the model for the figure in *The Paper Chase.* They seem similar because they use the same brutal teaching technique.

INTERVIEWER: And the subject is contracts?

TUROW: That's true, it's contracts in both instances. I did not happen to have contracts from Arthur Miller. As I say, this is one area that I will just stay away from.

INTERVIEWER: Were you surprised at the reception of *One L*? As I understand, they give it to first-year law students to keep them from going crazy.

TUROW: Either that, or to make them crazy. I don't know which. Certainly by the time I sent the manuscript back to the editor who had commissioned it, he had literally forgotten why he thought this book was a good idea. He called me up and said, "Remind me. Who did we think we were going to sell this book to?" So I literally had to do a sales pitch on the book, explaining how many people applied to law school every year. I thought that would be the exclusive market. After *One L* came out, it did extremely well, in relative terms, for a first book. It sold about forty thousand copies in hard cover. That's a hell of a lot of copies to sell for a first book. We were just amazed, and, of course, the other thing that is surprising about *One L* is that it has endured.

INTERVIEWER: Is it word of mouth that keeps it going?

TUROW: I would guess at this point about half of American law students read *One L* at some point in their career. Even before *Presumed Innocent* I had a very peculiar kind of localized celebrity because the book just kept being read by the legal community.

INTERVIEWER: What was the response to it at Harvard Law?

TUROW: Mixed. Those who were portrayed in a favorable light tended to think of it as a discerning and interesting work, and those who were less fortunately revealed had more critical things to say about it. I heard that Arthur Miller, who also teaches copyright, had given a test question that reads something like this: "You are an associate in a large law firm. The senior partner has introduced you to his dear friend and client, Rudolph Perini. Rudolph Perini has undergone the horrible experience of having a student, Ray Rip-Off, write a book about him. Please list all theories under which Professor Perini can sue Ray Rip-Off."

I think the people that frosted me the most were the *Law Review* types, some of whom reacted with utter indignation to the fact that I, a third-year law student, was suddenly receiving national publicity and some degree of prominence. They thought all earthly benefits flowed first to the *Law Review*, and only the remainder were then parceled out to the rest of the class. Some of them were deeply offended by this disordering of what they took to be the natural scheme of the universe.

INTERVIEWER: So you were a three-L by the time the book found its way into print. When did you actually shape the manuscript?

TUROW: I did it in the fourteen weeks between the end of the first year and the start of the second.

INTERVIEWER: So you really did it right after the year finished?

TUROW: I sure as hell did, and it was great writing. I was just really, really on point. Bang, bang. Everything came just right.

INTERVIEWER: In the afterword to *One L* you make a distinction between doing well and doing good.

TUROW: That came from a professor at Harvard Law School, Gary Bellow, and I think he borrows it in turn from Reinhold Niebuhr. One of the problems with law school is that it's a value-neutral education. Students learn very little about doing good. They're taught to do well. They're taught to shape the right argument, to score on exams, to get good jobs, and, prospectively, to make money. There's not a lot of thought about how a lawyer can do good. One of the reasons, to be fair to the legal academic community, is because there would be wide differences of opinion about what "doing good" means.

INTERVIEWER: I was a little bit surprised about this issue. In the layperson's viewpoint, the law has to do with right versus wrong.

TUROW: There's no attempt in law school to start by saying, "Okay, how would we design a society?" That's much too threatening a concept, and also, to defend what I attack, it's also beside the point. You and I can sit down and define a perfect legal system that would have nothing to do with what exists today.

INTERVIEWER: What about the notion in the nineteenth century, for instance, of utilitarianism, that you can legislate morality?

TUROW: You will get arguments about that today. Utilitarianism in the guise of economic analysis is now probably the dominant trend, given the success of the last administration in peopling the bench with judges of its own political persuasion. That is said by its practitioners not at all to be a way of legislating morality, but simply of making economically efficient decisions, that, supposedly, being a value-neutral way to do things. Of course, those who criticize it, including me, know that it's not.

INTERVIEWER: Do you think that a basic study of intellectual history by law students would help?

TUROW: There should be, in my judgment, a hell of a lot more of it, and there could be, particularly in the first year. The law is an amazing cultural artifact. It reconciles all kinds of different demands—economic, moralistic, philosophical, sociological—and it is an incredibly rich field of study.

INTERVIEWER: But that isn't the focus in law school?

TUROW: It's certainly not the focus. The focus of the first year can be said simply to be to teach students the principal form of legal reasoning, the kind of deductive argumentation that takes place in American courtrooms and legal literature. In the last two years you learn a lot of rules. Now, the education can get dressed up, especially at places like Harvard Law School. I took some very good, very stimulating courses in jurisprudence, and legal history especially, but the primary mission was to learn a bunch of rules about whatever it was you were supposedly going to go out and practice. At Harvard during my time everybody was encouraged to learn the rules about practicing corporate law.

INTERVIEWER: At what point after you got out of law school did you find the writing bug was still there?

TUROW: Well, I think it was still there throughout law school, but there wasn't a lot of time to write. Once *One L* came out, and was successful, I probably could have become a legal journalist but I was interested in doing two things at that particular time. One was practicing law, and the other was trying to write fiction.

After about a year in practice, I thought, "Gee this stuff (meaning the criminal justice system) is really great to write about. I can't do what I did with *One L* and write about my immediate circumstance. Nobody will ever talk to me again." I had spent three months as a clerk in the Suffolk County District Attorney's Office, while I was finishing law school and to some extent avoiding the contending forces about *One L*. Most of the beginning elements of *Presumed Innocent* are drawn from just what was going on in Boston while I was a law student. Garrett Byrne, an aging prosecutor, was challenged by Newman Flanagan, a former member of his office, and that's just exactly what is going on at the beginning of *Presumed Innocent*. There's Raymond Horgan, the veteran prosecutor, challenged by Nico Della Guardia. I started with that election campaign. The murder of Carolyn Polhemus resembles in many of its physical details the murder of a prostitute, the trial of which was the first jury trial I ever saw. Other elements were drawn from my experience in Boston. That was where the immediate setting came from, but I was able to write about what I wanted to write about.

I just wrote from interest and from inspiration and worried later about how the hell I was going to put it together. Then one day I found myself writing about this "B-file," having no idea what it related to. A hundred and fifty pages of manuscript, handwritten because I was writing every morning on the commuter train on the way into town. I had no idea where that was going, so I took two years off and just thought about the plot.

INTERVIEWER: What about the characters? When did Rusty Sabich come to you?

TUROW: One of the things I wanted to do was sort of kick back and write in what I took to be my own voice, and the thing that made me feel that I could do it was meeting the chief deputy prosecutor in Boston, who was not only a gifted trial lawyer, but also a poet. I thought, "Well, gee, not every voice in American crime fiction has got to be this hard-boiled voice that sounds like Sam Spade." Lawyers and prosecutors are more capable of expression than you would believe reading Raymond Chandler.

INTERVIEWER: It sounds like you started writing *Presumed Innocent* almost the way the law students learn law: they study cases, and from the details of cases, they learn to infer legal principles.

TUROW: I heard great stories. I had to repeat them. I had to commit them to paper somewhere. The last forty pages of the book were pretty much written as they now stand. I had my people, and I wrote the end of the book and then went back and wrote all over the goddamn book. I wrote the end. I wrote little pieces of the middle. I wrote back at the beginning. I filled in. I'd do a passage here and there. I'd do an interesting little story. Once I got that computer, I did not write in a linear fashion anymore. I think that my career as a writer owes a lot to the fact that the computer can organize all of it. You just move those blocks of text around. I couldn't imagine writing that way when I was younger. I used to read about Nabokov, who would write paragraphs out on index cards all over his books, and I thought, "How can the guy do that? You've got to have it all in order in your head." But I'll be damned. That's now the way I write.

INTERVIEWER: The obvious theme of *Presumed Innocent* is the question of truth. In the legal process as we see it in this book, the truth is concealed.

TUROW: It's not concealed deliberately. It's manipulated and certainly it's not fully discovered. One of the ironies is that this poor genre, the mystery, is so looked down upon, yet it enthralls people. It delivers answers that life and certainly the courtroom cannot. If the defendant says, "I'm not guilty," and goes on maintaining that until the very end, you try your case, the jury finds the facts, but all they're doing is making educated guesses in a criminal case. You know beyond a reasonable doubt, but you don't know beyond any doubt at all that that's what really occurred. Only in the mystery novel are we delivered final and unquestionable solutions. The joke to me was that the fiction gives you a truth that reality can't deliver.

INTERVIEWER: Was that the question in your mind when you began *Presumed Innocent*?

TUROW: I didn't know what the theme of *Presumed Innocent* was until I was finished. I was interested in resonance of the character, the story, the various digressive elements, the whole gritty courthouse world, that incredibly dense community with its extraordinary network of relationships.

INTERVIEWER: That very painful scene that Rusty has with his lawyer where he finally says, "I'm innocent!" and Stern gives him this look . . .

TUROW: That he's heard it before.

INTERVIEWER: Is that typical of what happens between a lawyer and a client? That the question is never asked, "Did you do it?"

TUROW: For me it depends. I do a lot of defense work now, and sometimes I ask and sometimes I don't. It depends on the client. There are clients who tell me things that I don't completely believe, and that's fine. It's mysterious to represent somebody accused or suspected of a crime.

INTERVIEWER: Because by law and the Constitution, they're guaranteed an adequate defense whether they are guilty or not.

TUROW: I'm very comfortable with that concept. Most laypeople find it to be absolutely incomprehensible and unacceptable.

INTERVIEWER: Is that part of the value-neutral thing that you were talking about?

TUROW: That to me is not value-neutral, and that's what I have a hard time explaining to people who are not familiar with the legal system. When you defend the concept that everybody is entitled to a defense, no matter how rotten they are or what they did, you're defending a certain concept of humanity. I regard it as extremely affirmative to say, "I don't care how big a crumb he is. The government is going to have to prove him guilty. And if they can't, he gets to go home." Notwithstanding the fact that if he gets to go home, it means that he may do it again.

INTERVIEWER: I guess one of the things that really took me away in this novel is the question of reconciling "not guilty" with "guilty." Rusty says to the jury, "Because if you can't find the truth, what is our hope of justice?" The vision of the world that you see in *Presumed Innocent* is "Man, everybody's guilty!"

TUROW: That has to do with the characters in *Presumed Innocent* and my own sort of dark view of compromised human nature. Yes, everybody is guilty of something. By the end of the novel, there's blame enough to go around.

INTERVIEWER: Is there ever a cathartic case—does Perry Mason exist?

TUROW: It's rare that somebody who is completely innocent is indicted. It happens. But it doesn't happen often. I can become outraged in representing somebody who has admitted to me that, yes, he or she is guilty, and yet I look at the government's case and say, "The government's got a thin case. Goddamn them. They had a hell of a lot of nerve indicting this person because they don't have enough evidence." But I can't go home and convince my wife that it's worth being outraged, because she just says, "Well, you know, what's the point? They're really right after all, aren't they?" Oh no, they're not right.

INTERVIEWER: Because that guy's presumed innocent.

TUROW: Well, you can go too far with that. The fact of the matter is that the trial in *Presumed Innocent* comes out exactly the right way. And that's not accidental. It's not for all of the right reasons, it never is, but in a rough, approximate way the justice system labors on. It's nearsighted, it's awkward, but it's not totally blind.

INTERVIEWER: I was curious why you didn't just go on and set this novel in Chicago, but it's apparent from what you've said that it isn't necessarily Chicago.

TUROW: No, Kindle County is not necessarily Chicago. I didn't want to get stuck with having a geography I couldn't alter. I find novels set in real places, involving fictionalized historical events, to be hokey. I'd rather make the fictional cut at the first level and just say, "This is a nonexistent place. These are nonexistent people. Now, we're all gonna sit around and agree it's real."

INTERVIEWER: The book has been described as a "Dickensian thriller." Are you comfortable with that comparison?

TUROW: God knows it's enormously flattering. I've read a lot of Dickens. Did I think of myself as a Dickensian writer? No. Do I see why people describe it as Dickensian? Yes, I do. I'm certainly, to say the least, thrilled and satisfied with the description.

INTERVIEWER: How aware are you of mystery writers such as Higgins and MacDonald, the ones that people consider to be really good?

TUROW: I've read a lot of those novels. There's a traditional structure in which the investigator usually investigates the crime, and he's got some personal trouble, a wife that he's not happy with, a girl he's pursuing. Something like that. The two worlds don't ever quite touch; they meet only on a level of values. Something is suggested by the crime being investigated that also goes to answer the personal problem that the investigator's having. *Presumed Innocent* took a one-eighty on that in the middle of the book and said, "Wait a minute, we're gonna connect it all. We're gonna draw the family troubles right into the middle of the crime. We're gonna turn the investigator and make him the investigated, indeed the accused. He's gonna lose the aloofness that he has." Usually the investigator enters the world of crime to learn something about it and to be transformed by what he learns. But he's always in control. Here's an investigator who completely loses control, who finds the whole world turning on him.

INTERVIEWER: How conscious were you of the crime novel as a genre when you shaped this piece?

TUROW: Moderately. I knew that the turn in the middle of *Presumed Innocent,* when Rusty is accused, was antigenre, that it was going against type. I knew the voice was antigenre. Those things were self-consciously done for those reasons. At the same time, I had a strong sense that the crime novel serves far more legitimate purposes than are sometimes attributed to it, that it has a philosophical purpose beyond what it often gets credit for.

INTERVIEWER: To what extent was the novel shaped in revision?

TUROW: What you see is pretty much what I did. There was some cutting in the first 247 pages, and there was one significant editorial change. I had written a single chapter describing Rusty's past relationship with Carolyn, and Jon suggested chopping it into three and interspersing it because it was a hard gulp.

INTERVIEWER: I read that Sydney Pollack, the filmmaker who bought the film rights to the book, took you to task for your treatment of women and caused you to expand Carolyn Polhemus' background.

TUROW: [sighs] I don't think that's true. What was written about Carolyn's background is what was in the manuscript that I delivered. I'm pretty much at peace with the fact that Carolyn is not a likable human being. I think that she, for better or for worse, resembles certain human beings I've known, and I don't regard her as a disparagement of all females. The fact that she is, in some ways, a nasty human being and in other ways a maimed human being just existed. Sydney helped me understand one thing. He made a remark about Rusty being attracted to Carolyn's pain, and I realized that pain was a currency between them. I didn't understand why the abused child was important to both of them. It turned out, of course, that both of them were abused children. There is a moment where Carolyn essentially tries to convert Rusty into a sadist and he succumbs. At that point their relationship is over. I didn't understand the significance of those elements. I didn't know why they hung together for me imaginatively, and Sydney did help me understand that, and that had some impact in what I said in the last few words of the book which were certainly rewritten. But he didn't cause me to import new material. Carolyn's background was there.

INTERVIEWER: The psychology of the novel is extremely interesting to me. How much of this came from your observations as a lawyer?

TUROW: God willing, we all keep our eyes open and learn a lot of things. I never thought that I'd be writing about child abuse. Yet one of the things Jonathan Galassi said to me when he got the book to edit was, "This is a book about a bunch of abused children." And he said, "The only crime in this book that is not forgiven is the abuse of children." Which is true. Those are my own values speaking out.

INTERVIEWER: Are you comfortable with Rusty's ease in sending Nat off to live with Barbara?

TUROW: I am. I am. I know that most people can't hack it, and they just don't believe he would do it. But I do. It's obvious he had to, wouldn't do anything different. You have to take the assumptions of the novel as given. Barbara's anger is not going to be directed at the child. She's a loving parent, and has never shown any indication of being anything other than a loving parent. I'm comfortable with it instinctively. It's not absolutely clear-cut. The notion of some self-sacrifice is important to me in Rusty's character. At the end there is some degree of atonement on his part.

INTERVIEWER: Did you have a sense when you wrote *Presumed Innocent* of another novel within that novel—Barbara's story? Could it have been told within this novel?

TUROW: Within this novel? I don't quite know the answer to that question. At the most superficial level the plot turn at the end ultimately depends on the fact that you are set up to believe throughout that the murderer is male because of the way the crime is staged. To turn around and write the book from Barbara's point of view creates problems. Some drafts of the screenplay make that mistake. You can't push Barbara too far into the foreground. Otherwise, the mystery is no mystery.

INTERVIEWER: So you had that ending in mind?

TUROW: When I began deliberating the ending, I said, "Now, there are only two people who could have done this, who had motive to do it and whose having committed the murder would make the novel meaningful within the range of the themes as I then understood them, and that was either Rusty or his wife. Did he really do it?" No, I ultimately decided he didn't. She did. How the hell could she have done it? I mean, I had it all set up. I had my first 150 pages. How the hell could she have done it? I had to figure out the mechanics of that.

Then when I drafted it, I actually wrote a scene very much like what's there. There's not the one conclusive line, and you didn't know for sure which of the two of them had done it. Then I began to think very much along the lines we've already talked about. "Well, what the hell is the point of a mystery novel if you're not going to know who did it?" Where I was at in my own thinking about it was, "Hey, you don't know in court!" You don't know. Yet one of them did do it, and the reader's entitled to know.

INTERVIEWER: How do you respond to readers who read for all the other things?

TUROW: I'm delighted, you know. I feel the same way. I hope those who read beyond the sort of first-level gimmickry are also my readers. But the solution is part of it. I really feel that fiction delivers truth that life doesn't. I'm pleased by those who say there is a hell of a lot more in this book.

The fact is if you get involved in *Presumed Innocent* in the way that I hope you will, you forget the question of who murdered Carolyn. You go through the trial, and the trial gets resolved. You're delighted to learn that Rusty's been exonerated, and then you have this scene between Rusty and Raymond, and you can hear the crank pulling when Raymond Horgan looks at Rusty and says, "By the way, who did murder her?" The elevator doors are closing and Rusty's got nothing to say.

INTERVIEWER: Some readers question whether a woman could have committed that crime. How do you respond to that?

TUROW: Whether Barbara would have committed the crime in that particular way I don't know. Obviously this is a sort of concoction. But one of the things that's interested me in contemplating why so many people like to read this book is that those that get the mystery, figure it out, are overwhelmingly female. I say, "How did you figure it out?" And they say, "Well, I just think, 'If my husband did that, I'd kill him and I'd kill her, too.' "

INTERVIEWER: The quarrels that I've heard center on the way the crime is executed.

TUROW: This is a sort of far-fetched story that I have done my best to make you believe. I don't want to sound too much like a magician who stands back and says, "Look for Christ's sake, I didn't really pull that rabbit out of that hat." Yet, this particular set of circumstances is devised. Obviously that woman is trying to set her husband up. Do people do that?

I used to stand up and argue as a prosecutor that it takes unbelievable nerve to lie about somebody else, to accuse somebody of a crime they didn't commit. The truth of the matter is I believe that. As much as people will try to exculpate themselves, they don't usually turn around and blame somebody else for what they've really done. But sometimes it happens, when people feel they have motive and reason to do it. I can accept Barbara's conduct. It's got to be viewed as at least half mad.

INTERVIEWER: To what extent do you write for an audience?

TUROW: Part of the answer goes to my own vulnerabilities as a reader. In the end, I really do like to be entertained at that primary level. I like a lot of plot. I like to get lost in the author's fantasy as well as to enjoy that tremendous pleasure of entering into another life, and to experience and admire luminous language. So I guess you really write to those elements you admire most in literature.

Now, I can also defend this ideologically. I don't believe that the role of literature has been historically, or ought to be today, to confine itself to a tiny professorial elite who are capable of understanding it. We all dream every night. We are in a constant process of telling ourselves stories and I am on the verge of rage when I listen to certain kinds of academics who believe that literature is really the province of a select few. It's not. Storytelling is as innate to human experience as music, and some of us who write may feel a fundamental responsibility to recognize that and to seek as wide an audience as is possible. I like the fact that I have had with this book an enormous readership, but that doesn't change the value of the book to me.

INTERVIEWER: Have you encountered the snobbish notion that any book with its own shelf in the airport can't be really good?

TUROW: There's some of it. There hasn't been as much in the United States as there was in England. Of course, you have to deal with the phenomenon that with a book that sold 5 million copies in the United States in hard- and paperback you make a tremendous amount of money. That is not something that I ever expected. It's not the widespread success of the book in the sense that a book that has an entire shelf of its own in the airport can't be any good, but a book that makes a lot of money can't be any good. I must admit that as a reader it's a rule I've long believed in too. I'm not sure I would have read *Presumed Innocent,* given my own prejudices.

INTERVIEWER: So why did you write it?

TUROW: It all comes down to impulse. I wrote it because I wanted to write it. I didn't see it as being simply a popular novel. I don't think it's a potboiler. I think it has a substantial theme. I admit that it's entertaining and I'm glad that it's entertaining. But you're asking me in the end if I think *Presumed Innocent* is a work of art? Yes, God save me, I do, and fortunately there are other people who share that judgment. Is it also popular entertainment? Yes, it is. Do I believe in trying to combine those elements? Yes, I do. Many of the writers I admire did it, sometimes without being noted for doing it. Bernard Malamud certainly did it. Joseph Conrad and Charles Dickens and Graham Greene all did it. They are aspirational figures, and I move in their shadows.

Margaret Walker

Margaret Walker has lived and taught in Jackson, Mississippi, since 1949. She has published ten books, including five volumes of poetry, one volume of essays, and a biography of Richard Wright, but is best known for her epic novel of the Civil War, Jubilee. *In 1942 she won the Yale Younger Poets Award for* For My People, *becoming the first black woman to win a major literary prize in this country. She was born in 1915 in Birmingham, Alabama, the daughter of a Methodist-minister father and a musician mother. After graduating from Northwestern in 1935, Walker worked at the WPA in the Chicago area for three years, where she was befriended by Nelson Algren, Jack Conroy, and Richard Wright, who introduced her to the South Side Writers Group.*

She also later became active in the black aesthetic movement of the sixties. In 1988 she wrote Richard Wright: Daemonic Genius, *relating the history of her very bitter breakup with him following his publication of* Native Son. *In a landmark "fair use" decision, the United States Court of Appeals ruled against the Wright estate, who had sued her and Warner Books over her use of Wright's letters and journal entries.*

Jubilee *(1966), a novel of the antebellum South, is much more detailed and frank about the suffering of people under slavery than most books, yet Walker retains an optimistic view about American history.* Jubilee *was important because it was the first large and serious treatment of antebellum-southern experience told from a black point of view. She became embroiled in another long lawsuit when she accused Alex Haley of plagiarizing parts of her novel in his later, hugely successful* Roots. *Although she did not win the case, many have noticed similarities between the two books, and some seven other cases of plagiarism against Haley were won in court. This interview was conducted in February 1991 in Columbia, Missouri.*

INTERVIEWER: Ms. Walker, when you were a teenager, after you'd finished two years of college in New Orleans, Langston Hughes told your parents that their daughter had talent and that they should get you out of the South. Why?

WALKER: Langston was saying that I couldn't get the kind of education I needed there. The summer before I went to Northwestern, some Jewish friends of my mother and father took my poetry to a professor of English at Tulane University, Richard Kirk. I dared not walk on that campus. At that time the only black people who could go over on Tulane's campus had to be maids and cooks and janitors. He wrote me a nice little note, said he thought I had talent, if I was willing to work.

INTERVIEWER: How did you decide on Northwestern?

WALKER: My mother and my father had gone there. It was a Methodist school and Methodist ministers could send their children there cheaper—they'd get a rebate. It cost about six hundred dollars a year, and they took off a hundred and some dollars of each semester for us. When I left school I still owed some of the money. I paid it though.

INTERVIEWER: After you finished school you stayed in Chicago for a time working on the Federal Writers' Project of the WPA. At the end of that time you made a most interesting statement. You said, "I felt the thing that I had to do then was to go to graduate school and get a teaching job back south." Why did you want to go back?

WALKER: The South is symbolic—the violence of the South, the protest, the struggle, all of that. The South is both an historic region and a mythic ideal. All my images, in my poetry, come from out of the South, where I was a child, where my imagination was formed, and where I was an adolescent. I never felt at home anywhere but in the South.

INTERVIEWER: And yet, why do you have to live there to write about it? Look at all the southern writers who have left.

WALKER: I'm one of the few black writers who lives in the South and writes there. Alice Walker told me she had to get out of Mississippi. She simply could not write there. I don't feel that I have to be in exile to write.

I wrote at Yaddo. I wrote at Cape Cod. I wrote in Virginia. I wrote in North Carolina. I wrote in New York. I wrote in Chicago. There is no place that I can live where I can't write. Maybe if I were in New York or Chicago my stuff might be considered better than it's considered as a southern woman living in Jackson. But I don't care about that. Those places were too cold, the pace was too fast. I just like living where I *live.*

INTERVIEWER: You began *Jubilee* in your senior year at Northwestern, worked on it for thirty years and published it in the sixties. Where do you think it fits on the continuum of twentieth-century African American fiction?

WALKER: *Jubilee* is a folk novel and an historical novel. In every sense of the word, regardless of period, time and circumstance, *Jubilee* can be defined in that way. I used folk ways, folk sayings, folk philosophy, folk ideas, folk everything. Vyry is a folk character. At the same time, no one can deny the historical accuracy of what I have written—the antebellum South, the Civil War, and the period of Reconstruction and reaction.

INTERVIEWER: How was it received when it came out?

WALKER: My southern salesman said if I had been a white woman writing that book I would be a rich woman. He went to a bookstore in Atlanta to get them to have an autograph party and when they discovered I was black, they told him no. He came to one of the church bookstores in Jackson, I think Southern Baptist, and although I had been a regular customer and had bought many, many books, they refused to have the book autographed in their store. But a big department store that has stores over Louisiana and Alabama gave me a wonderful autograph signing. The woman in that store said she sold more of that book than she had sold of any book in twenty years.

INTERVIEWER: Were black people buying it, or white people?

WALKER: Black and white. People in the South ate up that book quickly. In many schools it's required reading and it's on various supplementary reading lists. The book is twenty-four, twenty-five years old, I guess, and it has never gone out of print. Next year, *Jubilee* will be twenty-five years in paperback. That's where it's sold most.

INTERVIEWER: Did you have trouble finding a publisher when you finished it?

WALKER: My publisher was waiting for it when I finished it. I signed seven book contracts without an agent, but I tell all young people now that if they want to have a career, the best thing to do is to get an agent. I don't need an agent now. My books have made their own reputation.

INTERVIEWER: Beginning with the Yale Younger Poets prize after you got your master's at Iowa.

WALKER: I tried the Yale Younger Poets competition off and on about five years. Stephen Vincent Benet encouraged me. My book was rejected in '40 and '41 and I was not even going to send it in '42, but he asked me about it. He immediately gave it the award, but said that the publishers were not anxious to have a black woman published at Yale. I had not expected to find that kind of prejudice there. When I went up to Yale, I stayed first in the Y, and the woman told me that they had no discrimination there. I said, "Well, I didn't expect to find it here." She said, "Why?" I said, "Isn't this the cradle of democracy?" But I did discover there was strong prejudice and racism all over this country.

INTERVIEWER: Do you see *Jubilee* as a novel about African American experience?

WALKER: I take that for granted. I'm an African American woman, and I write about being a black person.

INTERVIEWER: Where do you see yourself in terms of that tradition?

WALKER: I was a child at the time of the Harlem Renaissance. I knew most of those people, read them as a child. But I belong to the school of social protest of the thirties. I was influenced by Wright, by what he wrote and what he said. I worked with him for three years.

INTERVIEWER: The social protest writers were pretty radical, weren't they?

WALKER: I'm in one or two anthologies that reflect that. One is called *Writing Red.* I said to someone once, "I didn't know I was that radical. I never published in any left-wing magazines. They wouldn't have me. I published in *Crisis.*" They said, "Yes, and that was black, wasn't it? But it was considered red, too." I didn't realize that, but I did know that was the decade of socially conscious writers. And that is where I belong. Despite the fact that *Jubilee* appeared in the sixties, it's influenced by the thinking that I acquired in the thirties. My poetry was written in the thirties and forties, published in the forties. But it's socially conscious poetry.

INTERVIEWER: During the mid-thirties, after you graduated from Northwestern, you stayed in Chicago where you worked on the WPA and were a member of Wright's South Side Writers Group. Did you know Jack Conroy during that time?

WALKER: The first time I saw Jack he had just come to Chicago to revive and organize the new *Anvil*, because the old *Anvil* had gone under, about that time. I thought Jack Conroy was a very, very wonderful person. He tried to help young writers. He tried to publish people in the movement—not just the labor movement, but basically the labor movement. He had a tendency to appreciate, shall we say, those with a leftist radical orientation. He had great, great stories of the working class, of mines and of the workers, the farmers, everybody.

INTERVIEWER: Conroy tells a funny story about having to send a rejection letter to J. D. Salinger. He and Nelson Algren had run out of money and were writing rejection notes on mortuary stationery, because it was all they had. J. D. Salinger wrote back and said, "Thank you for your nice letter, and I'm really sorry that you can't publish my work. I have to say, I hope it's the only rejection slip I ever get from a mortuary."

WALKER: They were very thick. I think Wright thought a great deal of Jack, too, and Jack liked Wright then.

INTERVIEWER: Jack Conroy said that he never really knew what happened to break up the friendship, that Nelson Algren just turned on him, and he never knew why.

WALKER: He didn't have to do anything. I knew Nelson before Jack came to the job. Nelson was a gambler. He must have made two or three fortunes, with the book and movies, and he gambled it all away. He even gambled away the money he made at the Iowa workshop.

INTERVIEWER: You and Richard Wright were very close during those years.

WALKER: I knew Richard Wright three years. I was always at his desk. Everybody seemed to feel that I was trying to marry the man, and that kind of thing. I don't think he ever asked me, and I don't think I was asking him. We talked about marriage, and I told him, "I hope when you're ready to marry the woman you want to marry will want to marry you, because I think that's what's important." I knew when our friendship ended that he had used me in Chicago. He had used me. He was not my sweetheart. We were never romantically involved. He was not a lover, as people have said. They saw us together, and put their own interpretations on it. What I have said in *Richard Wright: Daemonic Genius* is as true as if I had put my hand on the Bible and raised my hand up and said, "I swear to tell the truth."

INTERVIEWER: You have your journals, too.

WALKER: I have the journals. And I have his journals, too. That's part of the problem. Mrs. Wright sold Richard Wright's letters and papers and journals to Yale University for $175,000. In those papers she had forty pages of letters that I wrote to him, of which I have no copies. I had no idea I was going to write the biography. It so happened that I went to Atlanta, to speak for the Institute of the Black World, and there I saw Horace Cayton. He was going to Paris that month, December, and then he would be through with his research and ready to write his book about Wright. We spoke in a Baptist church that night, and I talked about Wright's negative treatment of women, and implied that his treatment in fiction was the way he felt about women. That caused a furor. I think I do the same thing in my book, although I didn't say in my speech that he was bisexual, that I had actually seen him on the bed with another man in New York. That was the reason for the breaking up between us, not my going there trying to get married to him, as Michel Fabre and Ellen Wright said. They didn't know what they were talking about. But I got it from the horse's head; I saw the two men in the room.

INTERVIEWER: You were set up. A woman took you up there, so that you would see, but she didn't know you were too naive to understand what you were seeing.

WALKER: I was stupid as the day is long. I didn't know anything about a ménage à trois, which was also going on then.

INTERVIEWER: You say in your biography of Wright that his work is a line of demarcation in African American literature. Can you explain what you mean by that?

WALKER: We had some very fine writers, like James Weldon Johnson and W. E. B. Du Bois, Paul Laurence Dunbar, and Charles Chessnutt, long before Wright. Wright comes after the Harlem Renaissance, when we had a great school of black writers, but the writers of the Harlem Renaissance believed that black people were really what white people said we were:

some kind of exotic, that we laughed in our suffering because we were not without laughter, as Langston Hughes wrote. None of those writers had the real conception of the problems of black people being basically economic and political. Wright wrote with the understanding that we are basically a powerless people because we do not own the means of production, and the political system is manipulated by those who do own the means of production. As a result we have very great difficulty with the system. All the problems we face—of substandard education, substandard housing, problems of health—all of these problems go back to the basic problems of politics and economics. That was his thesis.

INTERVIEWER: And what do you think then followed?

WALKER: After Wright we have a school of writers who not only were naturalistic, as he was, but who sought to deal with a consciousness that came out of an understanding of the problems. That school was most evident in the late thirties through the forties and fifties. In the sixties the black-nationalist revolution colored our thinking so that our best writers were the ones who understood the changes we had gone through. Both Ralph Ellison and James Baldwin were influenced by Wright, but I don't think they were as consciously naturalistic as Wright. A woman like Ann Petry, who wrote about the street, was doing the kind of writing, based on sociology, that much of Wright's writing was like.

Now, I'm very much refreshed with the knowledge that black women in the eighties were really the key to the best literature in the country, that we had a group. I don't know that these women were that much influenced by Wright, because I think Wright was very chauvinistic. Most of the black writers up to his time were chauvinistic. Langston Hughes and Countee Cullen and Sterling Brown belonged to the Harlem Renaissance, but so did Zora Neale Hurston, and she was a wonderful writer. Great imagination, marvelous storyteller, and just as talented as the men. But they gave her a hard time.

INTERVIEWER: It's interesting that you don't think the black women writers of the eighties were influenced by Wright. They were influenced by Zora Neale Hurston, who in turn influenced Wright, as you argue so persuasively.

WALKER: Zora Neale Hurston definitely influenced Wright, though he talked about her terribly. I don't know whether all male writers are like the black male writers, but they certainly have shown a jealousy of the black woman writer.

INTERVIEWER: Toni Morrison has said, "Nobody can tell me that those books that I grew up with, by people like Langston Hughes and Jimmy Baldwin, weren't beautiful. But those books were written for you, and I am writing for somebody else." Do you think there's any validity to that?

WALKER: Yes. Wright said that, after all, the critics were white and the audience was white. Their books didn't sell that much among blacks.

INTERVIEWER: Toni Morrison feels that now, because of their heritage, black writers are free to write . . .

WALKER: What they want to write. And to write for a black audience as well as for a white audience.

INTERVIEWER: The thing that strikes me about much African American literature that's come along in the last twenty to thirty years is a strong strain, like you see in Alice Walker, of Christian existentialism. I think you see it in *Jubilee* as well. Vyry's strength is that she refuses to buy into hatred. She elects choice.

WALKER: Vyry is conditioned by what she learned in the quarters, what she learned from black and white people, and she belongs in the Judeo-Christian tradition. *Jubilee* grows out of my family beliefs. I'm the daughter of a minister and the granddaughter of a minister. I'm a Methodist and my background is Christian. I think you can't get away from that when you're writing. Vyry didn't believe that hatred would solve any problem. I say exactly what Vyry says, "Yeah, a lot of white people are evil, but every white person is not evil." My father used to say, "We should respect a man's belief. If we don't, we don't respect him." I can't write a book that is not influenced by Christian theology and by Christian faith.

INTERVIEWER: What led you finally to write *Daemonic Genius*?

WALKER: After I was in Atlanta, Vincent Harding said, "Margaret, you better get ready to finish this book." I said, "What book?" He said, "This book about Richard Wright." I said, "Are you crazy? Why would I write a book about Richard Wright?" Well, he says, "Can't you see our brother Horace will not be able?" A month later, fifteenth day of January 1970, Horace Cayton was dead in Paris. That's the day I knew somebody had to write the book. I was sure Ellen Wright and Michel Fabre were satisfied that everybody was dead who had attempted to do this. Then they began to court me. Fabre wanted to come and see me. And I sent word I wouldn't be available.

INTERVIEWER: Was this after he had written his book, or while he was writing it?

WALKER: Before he had written it. His book didn't come out until '73, and Cayton died in '70. I saw him in Iowa in '72, and met him then. Then when his book came out in '73 he had all this mess in there about these women who were Wright's girlfriends.

INTERVIEWER: And you knew that didn't make much sense, given what you knew about Wright.

WALKER: Right, and not just what I knew. Both the marriages had failed. But Ellen Wright is mad because I put all that in the book.

INTERVIEWER: About the bisexuality?

WALKER: The bisexuality. The fact that his marriages didn't last. The first one was gone in less than a year. During his second marriage, to Ellen, Wright was moving around the world. In 1952 he was a whole year in England writing *The Outsider,* in '53 he went to Africa, in '54 he went to Spain. This kept right up till '57, and then they were going to move to London, but the English would not let him stay—he came back to Paris and she stayed. I said to Abraham Chapman, "Why would Mrs. Wright stay in England when her husband was denied a visa and came back to Paris?" He said, "But Margaret, their marriage was over two years before Dick died. That marriage was over." That's the first time it had even crossed my mind.

INTERVIEWER: What was the basis of Mrs. Wright's lawsuit?

WALKER: In 1971, Charles Davis asked me to come to Iowa to participate in a seminar on Richard Wright. "How I Wrote *Jubilee*" had been published in *New Letters* and included excerpts from letters Wright had written to me, which gave it great authenticity. When I began to write the book, I naturally planned to use that as a nucleus and core for the book. My essay was published in '71, published as a book in '72, and then in paperback. During those three publications she did not say a word. Fabre did not say a word. They didn't say anything until in '82 they heard that I was doing a biography. Then they began to say that I was using the letters and those had not been published, and therefore couldn't be used. I said they'd been published, and I can prove they've been published. I wasn't using any letters that were not published. The judge said I had a right to do everything I did. The case was decided on the nineteenth of September, 1990, and I won.

INTERVIEWER: Yet they're still fighting it, even though the book's already in print.

WALKER: I haven't gotten a penny out of the book, and probably never will because it's been tied up in that suit. They're using the royalties to fight the legal battles. This black woman has been through two copyright-infringement suits—lost one and won one. Now everybody figured that Ellen Wright was going to beat me in court because she was a white woman, and she was saying I couldn't use her husband's stuff. But the judge gave me the benefit of the doubt. Papers in the country headlined the fact that I had won that suit; they said this is a boon to authors.

INTERVIEWER: There seems to have been controversy about both of your very large books, the Richard Wright biography and *Jubilee.* Can you talk about the problem with Alex Haley and *Roots*?

WALKER: To tell the record straight would take three full, big books. In 1977, when I sued Alex Haley, I had never heard the term "fair use." I didn't know what the laws on copyright infringement were. I studied them for two years. I went through *Roots* and found every plagiarized thing. Fifteen scenes from *Jubilee* somehow showed up in *Roots.* I wish you could see the book, because it's all the way through.

There are six characters, most of them with the same names; Chicken George is born on a page in *Jubilee.* There are 150-some-odd verbatim expressions. Some part of four hundred pages of *Jubilee* appear in *Roots.* My friends said, well, so what? You wrote "Goose Island" and Richard Wright took it and made *Native Son.* You turned around and wrote a book about him. What's the difference?

Richard Wright was a demonic genius, and I won't say what I generally call Mr. Haley. We went to court and the judge said that I was wrong, even though he said in his opening remarks that it was a foregone conclusion that copying had gone on. Then he assigned us to magistrate court. The magistrate sent word back that there was every evidence of plagiarism, that there had been complete access, but she did not have the authority to declare it a case of copyright infringement. The judge must do that.

It went back to him and he said, "I'm going to make a ruling on this case in ten days, and then I'm going to retire from the bench." A man in midlife, in good health, federal judge for life, got off the bench after rendering the decision in that case. Then he said, "Alex Haley hasn't copied anything from anybody. There are similarities, but they're strained, and there's nothing there." Well, the public had seen what was there. They saw it on television in 1974, two years before *Roots* was published.

INTERVIEWER: Weren't there other suits against Haley?

WALKER: There are one hundred books, not just mine, where something has been copied out of them and used in *Roots.* A man named Harold Courlander hired lawyers, just like I had. Two months after the judge said that mine wasn't copied, another judge said there were three paragraphs copied out of Courlander's book, *The African.* That's all. And he won. They settled outside the court. It was rumored that he got $750,000. A month before I sued there appeared in a magazine called *New West* a story about an editor at *Playboy* named Murray Fisher who said he not only put together the book *Roots* for Alex Haley, but he put together *The Autobiography of Malcolm X* for Alex Haley. He said he did that one for free, because Malcolm X believed that all white people were devils, and he was proving that he was a white man who wasn't a devil. But he wasn't going to do *Roots* for free, because there was too much money in that, and they would either have to pay him or put his name on the book. Alex Haley wrote Doubleday and said, "You'll have to settle with Murray Fisher, because you can't let his name go on the book. People are going to say I didn't write this book anyhow." *New West* said Murray Fisher was paid a quarter of a million dollars, cash, flat, plus 10 percent of the net proceeds from the sale. What shocked me most was that here comes a man from England, named John Rolling, who said Kunte Kinte was his story. He had a book named *Kunte Kinte.* So, when people look at me like I'm crazy, an agitated old woman making up something, that's just the superficial stuff.

INTERVIEWER: I'm just burning with curiosity about some of the historical circumstances of *Jubilee.* How much did your great-grandmother tell you about her father, who served as a model for Randall Ware?

WALKER: I knew that he was Randall Ware, and I kept that name. His name is in the courthouse in Dawson, Georgia, now, as having owned practically the whole town of Dawson, a black man. It's very hard to separate fiction from fact, when you've worked with this thing imaginatively over such a long time. But my grandmother told me that her father was a rich man.

INTERVIEWER: In *How I Wrote "Jubilee"* you speak of the year that your father died, when you and your husband decided to cut back around through Greenville, and trace backwards your grandmother's journey as a child with her mother, from Dawson, Georgia, to Alabama. You found your grandmother's youngest sister who gave you Vyry's chest. Had your immediate family lost touch with these great-aunts who descended from Vyry's second marriage?

WALKER: Two or three of the half sisters had been down to see my grandmother when we were in New Orleans. The youngest was Martha. Martha lived to be ninety-nine years old. She was born when my grandmother was having her first child so Vyry was having her last child when her first child was having her first child. When Vyry died my grandmother said her mother's things had been sold all over two hills, Baptist Hill and Methodist Hill. Martha had done away with most of her mother's things, but she carried that Bible and chest with her to Detroit, where she died. When I went to Detroit, Uncle Henry's granddaughter had the Bible. I made Xerox copies, and got some information that I wanted. She would not turn loose that Bible under any circumstances. She resented my grandmother's side of the family because Martha was one of the second man's descendants. There was feeling there.

INTERVIEWER: Among the two sets of children. I wondered about that.

WALKER: My grandmother never said anything against any of her sisters, because they were all her mother's children. I'm the only one in the family, other than a cousin who died three years ago, who kept up with records and births and deaths. About three years ago, a white woman in Greenville called me on the telephone and said she had read *Jubilee* and people there remembered my great-grandmother, and that her people, her folk, had a farm nearby. This woman came to see me, in Jackson, and brought me three documents: my grandmother's marriage license, dated December of 1876, Jim's marriage license, and my great-grandmother's will. Vyry's will is documented in the courthouse in Butler County, Greenville, Alabama. They begin the sequel to *Jubilee.*

INTERVIEWER: How did she come by that stuff?

WALKER: It's in the courthouse. She said she was doing research and she was interested. I know what she was doing. She was hunting up that property, because her people had taken it over. She was looking me up to see if I had sense enough to know she has no business with that property. I'm not concerned about her people taking the property. That's happened to black people all over the South.

INTERVIEWER: How does it happen?

WALKER: Black people had land all over the South, just like Randall Ware had all that land. All of that land got taken over by wealthy white people in the town. They're wealthy now, they weren't wealthy then.

INTERVIEWER: You've said that you conceived *Jubilee* as a series of episodes with titles drawn from your grandmother's sayings. Did those sayings provide the concept for each episode?

WALKER: No. What I did was to write a sentence outline. If you wrote a complete sentence, and left it there, twenty-five years later you could go back to that complete sentence and the thought that sentence expressed would return to you. I wrote that outline in 1948, complete sentences. Some of them were things my grandmother had said. Some were not. When I sat down to the typewriter I had my topic sentence. But a sentence is not an idea. A sentence is a group of words expressing a complete thought. A thought is only the beginning of an idea. A paragraph expresses an idea. A concept can be symbolized by just one word. I know this for a fact: every artist begins with a concept. He begins with an idea, whether he's a painter, a graphic artist, a plastic artist, whether he's a musician, whether he's a writer. Creative thinking is nothing more than having the concept out of which the idea grows. It doesn't matter whether you're writing a poem or a piece of prose. It begins in the idea.

INTERVIEWER: What was your vision? What was the idea of *Jubilee,* to you?

WALKER: Oh, I don't think it was one big thing at all. It was a lot of little things that we put together which makes the big book.
Each chapter has what each poem has: unity. Unity and coherence, and emphasis, which I was taught as a child. What gives it lasting value is it's not a story you've ever heard before. It's a different story. It's unique. A lot of people, however, will say, "That's the same story my grandmother told me. I heard that story." But nobody had ever put that story down.

INTERVIEWER: Why did you want to do it?

WALKER: Because my grandmother talked about it all the time, and when I was a little girl, I told her, "When I grow up I'm going to write that story." I'd ask, "And where did you go, where did you live after that?" I had the feeling that it was an important story. The older I got, the more I realized that I had a very great story. And I had a document, a living document. I knew that the society in which I have grown up and lived, the segregated society, didn't want to believe that story. They had another story that they were always telling, *Gone with the Wind.* And that wasn't my story.

Linda Hogan

Linda Hogan is a prize-winning Native American poet, short story writer, and novelist living in Colorado. A mixed-blood Chickasaw, born in Colorado and raised in Oklahoma, she wrote four volumes of poetry between 1978 and 1985, before venturing into prose with the highly acclaimed novel Mean Spirit *(1990).* Red Clay, *a collection of stories and poems followed in 1991, and most recently a second novel,* Solar Storms *(1995).*

Hogan acknowledges a unity of theme between her poetry and fiction, believing the two genres are simply two ways of getting at the same story. She is drawn to the spirit of place, and in her work attempts to identify and decry cultural forces that she considers detrimental to the human spirit. She freely admits to being influenced by the works of Louise Erdrich and Jamaica Kincaid. But most of all, her work grows out of the oral tradition of her culture and the importance of storytelling in her family as she was growing up. Mean Spirit *is a chronicle of the stealing of oil rights and of murder in Oklahoma, in the tradition of* And Still the Waters Run, *Angie Debo's classic 1940 history. It is a lyrical but engaged novel, powerful in its evocation of place and its believability, particularly concerning its characters' day-to-day lives, which are simultaneously mundane and magical.*

This interview was conducted in January 1992 in Columbia, Missouri, after the publication of Mean Spirit *and* Red Clay, *and during the time that Hogan was working on* Solar Storm.

INTERVIEWER: Can we begin by talking about your background—where you grew up and the things that you did?

HOGAN: My family is from Oklahoma, near Ardmore. My father had a job driving a woman to Denver and he ended up staying there. He met my mother and they got married and I was born in Denver. At that time my father was a carpenter. He later went into the military to feed us, so we did some traveling around.

INTERVIEWER: When you were growing up, did you think of yourself as Native American?

HOGAN: I really did. There are so many Indian military people that having a military family did not in any way diminish that. I'd forgotten how many minority people were in the military until my father was in the army hospital last year. Among others, an Aztec woman was working there. In some very strange way the military became an equal opportunity employer. The only way that many people could buy a pair of shoes or eat was to go into the army.

INTERVIEWER: Did you grow up in a tribal community?

HOGAN: I was part of diverse communities. Most of my family still lives in Oklahoma. I try to maintain my connection with my relatives there, but we did spend much of our time traveling. My Uncle Wesley had moved to Denver before my father, and was working in the Indian community there. The community in Denver was mixed—there were some Navajo, but it was predominantly Lakota. During the 1950s relocation act a lot of Indians were moved into Denver and other urban areas like San Francisco, Chicago and L.A. In fact, Willa ManKiller grew up in San Francisco. She's the principal chief of the Cherokee Nation. During relocation her family had been moved out of Oklahoma to San Francisco. They moved people to the strangest places; the logic was really beyond me. There's a Choctaw community in Chicago for that reason—they were moved there in the fifties. It seemed that the intent was to break connections of the native people to their homelands and communities.

INTERVIEWER: So we're still living with the various relocation acts of the thirties and fifties. Any thoughts on the connections among them?

HOGAN: What the United States thinks about tribal nations is a problem, a conflict. I'm not a historian, so I couldn't really talk about the connections. I'm sure they are different in the case of each community. It's a complicated, large thing. Any attempt I would make to speak about it would be to minimize it, I'm sure. There is still an ongoing clash; now it's even come down to bingo, which is, interestingly enough, one of the few ways tribes have to make a living. Even where tribes are oil-rich or rich in other kinds of resources, like the Navajo people, the land and the coal mining has been leased out for pennies a year by crooked people. This is an ongoing problem that is still with us, in every aspect.

INTERVIEWER: I know you've had quite a varied work experience. What are some of the things that you've done?

HOGAN: I began working full-time when I was fifteen. I've been a nurse's aide, a teacher's aide, a cocktail waitress—I've done just about anything I had to do to earn a living. I worked my way through school, part of the time. I worked on weekends as a cocktail waitress and I worked during the week at various odd jobs, until I had work-study. I went to night school for a while and worked as a dental assistant. I worked at a credit bureau in Leadville, Colorado.

INTERVIEWER: When did you begin to write?

HOGAN: I was not interested in writing until I was an older person. I went back to school in my late twenties. At the time I was in Maryland. I was married, and working as a teacher's aide with orthopedically handicapped students. I started writing poetry on my lunch hour and decided to take a class from Rod Jellema, who just retired last year. That was my first class in poetry, my first introduction to contemporary poetry.

INTERVIEWER: Which school in Maryland did you go to?

HOGAN: The University of Maryland–College Park. I worked as a secretary there before I got the job as a teacher's aide at Montgomery County Public Schools. I just stayed at Maryland for one semester, then ended up in the writing program at the University of Colorado–Boulder and graduated from there eventually. I had to catch up by taking classes in literature. I took an American lit class at Maryland where we read Faulkner—*Go Down, Moses*—and there were Chickasaws in it. I got so excited, I mailed it to my Dad; he didn't have the advantage of having a teacher around. Faulkner wrote about the later removal period, about one of the women leaving with a horse and wagon. In the story she's dressed up in purple, and she's just finished selling some of her land. I don't know if he imagined that or really was a child witness to something like it. But it was important to me that at last in my life I saw something about us reflected—something true that had been denied in every other place and every other thing I'd been, done, read or seen.

INTERVIEWER: What led you to write poetry in the first place?

HOGAN: I think one of the reasons that I started writing was because of the split in my life—the dissonance between my background and the dominant culture in the United States. When I was young, there were no cars in our area. We still had horses and wagons. My grandparents didn't have water, electricity or plumbing. Finding myself in Maryland, in the suburbs of Washington, D.C., it seemed like my life had already spanned a century because of the changes I'd experienced. Poetry became the place where I somehow managed to come to terms with that, and put it in order.

INTERVIEWER: Had you read a lot of poetry before you began to write it?

HOGAN: The poet Kenneth Rexroth was the first contemporary author I ever read. Before that I really didn't know what poetry was or what it did. It was a mystery to me and I wasn't interested. But I found this book by Kenneth Rexroth. There was a poem about a cow, and I thought, "Wow, that's great. Somebody's writing about a cow. I could do that!" I started writing during my lunch hours. I think probably the next poem that really affected me was James Wright's "Blessing." When I discovered poetry I fell in love with it. I thought it was the most incredible thing in the world. It was not only a language, it was an emotion. It was something that moved me, and that I believed could affect change.

INTERVIEWER: Were your parents readers?

HOGAN: No, we had one book. It was a huge leather Bible that had belonged to my maternal grandmother. I liked that book; it had these terrific gold edges. You could feel the texture of them and smear them with your finger.

INTERVIEWER: You also wrote a play rather early in your career. Was the shift to prose a major change?

HOGAN: For several years I didn't write prose. I did a play before I started writing stories. I wrote the play because I had material I wanted to work on that I couldn't use in poetry. For years I'd been trying to write a poem about a birthday party when I was a child, but I could never bring it into a poem. When I tried to do it as fiction it came together quickly and easily because I'd been working with it so long. So I began to branch out into different forms, depending on what I needed to do with whatever it was I was working on. *A Piece of Moon* won the Five Civilized Tribes Museum Playwright Award in 1980, and was produced in '81. They did a really good job, but it was a terrible experience for me because as a poet I'd had control over all my work and, suddenly, with the play, I didn't. Here was someone who did not *look* like the main character, playing that role. People were saying things that were supposed to be tragic as if they were funny, and funny things as if they were tragic. It was a hard experience.

INTERVIEWER: Why did you make the movement into playwriting?

HOGAN: *A Piece of Moon* was written as a play because the subject seemed to lend itself to drama. It's about the occupation at Wounded Knee in the early seventies, among other things. A young woman who lost her children because she had personal problems is trying to have them returned to her. It wasn't something that I could find a way to put into a poem.

INTERVIEWER: And now you've moved on to an even longer prose form with your novel *Mean Spirit.* It's based on events that you had heard about originally through your family and later researched. How did these historical events come together for you as fiction?

HOGAN: It's set in Oklahoma during a time when the oil rights were being grabbed from the people in the Indian Nations. In some way, when you hear something from your family it becomes a part of your cell structure. I knew about oil, I knew about things that happened in the depression. I grew up with the depression even though I was born ten years later, because every time my family was together the stories came up in conversation. I didn't know about the murder of the Indian women in Oklahoma, and I hadn't read the history. I found the letter included in the novel in a book by Terry Wilson, *The Underground Reservation,* and when Carol Hunter, friend and Osage, talked about the murders, I began to see it. It became the center, about which everything started to whirl and revolve.

INTERVIEWER: At what point did it become a novel for you?

HOGAN: When I started making up the characters. I realized that I had to do something stronger than history to reach the emotions of readers. It had to be more than just a record of the facts, it had to get larger. That's when it became a novel—when it stopped being history. I taught a class in nature writing, environmental essay, in Minnesota at Split Rock. Another woman was teaching fiction there, and she talked about how she always had the structure and then embellished it to create and put the imagery to work. That made me think then that I could actually do it, too.

INTERVIEWER: It's almost like this case becomes a force compelling you to say all the other things that you really want to say. Not to minimize the importance of the murder mystery in the novel, but there's a lot more going on than just solving it. You're solving a deeper mystery.

HOGAN: And there are also the events that are historical, like the man being murdered in the hospital. I think a lot of people would not pay attention to those events, were they not in a kind of gripping story. It would be "only" history, without the power to deeply affect.

INTERVIEWER: How did you come upon those facts?

HOGAN: Some of the interesting things were actually written by the FBI. One of the agents wrote a chapter in another book about these incidents. Some of them I just happened upon.

INTERVIEWER: Why did the FBI center so much of their energy on that particular time and place?

HOGAN: You know, that's a very good question. It's a really good question. I don't know that. I don't know. But I can speculate that their interest had to do with oil. There are gaps in the information, and questions. Were confessions forced, for example. It is possible the conspiracy, like the Teapot Dome case, went all the way to the White House. Wars are still waged over oil today.

INTERVIEWER: Do you have any opinion about the Dawes Act? Most modern commentaries about the Dawes Act see it as a flip-flop. First they give Native Americans reservations, and then they decide in the 1870s or '80s to give everyone an acreage, make them a citizen, destroy the tribal governments and give the authority to individuals. A vast majority of the people in many of the tribes agreed at the time that it was a good idea. Tribal governments tended not to agree, of course.

HOGAN: The more traditional people did not agree because it was a move toward breaking up tribal sovereignty as well as land holdings. It also opened up more land for whites. Indian people ended up with less land. I think some people agreed because they had to, like Alexander Posey, the Creek poet. He has a book out that's a really interesting mix between what he learned in Indian school, which was a lot of Greek mythology and

European literature, and his own traditions as a Creek person. He also published a magazine, *Indian Baptist.* He ended up trying to convince people to sign for their allotment because the traditional people didn't want to sign or live like that. He realized that if they did not claim an allotment, they would end up with absolutely nothing.

INTERVIEWER: The Indians were made an offer they couldn't refuse. It's hard to resist when somebody offers you a quick two hundred dollars and 160 acres that you can call your own—even though not all of the Five Civilized Tribes were living in poverty. The Choctaws, for example, had a prosperous class living down on the Red River—planters and slaveholders in some cases.

HOGAN: The inability to refuse the Dawes Commission offer was about threat and having no alternative, not about money, although money became a necessity when the people were starving. It is true, I think that slaveholding was pretty common among southern tribes at that time, prior to removal. Chickasaws, too, "kept blacks" in those days. Even when the Civil War came, tribes were split; some people were antislavery and some people fought for the South. Some were told that if they didn't fight for the South they would be sent to Kansas. A whole group of Chickasaws were moved up into Kansas at that time from Oklahoma. They didn't have shoes. There was a blizzard; it was in November, terrible circumstances. One man who was freezing to death had only a handkerchief between him and the elements. He held it up trying to shield himself. This vision occupies me. It is an image of the loss, the desperate need.

INTERVIEWER: The characters in *Mean Spirit* also undergo great pain, yet despite the almost relentless tragedy, the book contains humor and laughter and joy. That seems remarkable given the strong feelings that you have. Yet, the writer in you was able to set those feelings aside and tell the story. When you're writing, do you ever consciously try to lighten things up? Do you ever find yourself laughing with your characters?

HOGAN: Well, yes, in a way. I think if I hadn't been able to do that, writing the book would have been unbearable. I was never depressed while I was working on it, even though I never got away from knowing the tragedy of the story. The humor was always there also, because even in desperate situations people are human. They still do funny things, and they still have their obsessions and habits. It bothers me when I read a book where everything is clear-cut and there isn't anything human about or in it. One of the things that often happens between cultures is the denial of common humanity.

INTERVIEWER: Is it true that *Mean Spirit* started out as a poem?

HOGAN: Actually, it was a screenplay. An Osage woman who wanted to become an actress was looking for a part. She asked me to create a role for her. Letty was originally a role that I created for this woman and I named the character after one of the woman's great aunts.

INTERVIEWER: She's a very interesting character because of the changes she undergoes. She has a unique dynamic about her; she seems to straddle the two worlds in ways that the other characters don't.

HOGAN: I was trying to work with all the characters on character change. I knew so little about what I was doing that it never would have occurred to me on my own to think about how a character changes when I was working on this novel. But I like to take classes on different things. I took a weekend screenwriting class in Denver, and we talked about character development—how you show it. The class gave me clues to what I could do with the characters in my book. Another one I like, whose change I think is really significant, is Martha. She evolves from being an Eastern non-Indian sort of society woman in the beginning, to going Indian by the end. Floyd is another one of those. In our community there are a lot of people like that, who are not Indians, but for some reason or other want to be. They're fringe dwellers. In fact, a few years ago, a lot of the young men did not want to be part of traditional ceremonies anymore because the older men were allowing white men to participate so often. Characters like Floyd and Martha interest me, as do the contemporary people who want to exist in an older culture. Why does anybody coming from a middle-class American background feel such an emptiness that they want to take up another culture? What are they missing?

INTERVIEWER: In a sense, it's completely understandable, though. After all, the Indian culture seems to offer a number of things that our culture doesn't.

HOGAN: It offers suffering, misery and the results of prejudice and colonizing forces.

INTERVIEWER: That's why I say "seems." In the novel something similar happens. The hill people finally have to conceal the pathway to where they live because so many people are finding their way up there. They're not going up to make trouble or cause problems, but the hill people are disturbed that so many outsiders have learned where they are. I don't see this laid out as some kind of dichotomy, or as a political document. Yet, I suspect you had strong political feelings about the issue. How do you adapt that—what you believe and feel and think about—to the demands of the novel and your characters?

HOGAN: One of the things that's really wonderful about creating a character is that you have a place to say things that you yourself could never say without being totally offensive to other people. You have a place to be opinionated. Characters are like mediums, in some ways. Or—maybe I'm like a medium for them. Sometimes I think that I'm possessed by the characters and by the story, but I also see that there's a bit of myself in every character—you know, the negative and the positive. The things that are like my highest self and like my lowest self: the poems I'm working on, for instance, about hunger and greed. People who write about wilderness and the environment are going away from themselves to do it. They don't look at the inner wilderness and what motivates people to be destructive. I think everything is connected, that I'm a part of the destruction; we all are. Investigating why we're sometimes apathetic is probably the best work we could do.

INTERVIEWER: Yet at the same time the novel presents a highly political situation about which I am sure you have a side to express or illuminate. The trick is to do it without seeming didactic or dogmatic. I know you said once before that what Native American writers are doing is telling the story instead of telling a story. Can you talk about what you mean by that?

HOGAN: Angie Debo was interviewed on television on her one-hundredth birthday, and she said, "I violated history by telling the truth." She was an Oklahoma historian who was threatened with murder because she named names and spoke about what happened to the tribes there during this same historical period I was writing about. There are all kinds of restraints that you have as a writer from a particular community. You can't just assume that you know another community. Right now I'm trying to work on a book that's set in the North, but it has to be from a Chickasaw point of view because I would never pretend to presume to understand tribes up in the North, or to speak for a person of another tribe. So I'm creating a totally fictional community, and yet the story is really about the truth.

It's about the history of the fur trade, and events taking place at James Bay, between the tribal governments and the Quebec government, which wants to build a dam there. It's also about the bias, and difficulties that tribes in Wisconsin are facing about spearfishing issues. Those are part of the story; they're not made up, they're not a story. It's a form of truth, not a story. It's in some ways a retelling of history. It's like Angie Debo saying, "I violated history to tell the truth." It's the story that's been repressed. In the case of *Mean Spirit,* a lot of the story will always be repressed because the FBI reports themselves are so thoroughly blacked out in order to protect national secrets. Some of it's just not there. But the content of the story is truth, fictionalized. Reimagined, I've created many characters that don't, in fact, exist. But the events are real, and some of the characters are real. Some of the characters retain their real names in the book.

INTERVIEWER: In *Red Clay* you're very meticulous in making the separation between fact and fiction—what's history and what's yours. Would it be accurate to say that in that book you're trying to strike a balance between the notions of story and history, of fact and creative impulse?

HOGAN: I was a lot younger when I wrote those poems and stories. I really didn't think that you could put something in a poem that wasn't absolute truth; I felt like you had to stick to the facts, somehow. Not that fact and truth are always the same.

INTERVIEWER: One of the points you make in *Red Clay* is that when you were a child your father gave you permission to see the story in your own way.

HOGAN: I think it's different way of raising children than a lot of Americans have. It has something to do with the difference between objectivity and subjectivity. My father instilled in me the idea that a person is more worthwhile and valuable than objective knowledge is. One of the problems I have working in the university is that the commodity is knowledge, and not the human value underneath it. People are evaluated on what they hold in their minds. When I was growing up my dad didn't want to rock the foundation by correcting me all the time. I do the same thing now with my daughter, Tanya. If she sees the dog out there with the coyote, when the dog is actually dead, what's to be gained by saying, "No, you know this isn't true," by putting her in a position of being not right? There are different ways of raising children, and I prefer the one that is not as damaging a lot of times to the integrity of the person.

INTERVIEWER: I see that same process at work in your fiction. In *Mean Spirit* no matter what the fact, no matter what the actual event, the needs of these characters as people are in the foreground; that's where the story is driven. The Nola in the novel has a real-life counterpart. But the Nola in the novel lives in a different place.

HOGAN: She does, and she responds differently, and she survives, too.

INTERVIEWER: We seem to be talking about the impulse to write fiction in order to get closer to the truth. You're not moved to write a political treatise, for example. You're moved to create a living thing.

HOGAN: Simon Ortiz says, "It's fiction and you'd better believe it." I always loved that line. Another way to say it is that fiction is a vertical descent; it's a drop into an event or into history or into the depths of some kind of meaning in order to understand humans, and to somehow decipher what history speaks, the story beneath the story.

INTERVIEWER: In *Red Clay* you give us the story as your father told it. And then you tell it again, making it your own story.

HOGAN: Well, actually that *was* my father telling it; that was his story. He wrote the whole thing; I didn't change one sentence, one period. Then I also wrote the story according to what I've heard from everybody else.

INTERVIEWER: So there really are two. There's your father's story and then there's your own.

HOGAN: Which really came from other people's story about the same Horse.

INTERVIEWER: In the introduction to that section you said that that was an illustration of how the oral becomes written, how life becomes the story. Can you talk about that a little bit with respect to what Horse does? He writes down the event, spends his whole life keeping a record, and finally comes down to the small, concise thing he wanted to say. What happens to the oral when it becomes fixed in a written form? What is the dynamic between the two?

HOGAN: When I was writing that, I thought things were easier than they are; but I'm never really sure what is meant by oral tradition. It seems to me that it's such a multifaceted concept because it takes into consideration ceremonial language, prayer, stories, gossip and all the other components—mythology. In this particular case I thought what was really important was what my father had left out of the story in the way he told it. It was also interesting to me to think about how the oral story translates into fiction. One of the problems is that a lot of oral tradition won't translate into contemporary ideas of what fiction's supposed to be.

INTERVIEWER: You were showing us the mirror of how you come to the idea, where and how you reveal the truth and fact, the art of the story.

HOGAN: Well, it's also about my hearing. For instance, the part about the people coming by on horseback and my grandfather going outside with the guns. When I was a child and people talked about that, told me history that was really significant to me, it stayed with me and grew very large. A few years before I was born, customs changed so much. People who had some kind of contact with something in my family, with my grandfather, would come through and stay, and it sounded very strange and mysterious. I heard the story of the horse trader when I was growing up. It was a language and a way that stayed with me.

INTERVIEWER: You've said that as a child you were blessed with the freedom to think of the stories you were told and suit them to your own needs at the time. If you changed them, then your father was not there to correct you and say that that's not the truth. That's a part of the oral tradition: the story changes with the listener. But when you've written it down, does it stop changing?

HOGAN: It's kind of funny that we're talking about this because my father, who never corrected me when I was younger, did when I started writing things down. I wrote a story about a man-fish because it came directly from the people. And my dad read it and said, "There isn't a fish called that, but there's a buffalo fish . . ."

INTERVIEWER: The poems in *Red Clay* struck me as being almost an extended farewell to something. In "Heritage," you say, "From my family I have learned the secrets of never having a home." Do you still feel that way?

HOGAN: No, I don't, though I still have a sense of reciprocal going out and going in that is reflected in the title poem, which is not just to a place, but to the center inside yourself. But I was younger when I wrote that book, and I hadn't thought things through very well. I believed that stories were vanishing, which isn't at all true. I used to think when my dad died he would be the last real Chickasaw, and there wouldn't be any more stories. That made it even more important to write them down.

INTERVIEWER: Despite a nomadic childhood, or maybe because of it, place seems to be a crucial element in everything you write. It anchors the story in *Mean Spirit,* for example.

HOGAN: Maybe this doesn't have to do with your question, which is about place in the book, but I've lived in the house that I'm in now since 1978, and I know the place intimately. I know where every kind of insect is, where one thing lives on the hill and where I'm likely to see a coyote. I walk every day, out around there, but I don't have the same connection to it that I do to the land in Oklahoma. I always say it's as if Oklahoma was my home before I was born. I feel a profound sense of connection to that place. The land that I resonate with is there.

INTERVIEWER: Do you have to make any special efforts to know it? Do you have to look things up, or do you know it in a deeper way?

HOGAN: I know it in a deeper way. And I know the stories. I know what happened there. Though it's not as it is with the Navajo people, who have lived longer in some of the areas in Arizona than Chickasaws have in Oklahoma. Their connection goes back longer and exists on a deeper bodily and spiritual level than ours does. When the stories of your people center around the name of one stone, one place, the whole land around you becomes a part of everything that you know: your religion, your mythology, your family history.

INTERVIEWER: You say you know the stories of the land. Are those stories that have been passed on through your family?

HOGAN: They are. A lot of the people in my family were and are terrific storytellers. What I used to do was I'd be sitting around with my family, listening, and run to the bathroom and write down all these great things, because members of my family had such a good way with words. My father could just tell what happened and where, and the event would be there in front of me, a real, living thing.

INTERVIEWER: You mentioned that one of the things you liked about the novel was that the animals could participate as characters, and that even the landscape takes on a dynamic, a personality of its own. Some people would say that's a definition of magic realism. I'm wondering if you find historical artistic antecedents or compatriots among Spanish American writers?

HOGAN: I really liked Isabelle Allende's *House of the Spirits.* I read Marquez when I was a student and *One Hundred Years of Solitude* is kind of the bible that I used to try to figure out stories and how to tell them. But I also think that their sense of indigenous people and the land is very limited. It has been pointed out that Allende uses this sort of mythos, the Indian people, as part of the novel, but they don't really appear in her work as people, as full beings.

INTERVIEWER: In your work the land becomes a character because you are so specific about it. It's not the land in an abstract sense; it's not "nature." It's a particular physiognomy. You take the time to know it so that it becomes magical.

HOGAN: Some people don't pay attention, so when you make them aware it's like magic. For example, in the book there's a cricket epidemic where the crickets invade for apparently no reason. Suddenly they're everywhere. That is a real incident, although it's more recent. The cricket epidemic that I know about took place in the 1980s in Martha, Oklahoma. And when my father talks about the locusts coming through, it could be magical realism if I wrote it in a book because it's so astounding. But they did come through and eat everything; he said that they even ate the shovel handle. That's how many there were.

INTERVIEWER: You still have the compulsion to save his stories. What about your own? Do you keep a journal?

HOGAN: I have two of them. When I'm mad about something at work or I'm not getting along with my daughter, I have a place for that. I like to write problems out of myself. But once I established myself as a writer I developed a fear that people might someday read my diary, that I couldn't write anything really personal. I also keep a diary of important historical information for Indians because this is a time when Indian people are undergoing yet another kind of change, confronting other kinds of difficulties. I keep files. I see my everyday life in a historical context. We are living in the midst of history; it's important that somebody keeps records. I keep track of all my correspondence for the same reason. Imagine what it would have been like if somebody had handed me a box of material from my grandfather, letters, records.

INTERVIEWER: Do you write from a need to pass those old stories on, so they don't pass out of history?

HOGAN: The older I get, the more I feel that way. Yes.

INTERVIEWER: Is that the inspiration, or the compulsion of your writing?

HOGAN: It has been until recently. Now I'm working on a very different kind of material than my own past or my family's past or things I feel are urgent to be told so they won't be lost. Right now I'm writing about tribal people's conflicts with social services, for instance. Conflicts within a tribal community. More contemporary kinds of issues.

INTERVIEWER: Do you see yourself moving more toward making your own story, rather than saving others'? Can you tell us about the novel you're working on now?

HOGAN: It's a complicated project. In 1978 the American Indian Religious Freedoms Act was passed because tribal people had gone to law school. Suddenly there were enough Indians to work on some of the legislation. In the same year the American Indian Child Welfare Act was also passed. It was important because in 1967, for instance, nearly every child born in the Indian Health Service Hospital in Pine Ridge was taken away from its family. Some of the Navajo children have been taken in by Mormon families—adoption is a very big issue for us. I had my own troubles with social services and I began to think that it was really important to write the story of what happens to children when they go home and try to search out their families, or when they are taken away from family and brought into another culture. I know a number of people who grew up without any contact with other Indians.

INTERVIEWER: When you're thinking about novel projects, do you think in terms of those ideas that you want to work with, or do you think in terms of the plot and structure of the novel?

HOGAN: I think about the events or incidents I want to include, and I think about place. In the last couple of years I've done a lot of programs on traditional hunting, fishing and treaty rights, things like that. I don't know if you know who Ada Deer is. Now she's an assistant to Bruce Babbit. She's been very active. She went to the spearfishing struggle in Wisconsin two years ago with a video camera and taped what happened to native people trying to do traditional spearfishing. There were bumper stickers, for instance, that said, "Save the wildlife, Kill a squaw," or "Kill a pregnant squaw and save two fish." The traditional people were singing and drumming and there were a bunch of white men in the background. Every time the Indians would say something, they'd scream out, "Bullshit!" Eventually to make peace, the tribe stocked fish for the white fishermen who felt like the Indian people were competing with them for fish that really belonged to the tribe. I felt like it was important to put that in the book.

INTERVIEWER: So you think about those episodes in terms of scenes within the book. Do you know from the outset how those scenes will fit together?

HOGAN: In *Mean Spirit,* I knew the end before I knew the beginning, and I do in the new one, too. But some of the events—for instance, the spearfishing—may not be in the book when I'm done. I can never predict how the story will evolve.

INTERVIEWER: You've talked to us about writing the novel, and at the same time talked about your new poems. Do you work on poetry and fiction simultaneously?

HOGAN: I always did until this last year. Then I found it difficult, for some reason. I know that the two genres are very connected in some way, because they're both doing the same thing. It's a descent into something older, deeper and more powerful than our everyday being or reality. But as far as the technical aspects of writing go, I've always been able to work both simultaneously and I even take notes for essays at the same time. Something will pop into my head when I'm working on one genre that doesn't belong there, so I write it down to use later in another. But in the last year—I don't know if it's something about being older or if it's about being in an academic environment—I'm less capable of doing that. I have to have things more neat and mechanical, and in their place mentally as well as physically. I think part of it is just being in the head so much. When you go into your mind you get cut off from the part where the creativity comes from. Being in a university keeps me in my head a lot.

INTERVIEWER: It often seems as though fiction writers and poets are two separate species, yet you and several other Native American writers aren't so genre bound.

HOGAN: Maybe when you're committing to a form instead of to the material, that becomes a problem. Certainly this goes back to the original question we started with, which is, "Are you telling *a* story or *the* story?"

If you feel like the material you're working with really has to be told, that people's survival and wholeness somehow depends on it, then you're committed to getting the material out in whatever form it will be. If you're committed to being a "poet," whatever that is, or a "fiction writer," then you're trying to find material that you can pull into your category. I would rather teach general creative writing than a workshop in poetry or in fiction because I think for some people to try to force material into a form is not the best way to work.

INTERVIEWER: You just finished a series of poems called *Hunger.* Why hunger?

HOGAN: *Hunger and the Book of Medicines* is the title, and the connection is that the medicines are somehow like a cure for the hunger, or a way to heal what our hunger and greed has done to us, and to the land and to the other species as well. I don't really know what started these poems, or even how I came to that name or to the idea of the book of medicines. I was merely thinking that the evidence of healing is all around us. A scar, for instance, is evidence that a wound has healed. But the poems are also about wilderness; they're about animals that live in the wilderness and humans who go into the human wilderness, and who also fear the wilderness outside them. In some ways the poems are an investigation of the depths of people, the history of land. John Hay, who is one of my favorite writers, wrote *The Immortal Wilderness* and *The Undiscovered Country.* He's an older man who's been around for a long time, and he said, "I used to believe that men were ruled by logic and rationality." And he said, "Now I know that people are motivated by fear and rage." These poems are about that—what's beneath our sense of logic and human rationality that really moves us and propels our lives through the world.

Robert Olen Butler

Of the Americans writing about the Vietnam War, Robert Olen Butler is one of the few who focuses on the Vietnamese people themselves rather than the effects of the war experience on Americans and the American culture or psyche. This interview was conducted in February 1994, shortly after Butler won the Pulitzer Prize for his collection of stories A Good Scent from a Strange Mountain *(1992), a book he recognizes as an artistic breakthrough for him. In the interview he talks about his development as a novelist, including the ultimate effects of studying theater and playwriting on his work. His theater studies led him to appreciate method acting, and his decision to adopt the first-person narrator in order to directly examine a variety of cultures and the experience of both genders is at the core of his development as a writer. He believes that fiction is a special kind of discourse that presents human experience as universally understandable and that the language and grammar of writing are sensual and emotional. Successful literature, to Butler, is not created through the development of ideas but through deep immersion of the artist's senses in a shared, unconscious pool of experiences with his characters.* They Whisper *(1994) is a controversial tour de force of sexual energy in which the first person male narrator lapses into the voices of "all the women he ever loved."* Tabloid Dreams *(1996), his most recent collection of stories, is written from the points of view of a series of characters imagined from the outrageous headlines of tabloid newspapers.*

INTERVIEWER: Your father was the chair of the theater department at St. Louis University and you grew up in Granite City, Illinois, the quintessential factory or blue-collar town.

BUTLER: I spent summers working in the Granite City steel mill. As I grew up I was every bit as comfortable talking Cardinals baseball with fellow members of the labor gang at the blast furnace as I was talking aesthetic theory with my father's colleagues at St. Louis University. Granite City is not a racially mixed city but it's full of exiles from the Deep South. There were forty thousand people in the city at that time and one high school, and I was the student-body president so I had good friends through the whole socioeconomic range. The sense of cultural collision that you find particularly in *A Good Scent from a Strange Mountain* I think flows from not just my experience in Vietnam but from my very childhood.

INTERVIEWER: You went to school at Northwestern University, first as a theater major, an actor. Eventually you took a master's degree in playwriting from the University of Iowa. What changed your direction?

BUTLER: I was more interested in acting than anything else when I was in high school. I went off to Northwestern in the fall of '63. Northwestern was, and still is, one of the premier training grounds for professional theater people. In that first year I was in four of the six major productions and had a major role in one of them, which was quite good. But into my sophomore year, I became restless with acting. I wanted to write, and since I was working in the theater I just assumed that the theater was what I should write for. On my twenty-first birthday, January of 1966, I was living at 626 Library Place in the top floor of a rooming house run by a very unusual old bachelor of a high school English teacher. I looked out over the snowy rooftops of Evanston and said, "Well, if you really think you're going to be a writer, you'd better write something." So I sat down and wrote, in the next couple of months, a full-length play called *The Rooming House* about that house and the people there. By the time I finished my master's at the University of Iowa, I had written a dozen full-length plays. The following eleven got worse and worse. I was a terrible playwright because I was in fact a nascent novelist trying to work in the wrong medium.

INTERVIEWER: What's the difference?

BUTLER: Plays and movies are collaborative art forms. The writer is responsible for two things only: structure, and to some lesser extent, dialogue. But even that is a collaborative process with the actors. If you don't understand and embrace your limitation as an artist you will write badly. I think artists write because they encounter the chaos of life on the planet Earth and yet have some deep instinct of order behind that chaos. If what you see about the world is deeply embedded in the moment-to-moment sensual flow of experience, then you're not going to be satisfied as an artist whose sensual access to that material resides in a different artist.

INTERVIEWER: John Gardner referred to fiction as the "whole hog": politics, history, anthropology, sociology, poetry; you get everything in fiction. Do you relate to that notion of the novel?

BUTLER: I was ready to embrace that idea, but when you started naming off those rational, abstracting sciences, I recoiled. I think fiction exists as a mode of discourse separate from any other because it resists and excludes the abstract and the rational and the ideational and the philosophical and the anthropological and sociological. All those things are the province of other modes of discourse. I don't think literature exists as a kind of elaborate word game where we sit around and talk rationally about what that work of art means. It's antithetical to the reason work is created and it's antithetical to the way the work should be encountered by a reader. There are 138,000 words in *They Whisper.* The only true answer to what that book means is to open the book up and read those 138,000 words again. The abstracting of our feelings, the interpreting, the analyzing, all those rational processes that we apply to our feelings are there in order to distance ourselves, to manage, to control, to shape, to vent off the direct, powerful hold these things have on us.

INTERVIEWER: How does the writer shape then? The artistic unconscious delivers, but the writer has to shape.

BUTLER: It's the interlocking, the weaving together of the deeply patterned motifs of the sensual world, that conveys a sense of order. That's why art is organic. Every sensual object, every moment, every word, every action, every metaphor in a true work of art resonates into everything else, links everything else. The tiniest example for you: in *Countrymen of Bones,* on page 2, Darell Reeves is out in the excavation site. He holds up his trowel, his basic tool. It's the thing that uncovers the past, and, in a way, uncovers himself to him. Now there are many different physical attributes he could consider at that moment, the heft of his trowel, the color of the blade, the texture of the handle, the pattern of earth clinging to the blade, but in fact he looks at it and notices that its blade is as strong and flexible as a Toledo sword. That's a very vivid sensual image. We see the thing clearly, and that's one of the levels at which art works. A hundred and fifty pages later, one of the ranchers gallops into the excavation site and takes Darell and the two young graduate-assistant workers hostage. That incident ends with Darell finally acting. And he does what?

INTERVIEWER: He stabs him with his trowel.

BUTLER: Exactly. He picks up the trowel and kills the man with it. Now, I wouldn't expect any reader to hold that initial image consciously in her head until that moment, but the vision of the book is manifest in the sensual impact of that trowel as he holds it, as he contemplates its blade, as the blade enters the flesh of a man.

INTERVIEWER: About eleven years ago you said, "I write novels to explore for myself and to reveal to others my vision of the fundamental patterns inherent in the flux of experience." Is that still your conviction?

BUTLER: *Explore* is the crucial word. I distinguish between literature and nonliterature in this way. Stephen King, Danielle Steel, even people like Jean-Paul Sartre understand ahead of time what effect they wish to convey, what ideas they wish to get across. Then they construct an object to do that. The artist responds to the world directly. He has some deep vision of order, but has no idea what that vision is until the object is created. The artist creates the object as much to explore as to express his vision. That's the fundamental distinction between what artists do and what entertainers or ideologues do.

INTERVIEWER: Anatole Broyard, the *New York Times* reviewer, spoke of you as a novelist of ideas, and Philip Biedler's study of the so-called Vietnam writers, *Rewriting America,* calls you the most political writer of your generation of Vietnam-era writers.

BUTLER: Everything I've been saying so far would seem to militate against both of those observations about me. But both men, I think, were on to something very important about the philosophical and political implications of art. The reason I can be so effective in the realm of ideas and the reason I can be so effective in the realm of politics is that I ignore both of those things when I write. I think it was Swift who said that you can't reason a person out of a position that he didn't reason himself into in the first place. The vast majority of the political beliefs that most people have are deeply irrational. We watch *McNeill/Lehrer* and read the *New York Times* in order to find some intellectual rationale for feeling the way we do. The work of art, because it ignores abstract ideas and touches the deepest irrational, sensual self, is better able to shape political ideas where they are truly formed.

INTERVIEWER: Three characters from *The Alleys of Eden* each went on to become central to a subsequent novel. Was that by design?

BUTLER: No. When I was writing bad plays, one of the ways I knew I wanted to be a novelist, at least in retrospect, is that I kept writing cycles of plays, with the same characters continuing on. Ironically enough, I got intrigued with a couple of secondary characters from the first novel I wrote when I got back from Vietnam in the fall of '72. I called it *What Lies Near.* David Fleming was the central character and Clifford Wilkes was a minor character. By the time *The Alleys of Eden* finally got published I had written six novels, including *What Lies Near.* On the fourth published novel, I went back to David Fleming and did him right. So the sense of characters going on was created backwards. Every character I create, no matter how small, becomes enormously interesting to me. They branch out into some other corner or pocket or vein in my artistic unconscious and begin to work there.

INTERVIEWER: Why did you move back to the past with *Countrymen of Bones* and *Wabash*?

BUTLER: I don't know. In a way going back to the fall of Vietnam was a kind of historical move, too. Going back to the energy crisis was a historical move as well, in a sense, because when I wrote those books we had gone past those events in some conclusive way. I've always been drawn to the large, external historical, cultural event that itself echoes the inner-personal pattern of the characters.

INTERVIEWER: Was a family story behind *Wabash*?

BUTLER: Oh, sure. My mother and my mother's mother and my mother's sisters were wonderful storytellers but there are no real-life counterparts to any of my characters. Graham Greene said that all good novelists have bad memories. What you remember comes out as journalism; what you forget goes into the compost of the imagination. All the characters in my work are creatures of the compost. Carlos Fuentes, I think, called the novel a pack of lies hounding the truth, and my books are the truest lies that I can tell. If anybody reads *They Whisper* looking for biographical details of me or my three wives or any other women I've loved or my son or my parents, they will be drastically misled. None of us exist in that book. On a deeper level, I am nakedly present in *They Whisper* and Ira Holloway. I would hasten to add, however, that *They Whisper* is not an attempt to find the unified field theory of human sexuality. It is a partial vision of myself and of what I see. *A Good Scent from a Strange Mountain* is deeply and nakedly me, as well, in every aspect of every character in the sense that I am pouring my most impassioned encounter with the world and my most ardent search for its meaning into every word, every image of that and every book.

INTERVIEWER: I read your novels in sequence and it seems to me that if there's a breakthrough book, a book where you found your voice, it was *The Deuce.*

BUTLER: I think you are absolutely right. It was the first book I wrote in the first person. The first five novels were my playwright self, from *The Deuce* on I've gone back to being an actor. I become the role, I become the character. In *A Good Scent from a Strange Mountain* it felt like I was speaking in tongues at times. I can't even imagine going back to the third person now. There's a great deal to explore with the first person. Look at *They Whisper*—the first-person voice of a man who lapses into the first-person voices of women, not as a kind of transsexual experience, but as the ultimate expression of heterosexual love.

INTERVIEWER: I'd like to talk about *They Whisper.* Why did you choose to center the book around a character as dysfunctional as Fiona in taking on the task of exploring heterosexual love and relationships?

BUTLER: Fiona is not the center of the book, as Ira keeps pointing out. Fiona is one very important, but only one, sexual and sensual and female influence in the book. All the women are equally important in certain ways. Fiona's presence in the book, however, is as strong and dysfunctional as it is because she is the dark counterimage to Ira. He sees sex as a kind of secular sacrament. Churches understand sacraments as a physical something that resonates into the cosmic sphere. For Ira, women's bodies are that. Though Ira loves many women, he loves them absolutely and individually. For him a woman's body is a sacramentally charged metaphor for the inner secrets of her unique personality, which he seeks even through hearing and taking on her woman's voice. For him there is a kind of holy grail that is unattainable: Karen Granger, the little girl that he loved one summer. For him, sexuality is a powerful life force. Fiona is the dark counterimage to that. She has had sexual encounters with many men.

But they were part of a constant search for reassurance that she is not loathsome. In place of Ira's holy grail, she has from her childhood the dark malignant influence of her sexually abusive father. Instead of being connected to the life force, sexuality for her is connected to death. Fiona and Ira are the yin and the yang; it's the life and death, wellness and sickness, connection and disconnection, that come together in that union.

A critical aspect of this book is the women's voices. I hadn't even conceived *They Whisper* until I wrote *A Good Scent from a Strange Mountain.* Notably enough, Ira Holloway and I are strictly heterosexual, exclusively so, and yet I could not conceive a book, I could not write a book about the essence of male heterosexuality—what it is, how it drives a man, what the dark sides are—with the complexity it required until I found the woman's voice in me. Ira carries an inner landscape around with him in which dwell all the women he has ever loved, and as he meditates on them he lapses into their first-person voices. It is the ultimate act of intimacy, to leave the self and to join the other in the inner self.

INTERVIEWER: But at the end of the book, he still feels incomplete.

BUTLER: *They Whisper* does not intend to discover a unified field theory of human sexuality. But it says things that I think are deeply true about our yearnings. And it is not just the man who continues to yearn for that deep connection where bodies are the way in. Women do too. Society has been much more efficient in suppressing that urge in women, but it is there. The question is, if sexuality is a kind of search for glimpses into the infinite, is it possible for any one relationship ever to be so complete as to exclude any other yearning or any other need for connection?

INTERVIEWER: Do you think that in any good story there is any such thing as a reliable narrator?

BUTLER: The work itself will encourage or discourage that half or full step back from the narrator. In *They Whisper* there is the tiniest little bit of distancing. We probably have our own independent sense—inevitably given the subject matter—of Ira's choices and decisions and priorities and so forth. But I think we trust him to be pretty thoroughly self-aware. He is prepared to feel guilty. He deeply regrets deception and pain and he tries rigorously to avoid deceiving anyone and to avoid inflicting pain in relationships and he is very conscious in trying to examine a profoundly mysterious impulse. Reviewers speak of Ira as if he were an acquaintance, a real person, and that's fine, that's good. To some extent to write about this subject matter you've got to build that into the process. If you get a half a dozen of your literary friends around a dinner table and say, "Let's name all the serious literary novels that we can about war," twenty minutes later you've got two hundred titles on the table. You say, "Okay, let's name all the serious literary novels we can about family relationships." It's going to take an hour and you'll have five hundred titles on the table. Then you say, "Let's name all the serious literary works of fiction that we can about the essence of human sexuality. Not just books with sex in them, but that really go at that subject head-on." There's going to be a lot of silence and you're going to stir your coffee and think and look out the window, and you probably won't get off the fingers of that one proverbial hand. There are reasons for that. This deeply personal reaction is one. Another is the limits of the language. Though the English language has more words than any other, the words for those most intimate of body parts involved in this most intimate of human activities don't carry with them the connotations of vulnerability and tenderness and cosmic resonance that many of us feel about those parts. They are either too clinical and scientific and bloodless or gross and trivializing and dismissive and pornographic. When I wrote *They Whisper,* with every word I felt as if I was reinventing the form of the novel and reinventing the language in certain ways.

INTERVIEWER: You've made it clear that you think we should trust Ira. But the big problem with first-person narrative is that by definition every human being is limited; therefore the reader is going to recognize things that the narrator cannot. What are some of the main things that you would hope the reader sees in *They Whisper* that Ira can't see for himself?

BUTLER: That's a difficult question because you are asking me to reconsider the whole book in exactly the kind of psychoanalytical abstracting terms that I have resisted in writing it. You trust him as much as any single human consciousness can be trusted. By and large we are led to distrust Ira in the same ways he distrusts himself. At any given moment, a reader might well be able to anticipate Ira's conclusions about certain things. For instance, we might well sense that Ira is not whole before he is able to declare it. He is so close to the women he loves that it is impossible for him to get a perspective on the dark side or incompleteness as soon as we would. He is deeply in love with and caught up in that glimpse into the infinite present even in the fading fingertips of a waitress on a cold wineglass. As much as he is able to evoke that for us, we are still a little bit separate. There can well be a range of personal reactions to him as a human being which I think still fit within the frame of a book about human intimacy and sexuality. To keep that range of human personal reaction within an artistic frame is the best that one can hope for and may be something quite special on its own.

INTERVIEWER: In her review of *They Whisper,* Jane Smiley wrote that men of the Vietnam generation live "the realities of imperialism, both abroad and in the home, without conviction." How would you respond?

BUTLER: On one level there is some validity to that but I think to limit it to men of the Vietnam era would be a big mistake. This is a universal and ages-old impulse of men that has existed since Solomon had two thousand wives and David lusted after somebody else's wife.

INTERVIEWER: But Bathsheba was not allowed to lust after a lot of men and that's the difference I am getting at. We have a whole generation of men who accept that women have sex lives just like them, but it's a reality that you don't often find reflected in contemporary fiction.

BUTLER: That impulse needs to be understood and accepted and embraced by and for women, and we have to take out society's reflex aversion to that impulse in men. Men who continue to love women throughout their life and feel that they might well be in love with more than one woman at once are treated as absolutely reprehensible. But there are many men for whom that impulse to continue to love women is deeply serious. They revere the individuality and the uniqueness of each woman and are seeking that connection to the cosmos. But Ira and men like him are terribly vulnerable. And for the men who feel that vulnerability and can't live with it, one defense mechanism is to coarsen and diminish the impulse. They turn it into the reprehensible thing which is the objectifying of women and womanizing for the sake of power and possession, and these men ultimately kill that deeper self. It is terribly important to realize that the impulse exists in both men and women and that it exists in a serious and beautiful way.

INTERVIEWER: It strikes a lot of your readers that you did a very, very nervy thing in writing not only *They Whisper* but *A Good Scent* as well. You took a lot of risks.

BUTLER: That's true. The books are full of risks, and that's the only way I can continue to write. I just have to think about going deeper and deeper and deeper in. I only write from the place that my inspiration and my deepest concerns lead me. In this case it's led me not only into other cultures, but into the other gender as well. My conviction is that artists are in the business of breaking down those barriers between us. Every human being on the planet, I think, carries around the fear that, in spite of appearances, each of us is utterly alone. And it's the artist's job to take us out of ourselves and into the other. One should come to a work of art nakedly, as you would to a new lover, and say, "Take me. Make me part of you."

INTERVIEWER: Was this your approach in writing *A Good Scent from a Strange Mountain* as well as *They Whisper*?

BUTLER: *A Good Scent* was really the book where I had to face down that inhibition that says, "I can't go there." I think that's best summed up in something that the great Japanese film director Akiri Kurasawa said, that to be an artist means to never avert your eyes. And if anything has guided me, that's it. With *A Good Scent* I found myself in that place artists must go in their unconscious where, lo and behold, we are neither Vietnamese nor American, neither Catholic nor Buddhist, neither Israeli nor Palestinian. We are all deeply, universally human. There is a place where all of us meet and share a self. And that's the place I think that all artists strive to get to. When you get there, you find that then you can project that common pool of experience from yourself, through yourself, but also from everyone else and through them. You can project back into characters and situations that on the surface seem far from you in those limiting ways of gender and race and culture.

INTERVIEWER: How essential is learning the language of another culture to this process of reaching that common pool of experience?

BUTLER: I did need, in terms of my Vietnamese, to spend a year knowing the language fluently and deeply submerged in the culture. I took every opportunity I could. For the seven months that I was in Saigon, for instance, I would go out virtually every night well past midnight and just wander the steamy back alleys, where nobody ever seemed to sleep, and I would crouch in the doorways with the Vietnamese people, who were as a group the warmest, most open and generous-spirited people in the world. And they would invariably invite me into their homes and into their culture and lives. And I fell in love more than several times in Vietnam. And I had a wide range of friendships, from my favorite leper beggar on the streets, who was by the way the most cheerful man I have ever met in my life, to the highest government officials.

INTERVIEWER: And you fell in love with the entire fabric of their culture and lives and language?

BUTLER: I was ravished by the sensuality of Vietnam. Fluency in another language, to really know another language is not just to develop equivalencies for words. You rename the world. And the sensual properties of that name echo into the object and the object echoes into the words and so with that other language, I was seeing the world afresh. I needed that.

INTERVIEWER: What has the response in the Vietnamese community been to *A Good Scent*?

BUTLER: The most common comment is that my understanding of the Vietnamese and their culture is so intimate they could have sworn that I was Vietnamese. In Orange County, California, home to eighty thousand Vietnamese—it's called "Little Saigon," and is the de facto capital of the Vietnamese in America—a wonderful man who's translating my work into Vietnamese arranged a luncheon with a dozen of the most prominent literary figures in the Vietnamese community in America. The thing they were so deeply grateful to me for was not the cultural accuracy of the book but the fact that I had portrayed the Vietnamese people as universally human. In Vietnam itself, an official in the foreign ministry, a fast-track young Communist, discovered my book and has translated some of the stories into Vietnamese. He wanted to do "A Good Scent from a Strange Mountain," the title story, but his superiors did not find that story politically acceptable. He went on to translate "Crickets," and his translation appeared in a weekly magazine in Saigon while I was there in '93 and caused quite a wonderful stir. Shopkeepers and cyclo drivers and so forth were stopping me on the street. "Crickets" has within it some pretty clear imagery.

There are two types of crickets: the large charcoal crickets, which are big and strong but slow; and the smaller fire crickets that are quick and wily. Even when a child had his own charcoal cricket in a fight, everyone, even that child, would root for the little fire cricket. Who was who was pretty clear in the story. Every morning I passed a man who sold lapel pins within a block of my hotel. I spoke a greeting to him in Vietnamese; and he spoke back. We had a lovely sort of very warm, passing-hello relationship. This man was in his mid- to late forties. He had a horrible mangled stump where his left arm had been. On the day after "Crickets" appeared, he waved the magazine at me and called me over. It turns out that he is a former Vietcong soldier. We had a lovely chat and he went on about how much he loved all parts of the story. He says, "But you know what the best part was," and he gave this great rich, deep laugh, "I used to fight crickets and what you say is true. When the fire cricket fought the charcoal crickets, we all rooted for the fire cricket." Kind of an eerie moment. Here literary symbol meets object of the symbolism, and he was responding, not in any intellectual abstract way but directly and emotionally to this imagery.

INTERVIEWER: Your stories seem to strike an accommodation between Buddhists and Catholics in Vietnam that I assume is reflected in Vietnamese life.

BUTLER: The Vietnamese are extraordinarily pragmatic and eclectic people. Everything you need to know about the Vietnamese people—their beliefs, their attitudes, their politics, their religion, their character—you can understand by learning how to cross the streets of Saigon. Those wonderful old wide French boulevards are filled at almost any hour of the day or night with ten, fifteen, twenty, twenty-five lanes of traffic in each direction. I say lanes but it's very amorphous. Virtually all of that traffic is motorcycles, motorbikes, bicycles, some cyclos—pedicabs, that is—a few taxicabs. To cross the streets in Saigon you stand on the corner and look across to the far side where you want to go. If you wait for an opening to get all the way across, you will die of old age on the curb. If you dash to an opening and wait and then dash to the next opening and so forth—you will die in the center of the street within seconds. In Saigon, what you do is this. You look to the left—the first small opening, you step into. And then you do not stop. You do not slow down. You continue to walk at a very moderate pace across the street toward the place you want to be. All those lanes of traffic bearing down on you will not stop, they will not slow down. But the vehicle that's about to strike you at any given second will at the last moment veer into the next lane. Without looking. Whoever is in that lane, understanding this process instinctively, moves into the next lane and so forth. You will continue to move through that traffic and it will ripple and flow around you until you are at the other side. If JFK had sent his chief of staff to Saigon in 1962 and said, "Learn how to cross the streets and tell me what you think," that general would have learned two important things. First of all, we could never win the war. Second of all, we didn't need to win the war, because as soon as the failures of the Communist system were clear to the Vietnamese, they would go around it—which is exactly what happened.

INTERVIEWER: In many ways the title story of *A Good Scent from a Strange Mountain* serves as a touchstone for the whole collection. Its function in the book echoes the structure of many of the individual stories: it makes you go back and think about the collection as a whole.

BUTLER: Yes, that story was written last, and it does indeed have a kind of overarching vision of life and the world and human aspiration and exile and choice of self that echoes through the whole collection. There's no question about that. John Clark Pratt did a very careful analysis of *Good Scent* in the *Colorado Review* last year. He sees it as a kind of quintessential postmodernist novel, working in montage. And I think he has got a point. Every story in the collection is carefully placed. "A Good Scent from a Strange Mountain" was consciously written at the end from a specific sensual inspiration, but it stands in the book as an overarching vision of the whole.

INTERVIEWER: How did you decide to order the rest of the stories?

BUTLER: It was a deeply subjective thing. I was looking for a rhythm of tone, of emotion, of gender. I positioned the stories so that there would be a kind of waveform, of hope and despair and cynicism and aspiration and so forth. It was a way of modulating the rhythm of emotion through the whole mosaic of voices.

INTERVIEWER: Certainly a story like "The Trip Back" is about the ways of memory. One of the first things the narrator says is, "I'm not a poet. I'm a businessman." Yet it takes a poet to tell this story, and the coming to be a poet is tied in with memory and action.

BUTLER: There's a certain paradox, yes. The narrator definitely feels that failure in himself; his potential to be a poet is latent, and the action he takes at the end of the story is the consummate artistic gesture.

INTERVIEWER: It says to his wife, "I'll be your grandfather. I'll be your brother, I'll be your friend, your father, everything to you." It's a great act of the imagination and it's also an embodiment of sensory memory.

BUTLER: Thanks. But part of me inevitably balks at analysis and generalization of that kind. We sit here to talk about the work like this, but ultimately the work is only itself. It is only the act. He puts his wife on his back and runs with her. The impulse to step back from it and say, "Ah, now he's telling her that he's everything to her" is a reductive act. When I teach literature we look at the subtext and articulate it in terms different from the terms in which they sit there on the page. But I always tell my students, "The only reason we are doing this terribly artificial thing is that the process may help you to thrum more completely or harmoniously with the next work of art that you read. In order to do that, when you leave here your last assignment is to forget everything we've said here." To be a real reader means to close the book and sensually resonate to the vision of order there and be at peace with that. That's enough. That's everything.

INTERVIEWER: Like many of the stories in the book, every detail in "Mr. Green" comes together and works perfectly with the ending. It answers the question "What then?" and also is a response to her grandfather's "Not possible" on so many levels. Every detail. What role does revision play in bringing everything to such a fine pitch?

BUTLER: There was very, very little revision in any of the stories. My editor did not change a comma in that book. I do not leave a sentence until it is as close to being finished as it can possibly be. I revise as I go, so there was, of course, revision from sentence to sentence, but there were no drafts of any story, nothing had to be pulled through the whole process again and again.

INTERVIEWER: Do you ever have fun writing? Was "Love" in *A Good Scent* a fun story to write?

BUTLER: Of course it was fun, and parts of *They Whisper* were great fun. The Karen Granger stuff, the synthesized voice at the grocery store checkout counter, the handwriting on the girls' rest room walls. There is actually quite a lot of humor in *They Whisper* and those things are fun to write. But there's a deeper fun, bound up with fear and trembling and pain. It's the deep satisfaction of going as far as you can into that utterly sensual unconscious and shaping it into a vivid and clear vision of the world. I walk away from my computer every day with an exhilaration. No matter how difficult, how troubling the vision is, the articulation of it is joyful.

INTERVIEWER: I know that you have in your head right now several more books. Can you please tell us what that means?

BUTLER: My unconscious is telling me that if I sat down tomorrow and began to focus entirely on one of the four novels and two books of stories I have in mind, eighteen months from now it would have an existence. It's an accretion of sensual details and relationships and localities and characters who yearn. You drive down a street at night and you know everybody on the block in some way. All the picture windows are open and you look to the left and somebody's sitting at a table and somebody is just moving into the room with her hair up in a towel and her bathrobe on and he turns and looks over his shoulder. Over in this house there's a child climbing onto the back of a father and down at the next house something else. You know that all you need to do is stop your car and go knock on the door and they would let you in and you'd sit in there for a year and a half and walk out with everything. It's images. It's that sense of lives together in a place that you can access.

INTERVIEWER: Now that a whole body of Vietnam War literature exists, is there anything productive to say about that literature and your place in it?

BUTLER: If one writes from the artistic impulse I've been describing, then to call me a Vietnam novelist is like calling Monet a lily-pad painter. Vietnam for me has always been simply a metaphor, a location, an instigator of action, a source of characters, a matrix of concrete sensual experience that holds the deep universal human issues I'm concerned with.

INTERVIEWER: You've been quoted as saying that to avoid madness, you had to turn yourself into your writing pad or computer and write, not think about prizes and fame and glory. Now you've won the Pulitzer Prize and you're one of the best-known writers in the country. I guess I would like to ask Mr. Green's question: "What then?"

BUTLER: The nice thing about the Pulitzer is that it will be there forever. I think the monkey's off my back now. I'm always the Pulitzer Prize winner now and it just makes it easier to write the books that I'm given to write. I was going to do that anyway, but the great and blessed difference is that people will actually buy the books and read them. I've always known that I would find a much wider audience someday. My books are devoted to the proposition that literary fiction does not need to disenfranchise itself from strong storytelling. Though the artist must focus ultimately on exploring and expressing his or her own deep vision of the world, the very act of expressing reveals a deep yearning to touch and to connect to others. It's also an act of lovemaking. When I write a book I am making myself naked to the world and saying I wish to touch you. I wish to connect deeply with you. The wonderful thing about the prize is that now others will respond.

INTERVIEWER: Earlier we touched on the question of wanting to make the reader see your vision of the world. If you were backed to the wall and had to say, "This is my vision of the world," what would you say?

BUTLER: The only true answer to that is to take my eight books and read them to you again. And then to read you every book I write from this point on. Ultimately, after all this talk, that is my vision of the world. It is irreducible.

Jessica Hagedorn

Jessica Hagedorn was born in 1949 and raised in the Philippines. At the age of fourteen she moved from Manila to San Francisco where she became a protégée of poet and translator Kenneth Rexroth. Her early career involved performance art, poetry, and rock and roll. For ten years she was lead singer and songwriter of the Gangster Choir. Her first novel, Dogeaters, *was published in 1990 after ten years of work. In addition to* Dogeaters, *Hagedorn's publications include poetry and short prose and multimedia theater pieces. She was also the editor of* Charlie Chan Is Dead *(1993), one of the most widespread and acclaimed collections of Asian American writing. Her second novel,* The Gangster of Love, *covering much of the same cultural territory, was published in 1996.*

In an era when many novelists have attempted to deal with the themes of multiculturalism, few have achieved what Hagedorn has managed with her first novel, developed as a pastiche of history, autobiography, song, and newspaper articles—sometimes authentic, sometimes invented. She presents a broad canvas of culture almost like a hip Dos Passos. Magical realism, her literary inspiration, is sometimes used to hide a mundane tale, but Hagedorn's technique conveys a multitude of voices and compelling incidents.

This interview was conducted in April 1994 while Hagedorn was continuing work on The Gangster of Love.

INTERVIEWER: Jessica Hagedorn, you've worked in such a variety of mediums: poetry, prose, theater, rock and roll—with the Gangster Choir—and also film. What medium are you busy with right now?

HAGEDORN: I'm preparing for a multimedia theater piece, *Airport Music,* that's coming up in New York City. And I've just finished work on a film, *Fresh Kill,* I actually wrote a couple of years ago—you know how long it takes to make a movie—for an independent filmmaker named Shu Lea Cheang. It was based on a story of hers, so in that way it was a real collaboration. Most of it is shot in New York City, which was really a crazy thing to do but we lived through it. And now it's making the rounds of festivals and looking for a distributor. And the theater piece which involves film and slides and soundtrack collages, I'll be performing in as well.

INTERVIEWER: *Dogeaters* begins at the movies. You seem to be fascinated artistically by film. Can you tell me why?

HAGEDORN: Because the movies really shaped my life. Growing up in the Philippines, I loved all kinds of movies. We had a very healthy film industry there when I was a child. It's now gotten very limited. They only make action movies and hardcore exploitation movies. Women get raped; men get shot. But in my childhood, they had all kinds of movies—to rival Hollywood's really—musicals, dramas, comedies. They were wonderful. I would go see those movies faithfully every week. It was my big treat. And I'd go see all the Hollywood movies that would come to Manila. We didn't have television until I was about eight years old, so it was either the movies or radio. A lot of radio drama. That was our television, you know. We had to use our imagination. So it was really those two things, and the comics, that I immersed myself in as a child.

INTERVIEWER: In *Dogeaters,* you make delightful use on many different levels of *Love Letters,* the radio serial that Rio's grandmother is so enamored with and that Rio listens to in the bedroom off the kitchen late at night while they eat rice with their hands. The servants come in too, and all socioeconomic lines are crossed.

HAGEDORN: Right. There were also horror shows on the radio. Very terrifying and thrilling to me as a kid. They had all these creepy sound effects. They would come on at ten o'clock at night, and I just would scare myself to death.

INTERVIEWER: Did they import any of the American ones like *The Shadow,* or was it all produced in the Philippines?

HAGEDORN: We produced our own. The radio was, and still is, a real instrument of communication there because a lot of people, in the villages way out in the southern regions, for example, can't afford TVs. There might be one TV per village, but with electricity being so scarce, the radio's still used in the home, or the community will all listen in to the one radio. Politicians use it. When I covered the elections there two years ago, the radio was really used as a primary medium for political campaigning. Can you imagine that here?

INTERVIEWER: You used that radio serial *Love Letters* in several ways: to comment on the story that's happening within the novel and just as a very blessed incident between the girl Rio and her beloved grandmother. Had you by any chance read *Aunt Julia and the Scriptwriter* at that point?

HAGEDORN: Yes. I had read it years before when it first came out, and I loved it. Did you notice the torture scene in *Dogeaters,* when the soap opera is used as foreground to a very painful happening in the background? That was the most difficult chapter to write for me. I think torture is so loaded, you know, that it's hard to make it effective. And the radio drama was the way I managed to get through it. For me, it worked really well.

INTERVIEWER: Absolutely. Vargas Llosa, too, in *Aunt Julia* uses the soap opera to great effect.

HAGEDORN: Well, I have been definitely influenced more by Latin American writers than by any other type of writer. They are very close in terms of voice—their humor, their fatalism, their . . . well, that overused term "magical realism." It's a wonderful term that's just been used so much we don't know what it means anymore. But the way they can use language and visions and surrealism without being corny, and the humor that's always there, is very close to a Filipino sensibility. More so than—now this is a completely personal perception—other writers from Southeast Asia.

INTERVIEWER: What is your particular ethnic background? I would like to talk about that a little bit because the whole question of what it is to be Filipino runs throughout your work.

HAGEDORN: I'm part Spanish. My paternal grandfather came from Spain via Singapore to Manila. On my mother's side it's more mixture, with a Filipino mother and a father who was Scotch-Irish-French; you know, white American hybrid. And I also have on my father's side a great-great-grandmother who was Chinese. So, I'm a hybrid.

INTERVIEWER: Assuming that it is you talking in one of your prose pieces from *Danger and Beauty,* you've actually described yourself this way: "I was born in the Philippines. I am a quintessential bastard. My roots are dubious." Where does the bastard part come from?

HAGEDORN: Well, there's always a bastard in the family isn't there? And certainly with the Spaniards; they left a lot of bastards around. I'm an underdog person, so I align myself with those who seem to be not considered valuable in polite society. I think for a lot of so-called postcolonial peoples, there's a feeling of not being quite legitimate, of not being pure enough. And to me that's the beauty and strength of the culture—that it is mixed.

INTERVIEWER: Can you tell us a little bit about the basic mix of cultures? In *Dogeaters,* you refer in one section to eighty dialects and languages spoken.

HAGEDORN: There are many, many tribes who speak their own dialect but who have no say in what's going on in government, for example. So we have to think about that too. But people speak Tagalog, which is also known as "Pilipino" now—the nationalists claim it's Pilipino. Many speak English, and some of the older generation still speak a very fluent Spanish, because that was part of the culture at one time, or a mixture of the three. For example, in my household sometimes a sentence could have all three languages in it at once. It's not like sometimes we spoke the whole sentence in English and other times in Tagalog. No, it was all in the language. Like a "Tag-lish" or something. And there are many, many more languages. When the Spanish came over to do their colonizing, these islands with disparate tribes suddenly got lumped together. And not everybody necessarily got along. There was, according to some Filipino historians, a matriarchal society which was wiped out. Animism was practiced. Some of the people are highlanders; some are lowland peoples. Some are Muslims because at some point in our history the Arab traders had come through there, so there is a very powerful Muslim faction in the southern region of the Philippines.

INTERVIEWER: With all the backgrounds that you've said are prominent in your family, why is it that you identify yourself with the Asian experience?

HAGEDORN: Because that's been my experience.

INTERVIEWER: Even though your father was Spanish?

HAGEDORN: Yes, but he was Filipino Spanish. There's a difference. When mestizos go to Spain, they are looked down upon. "Ah, you live in the

Philippines." You know, it's a class thing, even if you're rich. There's always this motherland-fatherland bit, and then there's the colonies. My identity is linked to my grandmother, who's pure Filipino, as pure as you can probably get. And that shaped my imagination. So that's how I identify. I also identify as a Latin person, a person who has Latin blood. Certainly, I'm exploring that now. And I've lived now in North America close to thirty years. In terms of my politics, I feel a political alliance too with the Asian community here.

INTERVIEWER: Can you tell us about the concept of "Kundiman" that you end *Dogeaters* on?

HAGEDORN: The novel ends on an ambiguous, ambivalent note. There's a lot of brutality in *Dogeaters,* and I think that especially with the suffering that the character Daisy goes through and the loss of the senator and all the other people who die or are tortured, and just the daily suffering of the poor there—which is enormous—the Philippines is still a beautiful country and I wanted somehow to convey that. So I decided originally that the Kundiman section was going to be the grandmother's prayer. I mean, actually, that was one of the titles I thought of, "The Grandmother Prays for Her Country." But I thought, no, I want to even lift it above a specific character's voice, and maybe it's my voice that speaks at the end. But how do I convey this sort of longing in this prayer, and the rage? There's a lot of rage in the prayer. So I decided on the Kundiman because it's music in a ballad form. It's very melancholy music. It's a love song often sung, it seems to me, in a way or played in a way as if the love will never be satisfied.

INTERVIEWER: And what tradition does it come out of?

HAGEDORN: "Kundiman" is a Filipino word that describes this music. But I'm pretty sure around the time it became popular there may have been a Spanish influence on it. We have little orchestras called *rondallas* and musicians play this banjolike instrument called the *banduria.* When I finally went to Spain, I found out the Gypsies play it there and the Spanish have claimed it. But actually maybe the Arabs brought it, the Moors. And so maybe that's how it came to the Philippines. Who knows?

INTERVIEWER: How did you come to the shape of this novel, of how you wanted to present this material?

HAGEDORN: It pretty much fell into place that way. It made sense as I was writing it. Whenever, for example, I'd come across a news clipping that really tickled my imagination I'd say, "Oh God! This really belongs here!" Rather than try to revise the clipping so that it would read as a narrative, I thought if it's a news item, use it as a news item, you know. You can have a novel that is like a collage, which I feel *Dogeaters* is. A lot of the ten years thinking about *Dogeaters* I worried about the structure. How could the structure also tell that story? A lot of novels about the Philippines or set in the Philippines don't cut it at all because they don't capture the crazy-quilt atmosphere and the hybrid ambiance that occurs twenty-four hours a day. Things happening all the time, and noise and crowds and beautiful animals and amazing flora. At the same time, pollution and urbanization and sophistication and, you know, the jungle. How do you do all that? You can't tell it in a traditional way because the language dies. And also the music of the language itself, the music of the streets. How do you convey that chaos? So, once I decided to go with it as I found it, I relaxed because at the risk of alienating some readers, this was the way the novel had to be presented.

INTERVIEWER: You've described the "memory of Manila" as "the central character of the novel I am writing." How much of the Philippines of *Dogeaters,* because you left at the age of fourteen, is the product of memory, as you've implied, and how much is the product of augmented memory and research?

HAGEDORN: It's both. I think it's very important that it's memory first because too much research and factual writing can kill a book. I wasn't trying to write the absolute "real deal" story of the Philippines. I was only writing about a certain time frame and also about a certain group of people in a city, you know. This is not the quintessential Philippines novel. I mean, I don't know who's going to write that. There are many writers there who have grappled with creating the epic Philippine novel.

INTERVIEWER: "I am the other, the exile within," you have also said. Do you think that in some cases, or in your case, it was an advantage to be an outsider as it were, writing from memory, in order to deal with such a large subject?

HAGEDORN: Having distance always helps. It gives you a certain overview that when you are right up against it, it's very difficult to make certain choices.

INTERVIEWER: How did you come to the characters that surely were not a part of your growing up in Manila at all, such as Joey?

HAGEDORN: But they were. I mean I didn't go to those bars when I was eight years old, but those people were always there. That's why the book jumps back and forth in time. When I was old enough and going back to the Philippines more often, it was the time of martial law when it was very repressive on the surface. At the same time there was a lot of corruption, and pornography was part of life even though you had this regime that was trying to present itself as being squeaky-clean. Well, it was the height of the worst moral decay. I was on my own then, so I could explore what I wanted to explore. And I already had the idea that one day I was going to write this novel, so I made myself open to a lot of different experiences and met all kinds of people. I wanted to get to that underbelly because I felt like those were the people who nobody cared about and nobody thought about and they were too easily dismissed.

INTERVIEWER: Characters like Domingo Avila, who is assassinated, begs comparison to Ninoy Aquino. And Santos Tirador, the handsome guerilla, has his equivalent too. What kind of a challenge was it for you to work in a purely fictive way and yet know that readers were going to recognize some of these people?

HAGEDORN: I hear that it's a wonderful parlor game back home for people to go "I know who this is!" It's funny to me because I really did combine people. Otherwise, it's too easy. I thought that Avila was the most difficult because he was the good guy, and good guys for me are hard to write about without making them saintly and boring. I tried very hard not to make it too obvious. He's killed in front of a hotel, for example, not coming off a plane. Anyway, there are so many people like him. That's another reason I did not name the president and the first lady purposely. It wasn't to be coy. It was that the Marcoses were symbols. They weren't the only dictators we've ever had. They just happened to have been around the longest, and they were the most public and the most celebrated and the most reviled. But there have been many victims, many assassins, and many political assassinations. You just don't hear about them because it's part and parcel of politics there.

INTERVIEWER: Were you conscious at all of this novel being able, at least on one level, to be read as a dual coming-of-age novel? It's Joey's coming-of-age, and it's Rio's coming-of-age.

HAGEDORN: Yes, but I didn't plan it that way. I'm not a writer who works off an outline. I don't do file cards. Some writers know where they're going when they sit down to write a novel. I know there are certain things I want to include, but I'm character driven and if the characters keep moving and living and growing on me, the story unfolds. It's like a puzzle which starts falling into place. But I never know where I'm going when I start. I knew it was going to open in a movie theater. I knew it was going to be from this young girl's point of view. I knew that sometimes the character of Rio, the young girl, would speak in the first person and sometimes she wouldn't, but I didn't plan for the character of Joey to be the only other character who speaks in the first person. Actually someone had to point that out to me. They said, "Oh, you have the two narrators."

INTERVIEWER: What do you think is going to happen to Joey after he finds himself up there in the mountains? Do you think about your characters that way at all?

HAGEDORN: Yeah, I do. But I didn't want to deal with whether he would become the good revolutionary or not. I think there's been so much disillusionment that's occurred with the Left in the Philippines. And I could see that the point was that Joey is taught something. Then where he goes from there wasn't my concern anymore. It was going to be very ambiguous because he could turn into a really awful person once again. This new knowledge that he has about what's going on around him doesn't necessarily mean that he's going to become a better person.

INTERVIEWER: It seems that where we leave off with the character of Joey, in that very ambiguity, you do have fertile ground for questions about the relationship between the personal and the political. What makes a person become a revolutionary in this world? There are any number of ways that can happen, and in Joey's case it was being the product of a horrifically abused childhood.

HAGEDORN: And then the accident of seeing something occur and realizing he's been used. But I'm not so sure that he gets to understand it all. That's why I wanted to leave it open. I did not want to go the easy way and make him go from antihero to hero.

INTERVIEWER: Is it a uniquely Filipino thing, or just something particular to him, that Rio's father is a person of Spanish background living in the Philippines for several generations and still feels like a visitor, that Spain was still really home? And, in fact, his mother does still live in Spain.

HAGEDORN: His mother lives in Spain, but she's not a Spaniard either. Is it a Filipino thing? I don't know. I really don't want to generalize like that because that's where you start getting in trouble. It's specific to this character, but there are many characters like him who are so caught up in the class garbage of feeling that they're the colonials in their own country. It's almost as if the Philippines is a stopping point and then life will go on once we get to the United States, get our visa and leave. Now, it's no longer about going to Spain. That was a particular generation. Now, it's like "We're going to get our visas and split and come to the United States." Because they have given up on the Philippines, they feel a certain hopelessness and despair, and they don't want to stay and try to fight it. They feel it's a situation that they have no power to change. Rather than even fighting or voting for someone else or something, they'd rather leave. So, it's a comment on that—about living there and always feeling like a stranger. And maybe that's a uniquely postcolonial condition.

INTERVIEWER: What do you make of the contrast between Joey and Rio, of how they both end up not having any control over their lives?

HAGEDORN: There are a lot of similarities between the two even though one came from pure poverty and the other comes from an upper-middle-class background and has access, she thinks, to many other things in the world and to material goods. But even she has no control on one level. But there is a point where the two of them realize they might have some control over their lives. They do, in their souls anyway. And she starts to come to grips with that as the book ends. And he . . . who knows? He's a pragmatist. Joey is a survivor, that much I'm clear about. Whether he goes back and hustles for the rest of his life or he really changes. Maybe he gets betrayed again? Because, hey, the Left, they're not saints either. Or he may end up working for the telephone company.

I based the Daisy character, for example, on a composite of several people, but one of them had been in the mountains, had fought, had really taken this idea of the revolution very seriously. But finally, she came down from the mountains, just got burned out and tired of being on the run. She was one of the most wanted people in the Philippines and by the time I interviewed her, she was working at a mundane job and seemed to be somewhat at peace with whatever compromise she had come to. It was completely bizarre because she had been somewhat of a legend.

INTERVIEWER: People know who she is?

HAGEDORN: Yes.

INTERVIEWER: And nothing's happened to her?

HAGEDORN: Not anymore, no. She's not living under an assumed name. It's kind of hard to do that in the Philippines. The city itself, you know, they would know who you were, so she couldn't do that. So, who knows, Joey could have ended up that way too.

INTERVIEWER: You've written that at one point you scorned yourself and that it was only later, after you had left the Philippines "to settle in the country of my oppressor"—which you have also said you never thought of as being the oppressor back then—"that I learned to confront my demons and reinvent my own history." First, what are the demons you're talking about confronting?

HAGEDORN: The demons of identity are certainly some of the demons I confront. God, I don't have to list all my demons, do I, Kay? But in that particular sentence I meant this sort of condition of "who am I"? I am of mixed blood. Where are my allegiances? Is there an easy answer? No, there isn't. I wanted to have clarity about what I was doing. Who am I as an artist, as a woman? Now whether or not I choose to answer those questions, I still get disturbed by them. Those themes permeate my work, so that's part of the demonology of my life. And I think about issues of morality and mortality. I'm starting to confront now living in the United States as opposed to living back in the Philippines. Why I've decided to do that. It's important to me to know why, and would I die here? That's my new question. Is this the country where I want to die and be buried? If so, maybe it's because this is a country that allows you to reinvent yourself.

INTERVIEWER: The two ideas are interrelated, are they not? Confronting your demons and reinventing your history in the sense of overcoming false things that are taught to you by the textbooks when you're in school? I was intrigued by the sense of correcting history in your work. Is that what you're getting at?

HAGEDORN: Even revisionists can be cloudy when they revise history, so I'm very suspicious of that too. It goes back to memory. What we choose to remember is also colored, don't you think? How, for example, I elevate the mother to this Rita Hayworth vision. And the father, who is a more troubled character, but still charming. The charming gangster. I have these archetypes in my memory. Even my memory is questionable, of course, but it's the memory I live with. So, there are things from your childhood that are always with you, and perhaps they were always an illusion anyway but, yet and still, you have to be fueled by something.

INTERVIEWER: At the age of fourteen, you were taken by your mother from Manila out of one very multiethnic culture into America, another multiethnic culture. What was that like?

HAGEDORN: It was terrible at first. Luckily, she chose to live in San Francisco and not in someplace where we would've stood out. There was a multiethnic community and, luckily, there was Chinatown, for God's sake, which we constantly went to. It was the closest thing to Manila we could find. I was at such a terrible age, so gawky and awkward, and I didn't know whether I was grown up or still a child. So it was a weird time. Also exciting. I mean, I had always fancied that I would travel once I was old enough, and live in many places in the world, so I had that adventurer thing anyway. It's just that it happened a little too abruptly. And I was uprooted in the middle of my schoolwork and I wasn't ready to go then, it was not the time. Too many adjustments too fast. But I was also flexible and we all were tougher than we thought. It took a turn for the better when I realized that one of the positive things about it was that as a female person, I suddenly had a sense of freedom that I never had growing up in Manila in that overprotected colonial environment—the girl with her chaperons and everything that still goes on, that kind of tradition. And even though girls are not discouraged from going to school, they're still expected to marry and have a family and that's the subtext of everything. In America, suddenly I was free from those shackles. And because my mother was preoccupied with trying to make a new life for herself, reinventing herself at age forty, she could not control me as much as she would have liked to. So there was a payoff for me.

INTERVIEWER: Was this when you started writing?

HAGEDORN: I started writing seriously then. I had always written. As a child, I loved to read and I always thought of myself as a writer. You know, I was very dramatic. I would write little poems and I loved to make little comic books. I would illustrate them, four-page comic books, and thought of myself as a writer. When I was fourteen, my mother gave me a typewriter, thank heavens, and I guess she thought that would be a healthy way to keep me at home. I would type poems and read.

INTERVIEWER: And then I've heard that somebody in your family sent them to Kenneth Rexroth? How did that come to happen?

HAGEDORN: We had a family friend who knew a lot of what was going on in San Francisco. He would come over and I showed him my poems because he was a reader, so it was nice to talk books with him. And he gave them to a journalist friend of his who thought to send them to Rexroth. Kenneth at the time was writing for the *San Francisco Chronicle,* I think, or the *Examiner,* one of those papers. He'd write about whatever he wanted, always about art and culture with a little bit of politics thrown in. He called up and said, "Why don't you and your mother come for dinner?" He had a daughter my age, and it turned out he lived in the neighborhood. So it all fell into place. I found out that he was this wonderful poet and semicontroversial, which of course appealed to my rebellious nature, and I thought, "Oh, yummy, you know. It's not some corny old guy." He became something like my mentor in that he had all these books, thousands of books. Poetry, novels. And he said, "Just come over here whenever you want. You can borrow books." He would invite me out with his daughter to go to readings and to do all these beatnik things like go to a book store at nine o'clock at night, which I was just so thrilled by. And he'd get me books and he'd say, "Here, you should read this." He wasn't didactic about it. He just said, "You should look at Mallarmé. Look at the French surrealists. Look at this." I guess he trusted my intelligence enough to know he didn't have to lecture me. And I would sit in on his classes at San Francisco State.

INTERVIEWER: Is there a reason why you didn't go on to college?

HAGEDORN: I don't like academic settings very much. I find them oppressive. I like learning in a much more unconstructed way. I also was very interested in the theater at the time. One thing Kenneth showed me by turning me on to all these writers who were not much older than me, who were writing what to me seemed very exciting at the time, was that you didn't need to have a college degree to be an artist. It was, you know, the sixties. So, I turned my back on it and went instead to the American Conservatory Theater, a two-year acting and theater-arts program.

INTERVIEWER: So you did go on to school. You went to a conservatory instead.

HAGEDORN: Yeah. There were no degrees, though. It was practical.

INTERVIEWER: What about that, being practical? Did you think at all in terms of writing and theater as something you could earn your living doing?

HAGEDORN: I was very naive. I always thought I would eventually make a living. And I had a very romantic notion of art, that it was a higher calling. I had all kinds of jobs. I worked at Macy's. I worked at the post office. But I always sort of had faith that one day I would make a living off the writing or the acting or directing. It didn't bother me. It was a great time when you could live with ten people in one room. It was wonderful.

INTERVIEWER: So where did the fiction fit in to your work? Taking on a novel is a very daunting, long-term task.

HAGEDORN: What made me want to write a novel was reading *One Hundred Years of Solitude,* by Garcia Marquez. I was turned on to that by a friend from Mexico who gave me the book. It was like Holy Communion or something. I said, "Yes!" Here is a novel that reads so lyrically and so poetically, and yet is a novel. It's a wonderful story. You want to know what happens to these people. And at the same time I saw the connection for me. It was like the Philippines was something I was carrying around and I didn't know what art form it would take to convey the story I wanted to tell, and I read that book and said, "That's it. One day I'm gonna do it." I started devouring all the other writers that were being translated at the time—Manuel Puig, Cortazar and others. I went on a frenzy. The early seventies was the Latin American boom in translation. And I would buy them as they came out. And I stored all of that away.

INTERVIEWER: Is there anything that you can identify that you bring from the poetry and from your love of music into the fiction?

HAGEDORN: Rhythm. And I think the love of language, the sheer wordplay. I love words. The sound of words, and puns. It's very Filipino too. Filipinos love puns and wordplays and they love language, the intonations and the nuances. They take it seriously. They also play with it.

INTERVIEWER: A subject that we've only touched on is the question of Hollywood and the movies, the American movie industry, on the culture that you grew up in. It seems as though the Philippines were really swept away by American movies in terms of expectations and a particular view of the world. And this has been noted as a phenomena that happened other places too, like in South America. And you've continued to have a great interest in the power of film.

HAGEDORN: I think it was a great colonial tool. Even if it was entertainment, and it was, an industry that was begun out of a desire to entertain and to make money. Somewhat innocent in that way, crass but innocent. Yet, I think it's a wonderful way to seduce the minds and the hearts of people. It's a very powerful medium. You sit in the dark. Everything is larger than life. It tells a good story in a short amount of time. It's very easy to be swayed by it. It's as close to life as you can imagine. And yet, there's something magic about it because everybody looks good. Everybody's a giant. And it's beautiful or it's hyper whatever-it-is. It's hyperugly, hyperviolent, hyperbeautiful.

INTERVIEWER: And it instructs us about how we are supposed to see ourselves and how we're supposed to see the world? In speaking of this very factor in *Dogeaters,* John Updike said, "A borrowed American culture [borrowed from the movies he's talking about] has given Filipinos dreams but not the means to make dreams come true." And that you as a writer are as good as anybody he's ever come across in showing the impact of the movies on, as he put it, "the young minds of the Third World." And you didn't have any corrective, any North American corrective when you walked out into the streets of Manila afterward. Can you say how this shaped the generation you grew up in? Do you think that the American movie culture had anything to do with keeping people from seeing what was really going on around them?

HAGEDORN: No, that's sort of minor. I think we all need our escapes. But I'm not going to say that just because you can run into an air-conditioned theater for two hours out of the day to escape from the heat and the oppression and lose yourself that, you know, the movie musical is the root of our problems.

INTERVIEWER: But is there a way in which Hollywood shaped Filipino cultural attitudes?

HAGEDORN: In our notions of beauty, okay? These gods and goddesses of the West were constantly being fed to us. They didn't look like us. We thought they were exotic. I remember the first time I saw a woman with red hair and blue eyes in the Philippines. I just couldn't stop staring. And even in our own movie industry, the big stars of the time were the people with the more refined features. You weren't going to get the pure Filipino look on the screen. They would always get the lighter mestiza. A lot of cultural shame is reinforced by these movies.

INTERVIEWER: As a writer you have made film a central part of your aesthetic.

HAGEDORN: For other people perhaps it was something else that brought them to certain conclusions about their lives and their identities. But, for me, film was truly one of the more powerful sources of entertainment, enlightenment, disillusionment. So, I use it a lot. In the writing of *Dogeaters,* especially, the movies were there because they were absolutely part of the fabric of my memory. Once I found that key, all the doors started swinging open in my imagination.

INTERVIEWER: In *Charlie Chan Is Dead,* an anthology of Asian American literature that you recently edited, you wrote that you were "eager to subvert the very definition of what was considered fiction." I'm interested in knowing what you meant by that. How do you feel your own work subverts the very definition of fiction?

HAGEDORN: In *Dogeaters,* the easiest way to answer that one is the way I use what are considered factual documents. For example, the McKinley speech is not a fiction; it's a real speech he made in 1898. There's also an Associated Press bulletin called "Insect Bounty" that's real as well as a fiction that I made up. And there are fake newspaper items along with real newspaper items with real people's names, and it all fits into this sort of novel form. I play with what is considered fake and made up and actual facts of history. I think, too, in the way I use language—in the fact that I use Tagalog without a glossary. The story is not linear. It doesn't follow the traditional form of a novel, and the time frame isn't clear. It goes around and around. I go back and forth between the fifties and the eighties, quite comfortably I think.

INTERVIEWER: Is there any sense in which you are writing for a purpose, to correct stereotypes or to reinvent history in a way that corrects wrongs?

HAGEDORN: If I were to write with that agenda in mind, then I'd destroy the writing. No, I write really because I have to and if the writing also destroys some of those myths and subverts forms and makes people question the very idea of the writer, the woman, the Filipino American, the whatever, great!

INTERVIEWER: Where does art have to come from to accomplish those kinds of ends? If you set out directly to accomplish them, you probably wouldn't have writing that is, in your opinion, worth reading? So, where does it have to come from?

HAGEDORN: It has to come from the deepest, deepest, deepest insides of your soul. And it's got to be brutally honest. It's like pornography. You know it when you are doing it and you know when you're bullshitting.

You know when you're being self-conscious and contrived and forcing something to be there because you want to make sure that people get the point. You know when that's happening. But if you just really listen to yourself and to your characters, you don't go for the easy stuff.

INTERVIEWER: The other major art form that we haven't talked about yet is your involvement in the world of music. As I understand it, for a number of years you had a band called the Gangster Choir. Is that right? Can you tell us about that, and what kind of an influence this experience has had on your life as a writer?

HAGEDORN: I formed the band in 1975 because I was a poet at the time, very active in doing live readings and starting to think about readings as performance. We didn't have all of those terms in the Bay Area like "performance art," which to me is a very East Coast kind of label. We just did it. But I knew there was something more I wanted to do than stand up there with a piece of paper or with a book and read. So I had an idea that maybe there was a way to work with a band. I had heard a little bit of the Last Poets, for example, who actually had a record. And I got very excited by the idea of the spoken word to music. So, you could call this rapping before its time.

INTERVIEWER: How did the band actually come about?

HAGEDORN: I called Julian Priester, a composer friend of mine, and asked him to help me get some musicians together. I didn't really think the musicians would go for it, but they all showed up. We started rehearsing. Julian and I wrote three things that had chorus parts, so we included singers. It was such a wonderful experience I decided to just go for it. Whenever I could, if there was a performance coming up or a reading where they could actually have the entire band there, I would include them and we became sort of a fixture in the Bay Area poetry-and-music scene. And the band in various forms grew to nine or ten people, full horn section, electric guitars, bass, backup singers. You name it, we had it. It lasted for around ten years and when I moved to New York, a couple of the people moved with me and we reformed again, dropped the "West Coast" from the Gangster Choir title and just called ourselves the Gangster Choir. And we worked in all the clubs. You know, there was the New Wave scene, CBGB's, the Mudd Club, all that. And we had to become more musical. And I just figured, if Sid Vicious can sing, I can sing too. It was very liberating for me, and the band became more streamlined and edgy. It was an interesting time to be around with a band in the eighties. Part of that will be covered in my next novel I hope, one I'm working on now.

INTERVIEWER: But all this was while you were working on *Dogeaters*?

HAGEDORN: My daughter was born in the eighties, and I really wanted to begin working on the novel. Maybe having a child made me realize that I might be old enough to attempt a mature work. And there was a point where I said, "I cannot be everything and do everything and write a novel. Something's got to go." I knew the novel was going to be a big undertaking, and I had to be alone to really focus. So the band was disbanded. But I still work with music when the occasion is right. Last year, I went to San Francisco for a music festival and they asked me to put a band together. They gave me a budget to hire local people. It was great. So now from time to time I'd like to continue performing because it's a different kind of high when you perform musically. It's just such great fun, and with good musicians it can elevate the words to another level and enhance the poetry, and it's marvelous!

Larry Brown

Larry Brown lives in Oxford, Mississippi, where he was born and raised. He joined the Marine Corps during the time of the Vietnam War. Though he was never stationed out of the country, he got to know and hear the stories of many returning disabled marine vets while he was stationed at Camp Lejeune and the Marine Barracks. After his stint in the military, he returned home and worked for the Oxford Fire Department for sixteen years. He resigned in 1990 at the rank of captain to write full-time in a kind of self-imposed apprenticeship that he compares to that of a carpenter. His novels are informed by his experiences with the marines and as a fireman, as well as by the acute kinship with place and family he has acquired living his entire life in Faulkner's South. Brown is the author of a memoir, On Fire *(1994), and five books of fiction,* Facing the Music *(1988),* Dirty Work *(1989),* Big Bad Love *(1990),* Joe *(1991), and most recently* Father and Son *(1996). This interview was conducted in June 1995, while he was finishing work on* Father and Son.

INTERVIEWER: You list your hometown as Oxford, Mississippi, where you're still living and worked as a firefighter for sixteen years. Did you actually grow up in the city or out in the country?

BROWN: I was born in Oxford at the old hospital up the street from the courthouse, but we lived about twelve miles out in the country. We moved to Memphis when I was about three years old. I lived there ten years and went to school in Memphis until the eighth grade, which was in '64, and then we moved back to Mississippi, and I've been out around here all the time since then, for the last thirty-one years.

INTERVIEWER: What took your family up to Memphis?

BROWN: My father came out of World War II in '45, and he farmed for a good long while, but he was having all of us, and just really couldn't make a go of it farming. He had a good job waiting for him at Fruehauf Trailer Company in Memphis so we moved up there. By that point there were six of us altogether, my mother and my daddy and my two brothers and my sister. We had a growing family in a short length of time. I was born in '51. My father came out of the war in '45, and my sister and one of my brothers are older than me.

INTERVIEWER: I understand your mother was a postmistress?

BROWN: She did that part-time until she retired. We had a little store out at Tula that Mary Annie and I ran for a couple of years. Mother would come in and take care of the mail every day. The Postal Service was threatening to close the post office unless we could move it into a building that stayed open all day long, so I went over and took all the stuff and moved it into my store, and nailed it all back together, and we opened the post office in the store. We've still got it out there, too.

INTERVIEWER: Is that the store you've modeled John Coleman's store in *Joe* and the store in the story "Old Soldiers" with Mr. Aaron on?

BROWN: Actually, ours was a relatively new building. The store that's in my books was torn down sometime around 1966 or '67, and had been there for a long time. It had the potbellied stove and the patches of tin on the floor, and all the bottle caps just ground into the sand, hundreds and hundreds and hundreds of them, and the old slick benches out front that had been whittled and had people's initials in them because they'd been used for years.

INTERVIEWER: Where did the love of books and reading come from?

BROWN: Mainly from my mother. One of my earliest memories is of seeing her reading. There were always books in our house. I just grew to love it real early, I guess—escaping into stories and discovering other worlds. When I was a child I was a big reader of Greek mythology. I actually read a lot of literature without knowing what I was doing, because Mother bought a set of encyclopedias, and there was a set of ten classics that came with it. There was Edgar Allan Poe, and Mark Twain, and Zane Grey, and Herman Melville, and *Grimms' Fairy Tales,* and Greek mythology, the

Iliad and the *Odyssey,* and Jack London. That's eventually what brought me to writing—loving to read.

INTERVIEWER: Was there a point when you started separating things out and making distinctions of taste?

BROWN: I don't think I did until around 1982. I had been writing for about two years, pretty much on my own. I had published one short story in *Easy Riders' Motorcycle Magazine.* That was my first publication. I was really desperate for some help. So I came out here and went to a writing class that Ellen Douglas taught at the university. She pointed me toward a lot of things that I hadn't seen before, like the work of Joseph Conrad and Dostoyevsky and Flannery O'Connor. It was around that time that I began to discover what kind of writer I wanted to be. I had read Faulkner when I was sixteen years old. I really didn't think too much about it, except that "The Bear" was a great hunting story. It was only when I got older that I could appreciate all the other things that story was about, like the encroaching of industry upon the forest, and the way things were changing and all this happening as this young boy comes of age. The gradual reduction of the wilderness, just by the railroad coming through, and people beginning to log the timber off. All that was real saddening once I grasped it later on, but it was only after I started writing that I was fully able to appreciate the value of that story.

INTERVIEWER: You must have recognized it because of the landscape.

BROWN: Very much so. It was all very familiar to me. It was right up my alley. When I was sixteen that's what I wanted to do—stay in the woods with my gun and hunt every day and half the night sometimes, too.

INTERVIEWER: I gather that you didn't much like school.

BROWN: No, I didn't. I was such a poor student that I failed English my senior year and had to go to summer school to get my diploma. I didn't graduate with the rest of my class. It was very disappointing to my mother.

INTERVIEWER: Why was that? Was it just attitude?

BROWN: It was probably a combination of losing my father when I was sixteen and never having any interest in school to begin with. The only interest I had was in getting out of school, getting a job and buying a car, because I didn't have any way to go anywhere. I always had to catch rides with somebody else. I was just itching to get out on my own and start making a living. I didn't think that the future looked very bright at that point anyway because the war was going on. All the boys I grew up with were worrying about it. We'd already had some friends who'd gone over and been killed. I pretty much knew that I was going to have to go into the service at the height of the Vietnam War. I didn't have any long-range plans. I didn't see too much reason to worry a whole lot about what happened in school.

INTERVIEWER: Is Walter James' story in *Dirty Work,* at least in terms of the going away, close to your story?

BROWN: In some ways. Of course my father was already gone, then. But one thing that struck me, and why there are references to my father in there, was I saw what a tremendous sacrifice he had made, and that veterans of the Vietnam War made. War is an awful thing, and I didn't understand exactly what his life had been like until I heard him talk about all the hardships that he'd suffered, and how lucky he'd been to come out at the other end of it alive. The guys in *Dirty Work* are actually based on some disabled marines that I met in the early seventies in Philadelphia where I was stationed—guys who were in wheelchairs, who had lost their arms and legs and had made that great sacrifice, too.

INTERVIEWER: You were in the marines during the period of the Vietnam War. Why didn't you get sent overseas? Was it just the luck of the draw?

BROWN: I just lucked out. Around the time that I went in, October of 1970, some of the troop withdrawals had already started. Now the marines' policy—I didn't know this when I went in—is, they're the first in, they're the first out, too. A lot of the people who were getting pulled back were in the Marine Corps. The troop involvement was winding down. There were still a few people getting sent over, but from my platoon of thirty-eight men, probably only four or five had to go.

INTERVIEWER: How did you spend your time in the marines?

BROWN: I went to the big base at Camp LeJeune, North Carolina, first. Then I got orders to go to Marine Barracks, which is the oldest post in the Marine Corps. It was founded in 1776. It's what they call a dress-blues station. They issue you a set of dress blues—you've seen these marines with blue pants and tunics? What you do is a lot of official duty. There's a big naval shipyard there. You christen ships, you march in parades, you have to be on all this spit-and-polish detail—things like that.

INTERVIEWER: But you met some disabled vets.

BROWN: We had an NCO club behind our barracks. These guys would come over in their wheelchairs, and there was a set of steps there, four or five high. We'd just roll their wheelchairs up those steps and push them back there with us. There were two guys I was most impressed by. One of them didn't have any legs at all, but he had a pair of artificial legs, with pants on and tennis shoes on the bottom. He would come in on a pair of crutches, and you couldn't tell he didn't have any legs. He'd sit up on a bar stool and order a beer. The other guy had the kind of injury that Walter has. He had been shot all the way through the base of his skull. To look at him, he didn't have any kind of disfiguring wound. He was a nice-looking young man about twenty-one or twenty-two years old. But he had blackouts, seizures. They could control it somewhat with medicine, but not to the point where he could remain on active duty. So here was a nice, good-looking young guy walking around, twenty-two years old, on a hundred percent disability for medical problems. All that stuff is based on these real people.

INTERVIEWER: How did you get to know them that well?

BROWN: We were marines, too. We were marines and these guys were all Marine Corps veterans, and they were attached to the naval hospital there. I guess they got passes to leave their ward—the ones who were mobile. My friend with the artificial legs had his car fixed up with hand levers. He'd drive himself around, wherever he wanted to go. He had a girlfriend and lived a pretty normal life. That's where all that came from. All the stuff about the weapons and the war I either learned as part of my training, or from talking to veterans of the war. The whole Marine Corps was full of them. The sergeants and everybody were all veterans. Everybody you talked to—the officers—had already been over there and served and come back and been decorated. They were all full of stories. The Marine Corps is full of history. It has a really proud tradition, and they teach you about the great battles the marines have fought in. They show you footage of the first day at Iwo Jima, when they shelled Mount Suribachi for two weeks, and then the first wave went out from those ships and there were three thousand U.S. Marines mowed down and killed the first day—in one day three thousand of them died. You see all that and you get indoctrinated into it. It just becomes a way of life.

INTERVIEWER: You said "I put my father in *Dirty Work*" in that scene between Walter and his dad. To what extent is the portrait of the father in that novel a portrait of your own dad?

BROWN: In little ways, here and there. My father never killed anybody and went to the penitentiary or anything. I make up all my characters out of little bits and pieces of real life. But I would like to think that if he and I had been allowed to have that conversation, if he had lived long enough to see me go in, the conversation would have been like that: he would have told me to be careful, and watch out, to try to come back home.

INTERVIEWER: What about the man that runs that country store in Tula—the John Coleman and Mr. Aaron character in "Old Soldiers"? Is that a tribute to, or a portrait of, somebody you know?

BROWN: Yes. His name was Norman Clark. He had the store there. He came out of the war just about the same time my father did and he never went anywhere after that. At one point he had a brand-new four-door 1962 Chevrolet Impala. That car sat right across the road and rotted into the ground. There was a period of twelve years when he never left Tula, and Tula's only a few hundred yards long. He stayed in that store every day for thirty-something years.

INTERVIEWER: Did he have sixty-thousand dollars in a bank bag? That's what John Coleman says he has in his bank bag when he goes off in the truck—to Joe Ransom's surprise he agrees to go for a ride with him.

BROWN: He had more than that! Somebody would bring a check in and say, "Can you cash this check for me, Norman?" He'd say, "Yes." They'd say, "Well, that's a pretty big check now. Sure you can cash it?" He'd say, "Yeah." It didn't matter how big the check was, he could cash it. He had the money in there. And he had that pistol, too. Everybody knew it. He kept his Budweiser in the candy case, too. He didn't mind drinking it hot.

INTERVIEWER: How often do you take people out of the community and out of your life, and transform them into your work?

BROWN: In this particular case it was somebody I cared a whole lot about, because I can remember being a little bitty boy and going in his store. He would give me a little pack of candy corn and make some kind of joke about a rooster pecking, or something like that. But then I grew up and spent a lot of time with him. If you went in there by yourself and nobody else was there he would sit down and talk to you and tell you stories. He would tell these great war stories, just like my daddy. But if one other person was there he wouldn't do it. It had to be you and him. I stayed up at the store a lot. It was a little bitty place we lived in. There wasn't much to do sometimes, in the summer. Then I went into the service and came back out. I married and began to raise a family, and he was there in the store. He just died a few years back, from a war wound. He got blood poisoning from a piece of shrapnel that was in one of his leg bones that they never got out.

INTERVIEWER: Is that a sensitive issue for you—using people in your fiction that are modeled on people out of your own life?

BROWN: Not really. Even though characters may sometimes be based on real people, what happens is that the story around them will be different. The events will be different and they won't do the same things in my story that they did in real life. They might have a similar lifestyle, but I will invent the rest.

INTERVIEWER: What about the family cemetery, the old house in *Joe*, where the Jones family is squatting. That's the Coleman Place. You figure that out as you're reading the book. Are that little springhouse and the well-tended grave site there real?

BROWN: They're all real but they're in different places. The log house was down on a place called Neal Hill many years ago when I used to hunt down there. It's since been bulldozed down. The grave was something that a friend and I found out in the middle of the woods one day deer hunting up in the national forest. There was no structure anywhere around, just these weird little plants like a little protective garden, right in the middle of all these big trees. Just one grave. And the springhouse is something that I remembered from years and years ago. I had a friend, an older fellow I used to coon hunt with all the time. He had an old springhouse on his place. It was ice cold. You don't see those things anymore.

INTERVIEWER: The interesting thing about the use of a detail like that in the novel *Joe* is the kind of atmosphere or reverberation that it helps to create in the character John Coleman. And by extension, in *Joe* as well. It makes the region and this community really sing.

BROWN: It's a way to establish history and give some depth to the background of the people. There are old cemeteries scattered in the woods out where I live. Some of the stones go back to the 1700s. These communities died out for some mysterious reason a long time ago. But it's fascinating to me to know that this country was being settled back when the Constitution was being written—that there were people down here in Mississippi, living and building homes and raising families and pretty much exploring this whole country, which was a big wilderness back in those days.

INTERVIEWER: You also move the story, explore character and, in the case of Joe, illuminate the landscape through the world of work. Larry Brown seems to be a person who is fascinated with the daily details of physical work.

BROWN: I think it's a hard thing for a man to have to get up every morning and work hard doing some kind of physical labor, like swinging a hammer, all day long. I've had to do that so much myself to support my writing habit. Writing didn't bring in any money. I was doing it all the time, but I wasn't selling anything. I couldn't just come home from the fire department and sit down and write because I had three children to feed. So I'd have to do stuff like build houses and tote bricks, and haul hay, and deaden timber and sack groceries and all the other things that I did. I'm well versed in what hard work is. I really admire the people who do it. A lot of people turn their backs on it, and lay out or become bums or something.

INTERVIEWER: It's interesting how you use it to illuminate character. You learn a lot about Joe Ransom's history from him banging out the fender on that old GMC truck. He says, "I used to be a body man." You wonder if it was in prison or not. The point is, that moves the relationship between him and Gary at that point in the story. It also shows keen observation of detail on your part.

BROWN: I listen to people, and I look at their lives and wonder what they're about. Then I begin exploring. I put a character in a situation and I know that I have to have some kind of trouble going early on to involve me in the story, because I'm interested in the way people get through their lives. Joe has had all this stuff happen to him. He's lost his family, his son won't even speak to him, he's been in the penitentiary. He lives by himself. And he's got this work ethic too. He believes that a man ought to get up and go to work every morning.

INTERVIEWER: And he makes a good living.

BROWN: He's lucked out and got this job which pays very well, but he has to think about what he's doing, which is killing a living organism, a living forest. He's not happy with what he's doing, but it's a job. I guess he looks at it maybe, "If I don't do it, somebody else will. It's going to get done."

INTERVIEWER: The narrator says, through his point of view, that he's thinking about what he's doing. What is it, in the larger sense of the word?

BROWN: The major thing, I think, is destroying the habitat for a whole bunch of wildlife. Hardwood forests support so many different forms of life: deer, turkey, squirrels, all the birds and insects and reptiles that live there. It's a renewable crop every year, this food that comes from oak trees and beech trees and all. The animals gather that up. Squirrels hide it. Predators find their prey there. Hawks and owls and all different forms of life are there. Man uses it to get food from, too. All that gets cut down, and you come back and plant a pine tree on it, and the only thing it bears is a pinecone, with a few little seeds in it. Once you lose that hardwood forest you've lost it forever, because they take so long to grow. You can have a pine plantation ready to harvest in about twenty years. You probably won't have even the first crop of acorns off of oaks until they're thirty years old. Once they're established, and they keep getting bigger and bigger, they provide a huge canopy from the sun. It's shady down there, right now, in the middle of the day, at three-thirty in the afternoon. Leaves fall year after year and choke out the small undergrowth. The big trees are left, and it's just like a floor. The beauty of a hardwood forest to me is unmatched. I think that's what Faulkner was talking about so long ago when he said that the land would accomplish its own revenge on the people. That's true. All that forest has largely disappeared, except for some privately held tracts of land in Lafayette County and what's available up on the national forest. It's gotten to the point now where if you want to hunt you've got to either own some land or be in a hunting club. Things have really changed from what they were when I was eighteen years old and could hunt anywhere in this county I wanted to, and nobody would tell me there's a posted sign over there.

INTERVIEWER: To what extent were you trying to call attention to issues like that in *Joe*?

BROWN: I used to do that for a part-time living. I'm not proud of what I did. I did it simply for the money, to feed my family. I deadened timber in the springtime and the summer, and planted the pines in the winter. It's brutal work. A lot of people can't do it. They come out one day and quit at the end of that day. It's a tough thing to get out there at daylight when it's ten degrees, and work all day setting those pine trees. And it's tough to get out there at six in the summertime, in May, and go down through the woods and run into snakes and yellow jackets and spiderwebs. *Joe* gave me a great opportunity to show the landscape, and to set my characters against it. And to have this larger thing, even larger than the lives that are going on, which is the land. The ground is so ancient. It's the oldest thing we've got. I like to have people picture what it looks like—that distant watershed where all the lines of trees fade into this little blue line that's the end of the horizon. That's what I love. This is my country, and I love this place. I try to re-create it on the page.

INTERVIEWER: In your book on fire fighting, called *On Fire,* you imagined a scene, or you saw this family walking down the road. It became the Jones family walking down the road in the opening pages of *Joe.* Was that the germ of the novel?

BROWN: Yes. I started writing it around 1984 or 1985, after I had already written five bad novels and thrown them all away. I burned one of them in the backyard. That was the first image that I had. The image of that family came before *Joe* came. Later on I invented my protagonist. But the opening shot that I wanted was that family walking down that hot blacktop road through a deserted landscape in the middle of the summer, with no place to go.

INTERVIEWER: Where did Joe come in? How did he get in the mix?

BROWN: He came as a way to try to save Gary from what his fate would have ordinarily been—probably something bad on down the road somewhere. The kid has never really been given a chance, and his father's not good. I wanted him to have a chance at a relationship with—not another father, but somebody who could take care of him for a little while. Joe was invented to do that. In the course of working on the story about him, I began to find out that his story was important, too. He had to have a background, a history, a future. This timber job was a logical thing for him to have. He'd lived a good bit of his life already. He'd already had other jobs. He'd had family. And now this is what he was left with. He was left with this job and a dog. That's really all that he has. Once in a while he has a woman, but he doesn't care too much about that. He cares about taking care of the future and trying to get through his life without going back to the penitentiary.

INTERVIEWER: Which he probably fails at, ultimately.

BROWN: Yes.

INTERVIEWER: What fascinates me about the Jones family is that in spite of the horribleness of their background and their history, and all the things that have been going on throughout their life, they're a family. That's what pulls Gary back, tragically, into that milieu. The question of family and community is apparently very important to you. It's underneath everything you do, in your short stories and in the novels.

BROWN: I'm concerned very much with family connections, relatives, and all that. That's like a nest you go back home to every night. You have these people around who are going to be with you all your life—the person you picked to marry, and your children. Your grandchildren are going to come from them, and you had the family that you came out of. And your mother had the family she came out of, and your father, on down the line. The Joneses are dysfunctional as a family, but still they're a unit. Fay takes it as long as she can, and then she goes. She's seen some of the others leave, too. Gary is young enough to remember Calvin. What happened to him and all. Putting all that in just illustrates how hopeless Gary's case is. I wanted him to have a chance. When you're writing something you never know how these things are going to turn out. When it came time to finish this novel, I wrote the ending of *Joe* about five different times.

INTERVIEWER: You rewrote the ending five times? Different outcomes?

BROWN: Different outcomes. One was a happily-ever-after where everything was hunky-dory. But the question that I ultimately had to ask myself was: Do the guilty always get punished in life, or do the innocent sometimes have to catch some stuff? And I said, in the real world they do, and if your fiction really imitates life, that's what you have to go with. I build my stories, and I try to be authentic in them. I sometimes get accused of being brutal and having a dark vision. That may be true. I don't know why my stuff is so dark. Except that I believe the whole process is just an attempt to pull the reader into the story, like I said a while ago. To make him forget that he's reading. Tragedy is inevitable in my stories, because of the circumstances people live in. I think my characters—most of them—know the difference between right and wrong. Certainly Wade knows the difference between right and wrong. So does Joe. But doing those things—that's where you come to grips with your characters, how they react in certain situations.

INTERVIEWER: Along with family, community is extremely important in your work. But the community is implied. It's interesting that you look at community from the points of view of those who are in fact, as you said in one of your short stories, living separate in the same house on badly eroded land, in a house of poor quality. I'm curious about that. Why do you choose to look at the issue of family and community from the broken side?

BROWN: If Joe was a regular family guy he wouldn't have been involved in all this drinking and fighting and messing around with the police—all the things that he's done that have given him such a reputation and made every lawman around know him. He has a code of his own that he goes by. You have to respect him or fight him if you're going to tangle with him. I made his life the way it is to give the reader a sense early on of the brokenness of his life, and the amount of time he spends alone in that house listening to the tape player over and over again, watching junk on television that he doesn't even like, eating poorly, drinking way too much, smoking all these cigarettes, and all the carousing that he sometimes does. He has periods when he can do fine. He can go to work every day and go home and sleep every night. Then he has other times when he starts drinking and he gets in trouble. He starts running into people and making mistakes, and he has to start paying for all his mistakes again. Then he becomes partially involved with this kid, Gary. He becomes concerned about him and sees what the old man's doing to him, sees it the first day that he pays the kid off. He knows that the boy's old man, Wade, is going to take every penny the kid made that day. The way he looks at it is that there's no sense in paying him to work if Wade is going to take it anyway. "It's too painful to watch and I don't want to have to watch it because I know what's going to happen." But a little later he thinks, "If he won't bring his old man back, maybe he'll have a chance." Things get a little better and he says, "Maybe I can sell him my truck. He'll have a ride," and all this. Then he begins to find out more: how the kid can't read, doesn't know what a church is, how ignorant he is of the world around him, the things that other boys around him take for granted.

INTERVIEWER: One reader has pointed out that another tragedy is that what Joe passes on in his initiation—such as it is—to Gary is the torch of some of his most destructive and worst habits, especially alcohol. I assume you would say, "That's the way it goes. That's the way things do tend to work themselves out." Nothing's wasted in this book, so you must have been keenly aware of the irony there.

BROWN: Yes. Whatever kind of deal Gary is going to get out of Wade is going to be rotten. His father won't even defend him when some guy is beating him up. Even though he's in kind of rough hands, with Joe I feel like he's in better hands. There's hope towards the end that things are going to work out for him. But all these wheels have already been set in motion a long time ago.

INTERVIEWER: The rule of inevitability.

BROWN: The rule of inevitability. It's got to drop off like ripe fruit in your hand, to be unexpected and inevitable at the same time. That's what Katherine Anne Porter said, and I believe that. Some readers have a problem accepting that life goes like this sometimes.

INTERVIEWER: I'm intrigued by the sheriff—that scene towards the end of *Joe.* The sheriff comes in as the voice of sanity and says, "You can't take your dog into somebody else's house and let them kill another dog. Joe, you just can't do things like this." Joe's wife tells him, "I can't have a social life because you'd go out and beat the guy up." And he says "Me? Me, do that?" At that point in the novel, which is towards the beginning, you don't really know if in fact he's capable of it. But you find out yeah, he probably would do something like that. The sheriff's a guy who's been wild in the past and he's straightened around. You're not curious about a character like that? I think his story would be interesting.

BROWN: He's the last voice of reason trying to speak to Joe. He's already witnessed Joe's descent into the place he got to when he had to fight with all the police officers uptown. He knows full well what is going to happen. He's got his ear on what's going on in the county. He knows Willie shot Joe. He knows what's coming. He says, "How long do you think you and Willie Russell can keep shooting at each other before one of you winds up dead?" Joe just laughs and says, "Huh, somebody ought to do the world a favor." That's what he means, too. The world would be better off if that son of a bitch was dead.

INTERVIEWER: He's right. But the sheriff knows something that Joe doesn't know about reality.

BROWN: And the sheriff has to operate on the right side of the law, but Joe doesn't. There's nobody to take care of it but Joe. It just falls into his lap. If somebody doesn't take care of these people right now—Willie and Wade—this is going to happen again, and no telling how long it's been happening. They stole Gary's truck, Willie's beaten him up, now his dad's selling his little sister, took his money. How much more am I going to let him get away with? That's Joe's question.

INTERVIEWER: You still haven't answered my question about writing a novel from the point of view of these members of the community.

BROWN: The novel I'm working on now is about a guy, Glen, getting out of the penitentiary after three years, and coming home. I was pretty sure that this novel was going to focus on him. But he gets met at the cemetery—his mother has died while he's in the pen—he gets met at the cemetery the first day he's home by the sheriff, a guy that he grew up with. And slowly the focus, as I wrote, began to slide over to Bobby, the sheriff, and his home life. Bobby is a really good man. He's that voice of reason in the book I'm working on now. But these two characters have something between them, and that is they both want the same woman. She has had Glen's illegitimate child before he went in, so the child is between three and four years old now. But in the three years he's been down, the sheriff has been out and she's been unattached. They haven't actually been lovers, but they've gotten to feeling very, very strongly about each other, and she's going to give Glen one chance to come back, claim this baby and give it a name. She's still unmarried. Bobby wants her. He's willing to take the baby too, give it his name, do everything. All he wants is family. He wants them for his family. Glen doesn't really care if he ever has a family or not because he's very estranged from his own family, from his father, from things that have gone before. He has a lot of hatred. He blames a lot of people for the mistakes that he's made. The one thing that he's going to do when he comes home is take care of his enemies. He begins to do that as soon as he gets home.

INTERVIEWER: A lot of people who study the lives of policemen say that they have difficulty in their personal lives because their world vision gets skewed from what they're seeing all the time. In reading *On Fire,* I couldn't help but wonder if you think that all those years you spent on the Oxford Fire Department intensified that attention to the darker side. You talk in there about how mainly in your work you see people over and over again that have been out driving drunk, decapitated on bridges, young lives snuffed out, people burned to death from doing something totally stupid like driving while drunk, people who get drunk and burn the apartment down. Was it just a good source of material, or do you think in fact it shaped your view of the world?

BROWN: What it showed me was that poverty causes many of these terrible tragedies, because the people who are on the lower end of the economic scale are the ones who have the lousy housing, who live in the firetraps. Why? Because the wiring is bad, because somebody's been careless, somebody's put a penny in the fuse box and there's a wire under the rug, or the smoke detector doesn't have a battery in it, or their child has never been told not to play with matches and catches the curtains on fire, then catches their pajamas on fire. Of course, it can happen to anybody. Some fellow can go out and have a car wreck in his big Cadillac. But so many times you may go from the biggest mansion in the city of Oxford that morning down to the most squalid shack on the other side of town that evening. You can figure which one's going to be the worst. It's because of the conditions that poor people live in. You get your eyes opened to something like that, and it makes you appreciate the life that you have, and the things that you've been taught, and your children. Even though they might get a little wild sometimes, at least they're not out selling drugs or robbing folks on the street. It also tends to make you appreciate family even more. Many of the things that I saw in the fire department were so bad, and the memories of them wouldn't let me sleep sometimes. All that stuff is what I write about—what I saw and the way it made me feel.

INTERVIEWER: Everybody who talks to Larry Brown hears that when he was twenty-nine he decided to start writing. But somehow there's got to be more to it. What happened? You'd been on the fire department seven years at this point. You were married. You had at least two or three of your children.

BROWN: Right before I turned thirty I looked at my life and I said, "Okay, what are you going to do with it?" I think I just wanted to make something more out of myself than what I was. Being a firefighter was, and is, I still think, a very noble, honorable profession because it's in the business of helping people. But I said, "Isn't there something else you can do with your life that might be even better?" I said, "Well, what about writing?" As much as I loved to read, I wanted to know how people went into a room and sat down and created a book out of their imagination or memory or whatever—created this book where nothing had existed before, a tangible object you could pick up and hold in your hand. How did people do that? I decided, "All it's going to cost is a typewriter and paper, a very basic thing. I'm going to write a novel."

INTERVIEWER: It could have also cost your family life, your personal life, as you illustrate so well in some of your stories about writers.

BROWN: For many years nobody understood what I was doing or why I was doing it. I'd had a project not too long before that where I was going to disassemble a '55 Chevrolet and put it back together. I had it up on blocks in my pasture. The whole thing lay in pieces and never got put back together. Somebody finally came and towed it away. Mary Annie probably thought writing was just another little whim like that. But a couple of years later I was still working hard at it. She began to see that I was dedicating myself to changing careers, to stopping the job as a firefighter to become a writer. I think the years that a person goes through learning to write are just like the years that a journeyman carpenter goes through, or a brick mason goes through, learning how to lay an even course. It's an acquired skill. I don't think people are born with talent. The reason I say that is because if you went out to the house and climbed up in the attic and looked at all those bad novels and stories that are up there gathering dust, you would say that Larry Brown has no talent. You would have to.

INTERVIEWER: That's interesting, because I know people who after twenty years think of themselves as aspiring writers and the stuff they're writing is still bad. I guess it's a question of learning from your mistakes. How did you identify the mistakes in the first place, to learn from them? Writing is so solitary. You don't have a steward over you saying, "You didn't tie that knot right. Here's how you do that."

BROWN: One thing you have to do is lose all your sentimental feelings about your characters. You also have to get a certain amount of bullshit out of your system to tell what's genuine from what's fake. There are two ways you can go. You can be sentimental, or you can be hard-hearted. The perfect place to be is right in the middle. You walk a fine line between weeping over the stuff and turning a cold eye on it. You can't fool people. You have to be honest with them. I think that you go into a room and you believe in yourself. You must have this unshakable belief, no matter if you can prove it today or not, that you're going to make it. That's the only thing that kept me going. I told myself, "If I do this thing long enough,

I will eventually learn how." It takes discipline to actually commit to sit down and do the work, to invent all these hundreds of stories and ideas that you come up with that don't even get finished, that get thrown away. It's mainly up to you. I don't think that I was born with any talent. I think it's more just a way I have of looking at the world that's different from how most people look at the world, but that people everywhere can identify with.

INTERVIEWER: You said you came to Ole Miss to take a writing course from Ellen Douglas. What did that teach you?

BROWN: She told me, "I don't have any problem with the way you construct a sentence. It's your subject matter that you need to learn about—what the things are to write about." My first novel was about a man-eating grizzly bear in Yellowstone National Park. The next one was about a couple of guys who were going to raise a big patch of marijuana in Tennessee and sell it. The third novel was a supernatural novel. The fourth was a boxing novel. I don't know anything about boxing. I've watched a lot of it, but I never have done any of it. The fifth novel was about some guys who lived out in the woods around here, and it almost got published. Then I started writing *Joe* and *Dirty Work,* and I published both of them.

INTERVIEWER: You took six years to write *Joe.* How long did you take to write *Dirty Work*?

BROWN: I wrote *Dirty Work* in two and a half years of very hard work. I didn't do anything else for those two and a half years.

INTERVIEWER: What started that?

BROWN: I took six months off from writing in 1986 to build the house that I live in now. *Joe* was already under way, but I said, "Okay, I can't go drive nails for twelve hours and then write at night, too, so I'm just going to drop it for six months, get the house built and move in it. Then I'll start back writing again." During the time that the house was under construction, I got an idea about a guy whose face was disfigured from a rocket attack in Vietnam and he wouldn't come out of his room. That was all I had. It was just driving me crazy to get to work on it, but I couldn't until I had all the sheetrock hung, and the wallpaper and paint, trim, the cabinets, all the million things that go in a house. But the day that I had a table to put my typewriter on, and a chair to sit in—we hadn't even moved in yet—I sat down and started writing *Dirty Work.* That idea had grown and festered in those months and I just had to get it down. It turned out that I had to write it five different times and throw out six hundred pages. It went through five complete revisions.

INTERVIEWER: At what point did the two voices come in, of Walter and Braiden?

BROWN: After the third draft, when I finally showed the manuscript to my editor, Shannon Ravenel. She wrote back and said, "Larry, the bad news is your novel starts on page 160." I said, "Oh, no. That's unacceptable. I'm just going to throw it away. I've put in too much work. I'm not going to go through all that." She wrote me a letter and said, "You have worked by yourself all this time. You haven't had any guidance, I understand all of that. But this is too good an idea for you to throw away. Just trust me and work on it with me. I'm going to help you." And she was right. We started working on it again. I started writing the fourth draft. We sent things back and forth. We'd argue sometimes. We'd have our disagreements. But in the process I discovered that she was right about all that stuff. She was the one who taught me so much about characters' histories, their relationships, their feelings, their memories, their childhoods, their concerns, and how characters had to be so well fleshed out.

INTERVIEWER: To what extent do you accept or are you comfortable with *Dirty Work*'s identification as a novel of the Vietnam era, and of you as a novelist of the Vietnam era?

BROWN: The word *Vietnam* is never mentioned in that book. It's about the aftermath of the war more than the war itself. There aren't a whole lot of combat scenes. There's a little bit about the war in there. But it's mainly about what happens to people years and years on down the road. That's why it carries the dedication that it does: "This book is for Daddy, who knew what war does to men." He saw and went through so many terrible things. The guys that I met did too. I wanted to say something about the people who make these sacrifices for us, the veterans—the guys who we honor every Memorial Day. Sometimes what happens to them is not pretty. Many people's lives are not right, and are never going to be right. Those are the people I explore over and over. If you don't have problems in your characters' lives, then you don't have a story. The way to hook your reader is to give your character some trouble early on, and then find out what's going to happen, and sandbag him and put all this pressure on him and see how he's going to react when things really get tough.

INTERVIEWER: *Dirty Work* also seems to me to be a book that's about the question of how God works in this world. There's a real dialogue that's taking place at a philosophical and a spiritual level between Walter and Braiden throughout the book. Were you conscious of that as being one of the questions you wanted to address?

BROWN: Certainly. I wanted to address what I felt God would say about Braiden, the situation that he's in, having lived for twenty years without arms or legs. He's reached a point where he just wants to die, but he has to persuade someone to do that for him. Jesus comes down and explains everything very straightforwardly to him: "I can't take your life. This guy over here, that's something else, but you're treading on shaky ground." It's not exactly suicide, but in a way it kind of is, too. But I also believe that God is very merciful and compassionate, and would not blame Braiden for wanting to leave, even though life is what he gave you—"all of us," that's what he says. That's very much true. Life is what he gave us. But some lives get to the point where they're unbearable, and Braiden's life has gotten to that point.

INTERVIEWER: Braiden says at one point about the question of suffering in the world, "God doesn't work like that. God doesn't visit suffering on the world. Things just get out of hand." So what do you think, philosophically? Is Braiden speaking for you?

BROWN: I don't know if he's speaking for me. I've got a very deep faith. I'm not a compulsive churchgoer. I was for many, many years. I was raised in a church. I don't go like I used to, but I still have this faith. I believe that the world is a hard place for a lot of people, but there are also many, many good things about it. You hardly ever hear about the good things. I think in some ways I was trying to create a situation that most people would never encounter, but I wanted those people to know what Braiden had been going through and what a good human being he was, and what the loss of him was. We lost a schoolteacher, we lost some guy who was going to try and help other people with his life. He was really a kid, and then he lost everything that he had. The world's forgotten about him. All the medals have been pinned on and the TV's turned to another channel. He's still here, and he's going to be here unless somebody can do something for him.

INTERVIEWER: You've talked quite a bit about the struggle you went through to establish yourself as a writer. How do you feel about it now that you have published five books?

BROWN: Many times it's still a complete shock to me to just see a finished book and say, "How did you ever manage to accomplish that?" But it's an accumulation of time. You spend every day doing it, and you spend enough days together in a row, then you've got a book. It's like building a house. It may be real hard—the days may be real hot or real cold when you're doing it—but after the house is finished, no matter how tired your muscles have been on all those other days, the memory of the work is something that goes away. You're left with the finished product.

Principal Works

Larry Brown

Facing the Music (1988)
Dirty Work (1989)
Big Bad Love (1990)
Joe (1991)
On Fire (1994)
Father and Son (1996)

Rosellen Brown

Street Games (1974)
The Autobiography of My Mother (1976)
Tender Mercies (1978)
Civil Wars (1984)
Before and After (1992)

Robert Olen Butler

The Alleys of Eden (1981)
Sun Dogs (1982)
Countrymen of Bones (1983)
On Distant Ground (1985)
Wabash (1987)
The Deuce (1989)
A Good Scent from a Strange Mountain (1992)

They Whisper (1994)
Tabloid Dreams (1996)

Robb Forman Dew

Dale Loves Sophie to Death (1981)
The Time of Her Life (1984)
Fortunate Lives (1992)
The Family Heart: A Memoir of When Our Son Came Out (1994)

Louise Erdrich and Michael Dorris

ERDRICH

Love Medicine (1984)
The Beet Queen (1986)
Tracks (1988)
Bingo Palace (1994)
Tales of Burning Love (1996)

DORRIS

A Yellow Raft in Blue Water (1987)
The Broken Cord (1989)
Working Men (1993)
Cloud Chamber (1997)

ERDRICH AND DORRIS

The Crown of Columbus (1991)

Jessica Hagedorn

Dangerous Music (1975)
Pet Food and Tropical Apparitions (1981)
Dogeaters (1990)
The Gangster of Love (1996)

Jim Harrison

Wolf: A False Memoir (1971)
A Good Day to Die (1973)
Farmer (1976)
Legends of the Fall (1979)
Revenge (1979)
Warlock (1981)

Sundog (1984)
Dalva (1988)
The Woman Lit by Fireflies (1990)

Linda Hogan

Eclipse (1983)
Seeing through the Sun (1985)
The Stories We Hold Secret (1986)
Savings (1988)
Mean Spirit (1990)
Red Clay (1991)
The Book of Medicines (1993)
Solar Storms (1995)

Jamaica Kincaid

At the Bottom of the River (1983)
Annie John (1985)
A Small Place (1988)
Lucy (1990)
The Autobiography of My Mother (1996)

Peter Matthiessen

Race Rock (1954)
Partisans (1955)
Wildlife in America (1959)
The Cloud Forest (1961)
Raditzer (1961)
Under the Mountain Wall (1962)
At Play in the Fields of the Lord (1965)
Sal Si Puedes (1969)
Blue Meridian (1971)
Far Tortuga (1975)
The Snow Leopard (1978)
Sand Rivers (1981)
In the Spirit of Crazy Horse (1983)
Indian Country (1984)
Midnight Turning Gray (1984)
Nine-Headed Dragon River (1985)

Men's Lives (1986)
On the River Styx and Other Stories (1989)
Killing Mister Watson (1990)

Tom McGuane

The Sporting Club (1968)
The Bushwhacked Piano (1971)
Ninety-two in the Shade (1973)
Panama (1978)
An Outside Chance (1980)
Nobody's Angel (1981)
Something to Be Desired (1984)
To Skin a Cat (1986)
Keep the Change (1989)
Nothing but Blue Skies (1992)

Robert Stone

A Hall of Mirrors (1966)
Dog Soldiers (1974)
A Flag for Sunrise (1981)
Children of Light (1986)
Outerbridge Reach (1992)
Bear and His Daughter (1997)

Scott Turow

One L (1977)
Presumed Innocent (1987)
The Burden of Proof (1990)
Pleading Guilty (1993)
The Laws of Our Fathers (1996)

Margaret Walker

For My People (1942)
Jubilee (1966)
How I Wrote "Jubilee" (1972)
Richard Wright: Daemonic Genius (1988)
This Is My Century (1989)

John Edgar Wideman

A Glance Away (1967)
Hurry Home (1970)
The Lynchers (1973)
Damballah (1981)
Hiding Place (1981)
Sent for You Yesterday (1983)
Brothers and Keepers (1984)
Reuben (1987)
Fever (1989)
Philadelphia Fire (1990)
The Stories of John Edgar Wideman (1992)
All Stories Are True (1993)
The Cattle Killing (1996)

About the Editors

KAY BONETTI is founder and Director of the American Audio Prose Library.

GREG MICHALSON is Managing Editor of *The Missouri Review.* His fiction has been mentioned in *Best American Short Stories* and in the Pushcart Prize anthology. He also serves as General Editor of a prize-winning novel series published by MacMurray and Beck.

SPEER MORGAN is Editor of *The Missouri Review* and Professor of English at the University of Missouri–Columbia. He is the author of four novels, most recently *The Whipping Boy.*

JO SAPP has recently returned from a four-year stint in Malaysia, where she studied the literature of the region and wrote short fiction. Her stories have appeared in numerous magazines and have been included in *The Norton Anthology of Short Fiction.*

SAM STOWERS is sound recordist, audio editor, and coproducer of numerous American Audio Prose Library audio cassettes and radio programs.